Teaching Primary Programming with Scratch

Pupil Book – Year 6

PHIL BAGGE

A research informed scheme of work by Phil Bagge HIAS Computing Inspector/Advisor
Part of the HIAS Teaching Primary Programming from Scratch Series

Published in 2023 by University of Buckingham Press,
an imprint of Legend Times Group
51 Gower Street
London WC1E 6HJ
info@unibuckinghampress.com
www.unibuckinghampress.com

Published by arrangement with Hampshire Inspection and Advisory Service (part of
Hampshire County Council)

ISBN 978-1-91505-4-289

CONTENTS

Book resources can be downloaded from https://computing.hias.hants.gov.uk/course/view.php?id=5

3

INTRODUCTION & PROGRESSION

INTRODUCTION

Scheme

This book is a complete scheme of work for teaching primary programming using Scratch in Year 6 for 10–11 year olds.

Part of a Series

It is part of a five-book series. Three other books include projects for other year groups.

> *Teaching Primary Programming with Scratch, Year 3*
>
> *Teaching Primary Programming with Scratch, Year 4*
>
> *Teaching Primary Programming with Scratch, Year 5*

If you are interested in the methodology and research-informed practice behind this series as well, as well as a wealth of other insights gained from teaching block-based programming for thousands of hours, then this will be an informative read:

Teaching Primary Programming with Scratch – Research-Informed Approaches.

Permissions

It includes permission to photocopy the pupil worksheets and answer sheets for your class and school. These are clearly marked.

It includes links to example code, project templates and slides to introduce new programming concepts.

Progression

There is a clear, research-informed progression through the series, and the graphic on the next page on a grey background shows which programming concepts are introduced in this book.

Pedagogy in a Few Paragraphs

Introduction to Programming Concepts Away From Code

Pupils are taught key programming concepts away from programming to lower cognitive load and make it easier to transfer these ideas from one programming language to another.

Paired Programming

Pupils are encouraged to work in same ability pairs for some parts of the projects, because this has shown to be particularly helpful for pupils working within or below the expected outcomes.

PRIMM

Pupils are encouraged to read and understand code before they create their own code. We use the PRIMM method in this book.

Predict

Run

Investigate

Modify (change)

Make

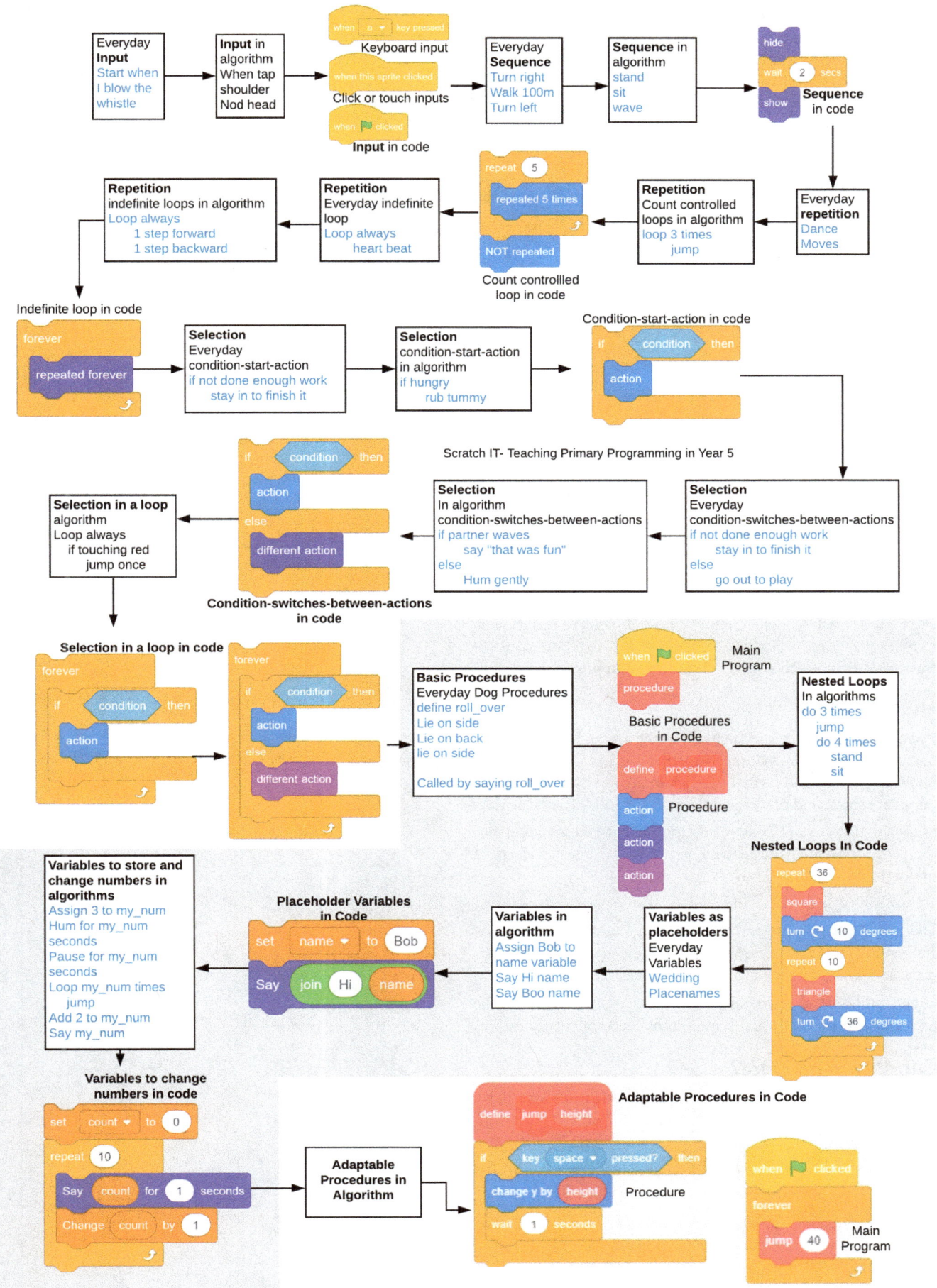

Everyday **Input**
Start when
I blow the whistle

Input in algorithm
When tap shoulder
Nod head

Keyboard input

Click or touch inputs

Input in code

Everyday **Sequence**
Turn right
Walk 100m
Turn left

Sequence in algorithm
stand
sit
wave

Sequence in code

Everyday **repetition**
Dance Moves

Repetition
Count controlled loops in algorithm
loop 3 times
jump

Count controlled loop in code

Repetition
Everyday indefinite loop
Loop always
heart beat

Repetition
indefinite loops in algorithm
Loop always
1 step forward
1 step backward

Indefinite loop in code

Selection
Everyday
condition-start-action
if not done enough work
stay in to finish it

Selection
condition-start-action
in algorithm
if hungry
rub tummy

Condition-start-action in code

Selection
Everyday
condition-switches-between-actions
if not done enough work
stay in to finish it
else
go out to play

Selection
In algorithm
condition-switches-between-actions
if partner waves
say "that was fun"
else
Hum gently

Condition-switches-between-actions in code

Selection in a loop
algorithm
Loop always
if touching red
jump once

Selection in a loop in code

Basic Procedures
Everyday Dog Procedures
define roll_over
Lie on side
Lie on back
lie on side

Called by saying roll_over

Main Program

Basic Procedures in Code

Procedure

Nested Loops
In algorithms
do 3 times
jump
do 4 times
stand
sit

Nested Loops In Code

Variables to store and change numbers in algorithms
Assign 3 to my_num
Hum for my_num seconds
Pause for my_num seconds
Loop my_num times
jump
Add 2 to my_num
Say my_num

Placeholder Variables in Code

Variables in algorithm
Assign Bob to name variable
Say Hi name
Say Boo name

Variables as placeholders
Everyday Variables
Wedding
Placenames

Variables to change numbers in code

Adaptable Procedures in Algorithm

Adaptable Procedures in Code

Procedure

Main Program

Scratch IT- Teaching Primary Programming in Year 5

Creative

Each project provides time and stimulus to be creative in code within the zone of proximal development provided by the taught concepts and explored projects. In other words, it has reasonable projects that can be created independently or with minimum teacher support.

Knowledge

Key knowledge is introduced in the concept introductions and reinforced in each of the activities.

Revisiting Learning

It is important to revisit prior learning, so some modules have questions and activities which revise learning from Year 4 on loops and conditions in Year 5.

Assessment

Summative Assessment

Summative assessment is baked into every stage of the PRIMM process, providing a wealth of data to determine progress.

If you have used earlier versions of these resources on the code-it website, then you will enjoy the new project assessment grid that combines pupils self-assessment and quick teacher assessment, ideally within the lesson.

Self-Assessment

Pupils self-mark to help them see how they have progressed, reducing teachers' workload and enabling teachers to concentrate on the pupils that might need more support.

Hints & Tips

Every pupil's resource also includes a copy of the resource annotated with extra information to further teachers' programming knowledge, hints and formative assessment opportunities in case pupils are stuck, and tips to adapt or support whole class teaching.

Many of these extra hints and tips will not be needed, but the more informed the teacher is the better quality learning opportunity pupils will have.

Yellow highlighted hints and tips are whole class suggestions

Lilac highlighted hints and tips are information to help teachers extend their programming knowledge and sometimes explain why something has been included.

Green highlighted hints and tips are suggestions to help the teacher support individual pupils stuck on a specific question.

Can We Start Here?

If pupils have never programmed with Scratch before a basic introduction project, *Teaching Primary Programming with Scratch, Year 3* is a must.

I would also recommend a single module of count-controlled loops and one on indefinite loops found in

Teaching Primary Programming with Scratch, Year 4

I would also recommend covering conditions using Making Choices and one of the gaming modules found in

Teaching Primary Programming with Scratch, Year 5

Many of the projects include revision questions to remind pupils about prior learning.

Committed to Improvements

HIAS, Hampshire's Inspection & Advisory Service, is committed to developing and improving these resources. We recognize that primary programming is still its infancy in comparison with other subjects, and that new research and primary practice will refine and improve teaching and learning in this area. All royalties earned from this series will be used to write more computing books and revise these resources as needed.

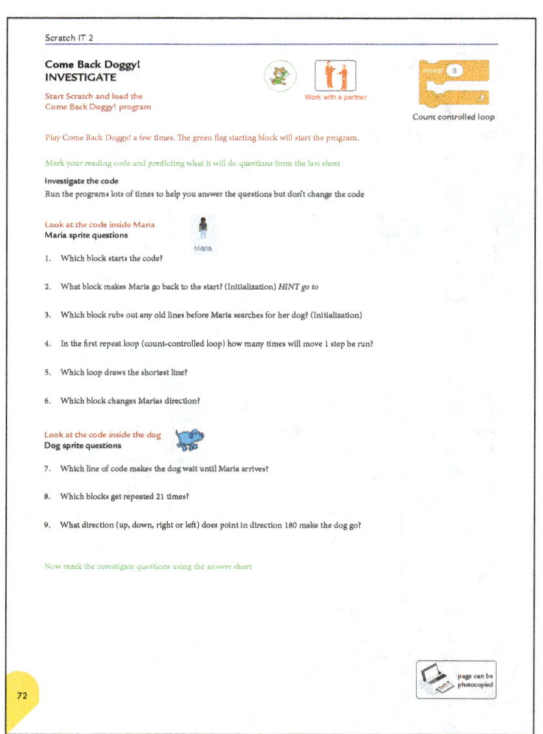

Photocopiable resource for pupils

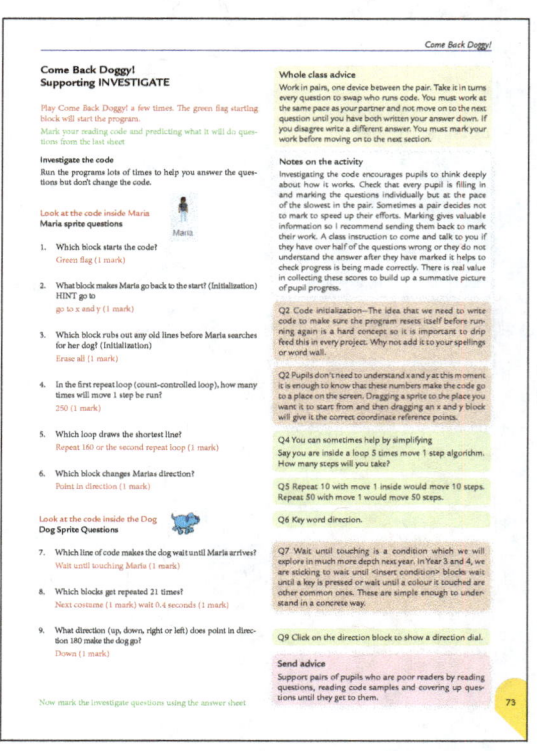

Teacher Hints & Tips on the same photocopiable resource

WE ARE LEARNING ABOUT PROCEDURES AND VARIABLES IN PROGRAMMING

Variables are used to store information to be referred to and changed in a computer programme or algorithm

Variables

Have a name and a value

Algorithms and programs read the name but act on the value

Values can be changed during the algorithm or programme

When writing the value of a variable, we call it assigning

Assign 30 to length variable

Pen down to start drawing

do 4 times

    Move length steps

    Turn right 90 degrees

Pen up to stop drawing

Naming

Always name a variable after the data that it stores or the task that it does

Avoid naming variables with spaces; use teamScore (camelCase) or

user_name (underscore)

Avoid using the same name as a procedure

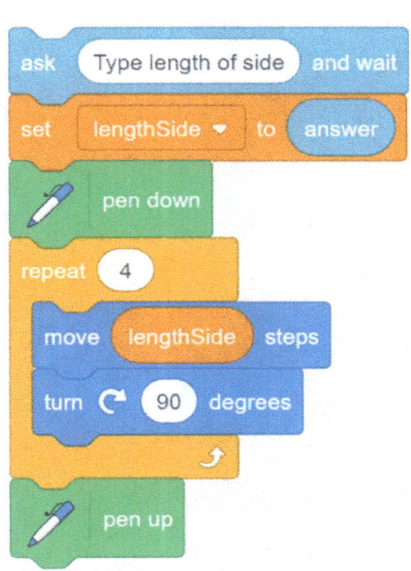

Year 6 Algorithm & Programming

Variables Algorithm

Define walk
Move right leg forward
Wait
Move left leg forward
wait

Everyday Procedures

Loop always
    breathe
    if need to go somewhere
      walk

Main Algorithm
Calls Procedures

Simple Procedures

Have a name

Are called or run by the name

Can be run many times in a programme

Found in My Blocks in Scratch

In Scratch has define first

Naming

Always name a procedure after the task that it does

Avoid naming procedures with spaces

Avoid using the same name as a variable

Procedures are a set of instructions bundled together to complete a part of a program

Define **breathe**
Breathe in
Breathe out

Procedure Algorithm

Variable Vocabulary assign, value **Procedure Vocabulary** define, sub-routine, sub-programme

INTRODUCING NEW CONCEPTS

Introducing Simple Procedures

These slides can be downloaded from the HIAS website https://computing.hias.hants.gov.uk/course/view.php?id=51.

Delivery

They are designed to be delivered to the whole class before pupils move on to using the basic procedures module.

They can also be delivered to a small group or pairs of pupils if they are working independently through resources.

Format

Slides are provided in PDF and PowerPoint formats, and teachers who purchased the book are authorised to adapt the resources within their school or on closed learning platforms such as Seesaw, Google Classroom or Teams, as long as they are not shared outside the school community.

Hints

Extra hints and tips on usage are provided alongside each slide on the following pages.

Resources

Pupils will need whiteboards and pens or paper and pencils.

Knowledge Summary

There is a sheet that summarizes the knowledge gained through these slides and provides a space for pupils to write their own algorithm and flow of control. It can be found on page 11.

Programming Concepts Simplified

Simple Procedures

You will need pen and paper or pen and whiteboard

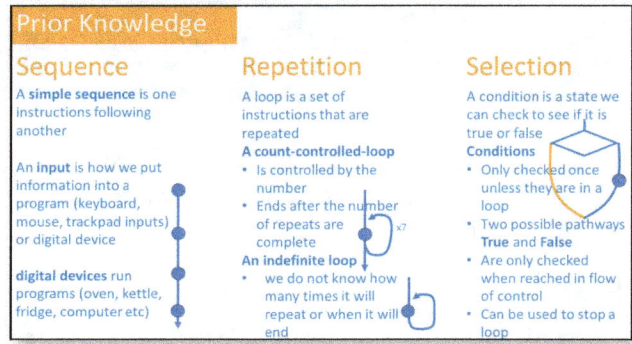

Remind pupils what has been learnt in past years and say they can use this understanding when they come to make things independently. Can they remember the projects they created?

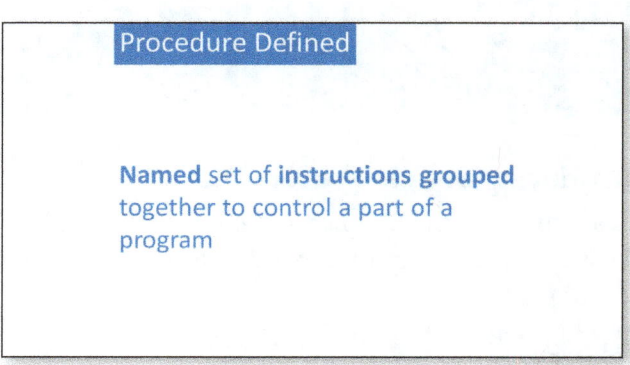

Define what a procedure is before we unpick it in the following slides. Note name and groups of instructions.

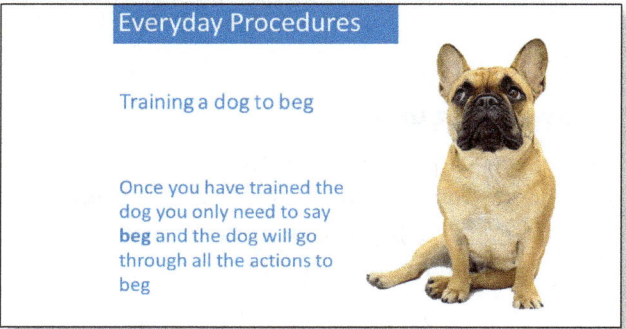

We train our dogs to carry out simple procedures.
These tasks are called by using a single word, in this case beg triggers a complex set of commands that the dog knows.

The beg procedure can be used with your dog as many times as you want. Sure it will get bored eventually or hungry, but other than that it will keep doing it triggered by the word beg.

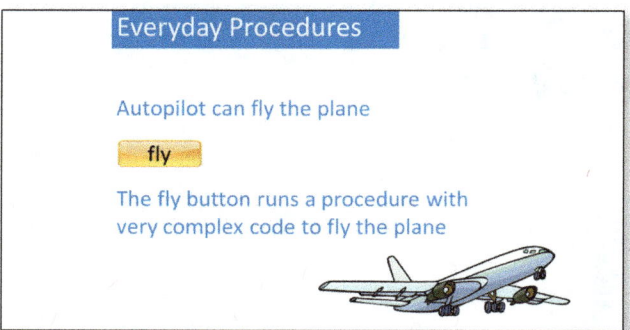

Autopilot is an everyday example of a procedure that they may have heard of. There is a complex programme that controls what airplanes do, but a sets of these instructions are grouped together to keep the plane level. Behind the buttons that start this autopilot is a complex procedure made up of many instructions. To the pilot, it is called by pressing one button.

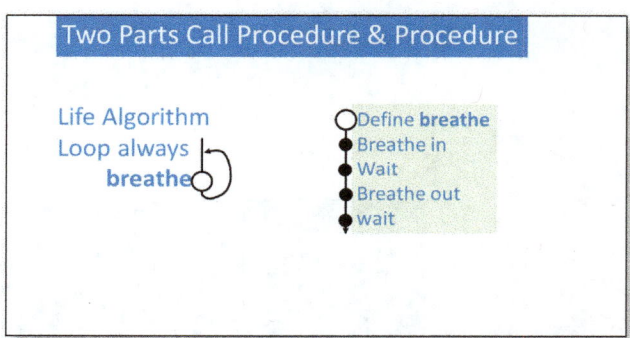

Here we have a simple loop with one command, breathe. This calls the breathe procedure on the right.

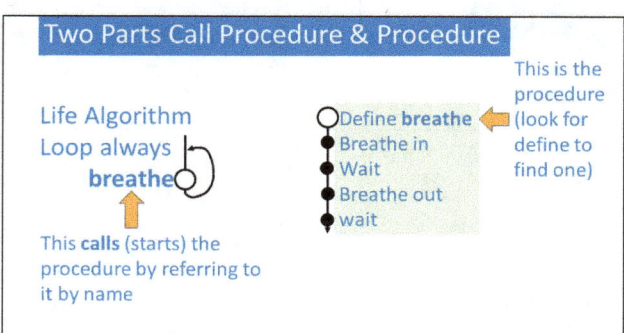

We have chosen to use circles to show where our procedure is called in our algorithm on the left (point to it) and where the procedure it written on the right (point to it).

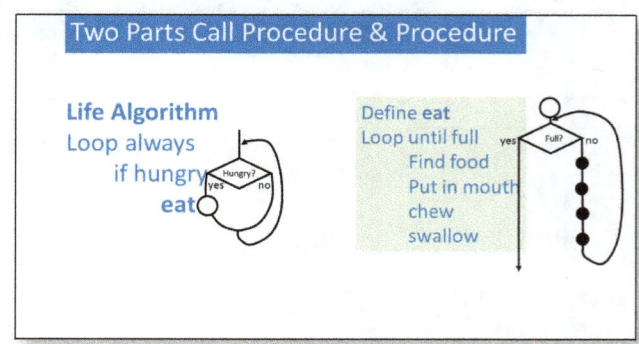

In this example that uses conditions we can see our life algorithm on the left checks if we are hungry. On the right our eat procedure uses a loop ended by a condition. Run through it starting with loop always. Once you have finished the procedure, go back to the life algorithm starting after the procedure and go back round the loop again.

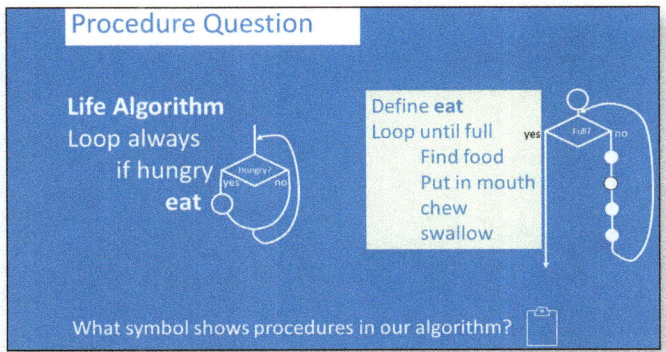

Now for a few questions to see if you were listening.
What symbol shows procedures in our algorithm?

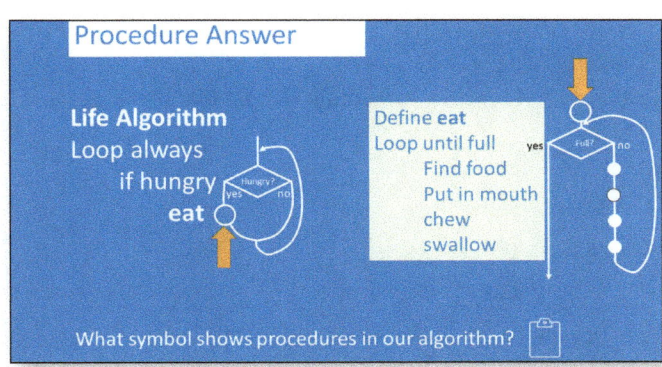

That is right it is the hollow circle.

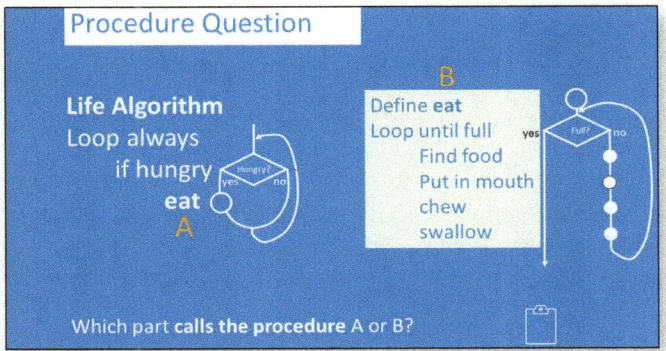

We know there are two parts to a procedure. Calling the procedure and the procedure itself.
Which part calls the procedure A or B?

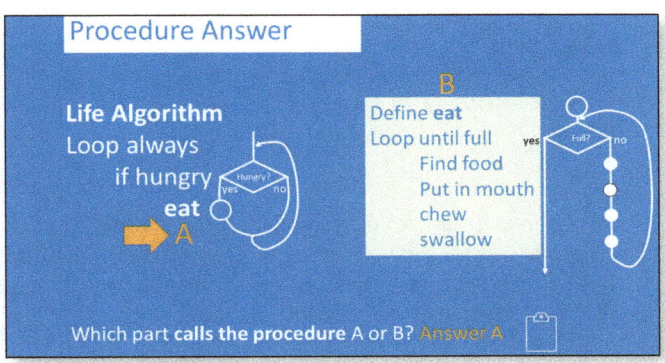

A is the correct answer.

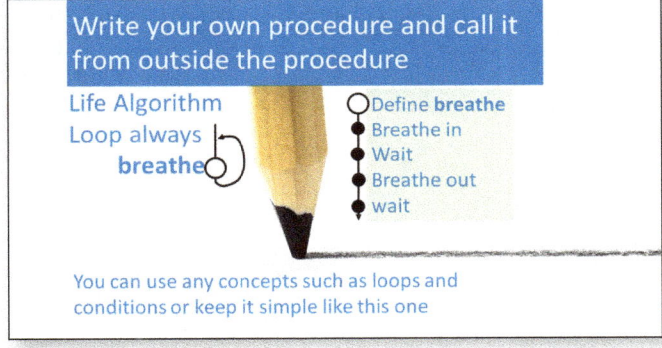

Now write your own algorithm. Make sure it calls the procedure and has a procedure started by define.

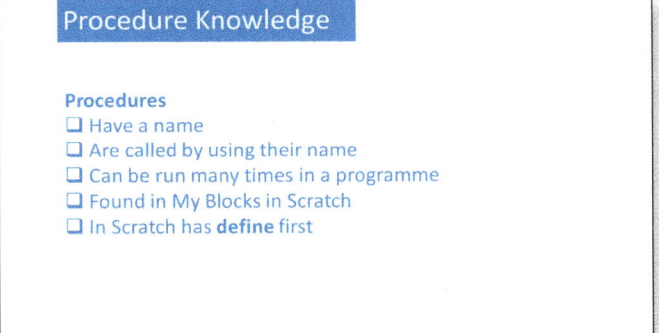

This summarizes the knowledge learnt.

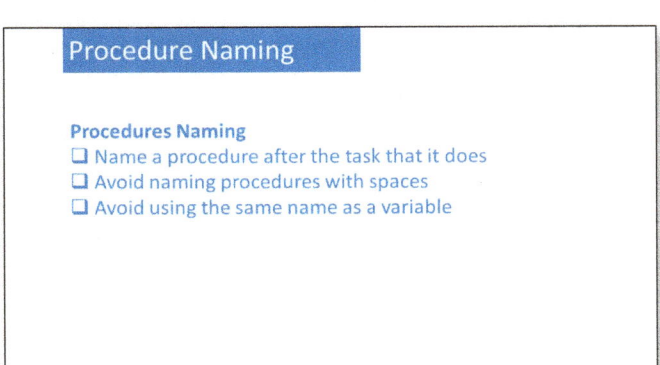

In Scratch you can get away with lots of bad programming practices, but to help us in the future we encourage you to follow these procedure naming practices.

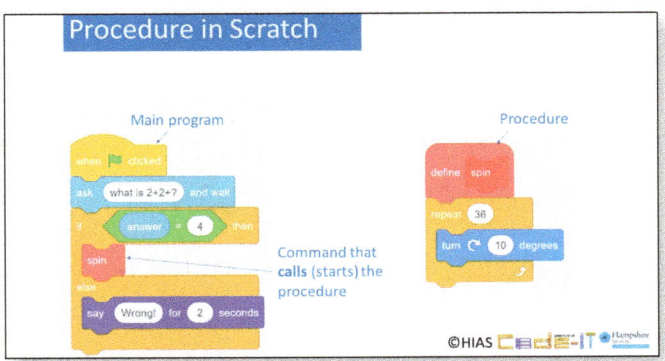

This slide shows what procedures look like in Scratch. Make sure you say how the spin procedure block starts the define spin blocks on the right.

I really recommend that you show the whole class how to make a procedure at this point.

Make sure you make something simple like the example on the right.

To make a procedure

- My blocks
- Make a block
- Where it says block name, type in a name like square.
- Ignore the options at the bottom; they are for more complex procedures.
- Click OK

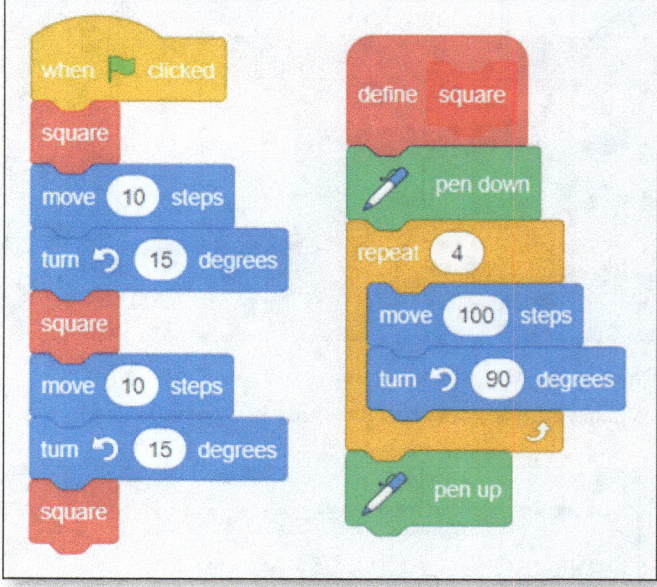

Another way to reinforce procedures is to give a few pupils simple commands to follow every time they hear your trigger word. For example every time you hear the word chicken, stand up and cluck, or every time you hear spin, stand up and spin around once before sitting down. You then speak and occasionally use the keywords calling the procedures. This is good for communicating that procedures can be called more than once.

CHAPTER 2 Nested Loops

Nested Loops

These slides can be downloaded from the HIAS website https://computing.hias.hants.gov.uk/course/view.php?id=51

Delivery

They are designed to be delivered to the whole class before pupils move on to using a nested loop module such as: Nested Loops with Procedures.

They can also be delivered to a small group or pairs of pupils if they are working independently through resources.

Format

Slides are provided in PDF and PowerPoint formats, and teachers who purchased the book are authorized to adapt the resources within their school or on closed learning platforms such as Seesaw, Google Classroom or Teams, as long as they are not shared outside the school community.

Hints

Extra hints and tips on usage are provided alongside each slide on the following pages.

Resources

Pupils will need whiteboards and pens or paper and pencils.

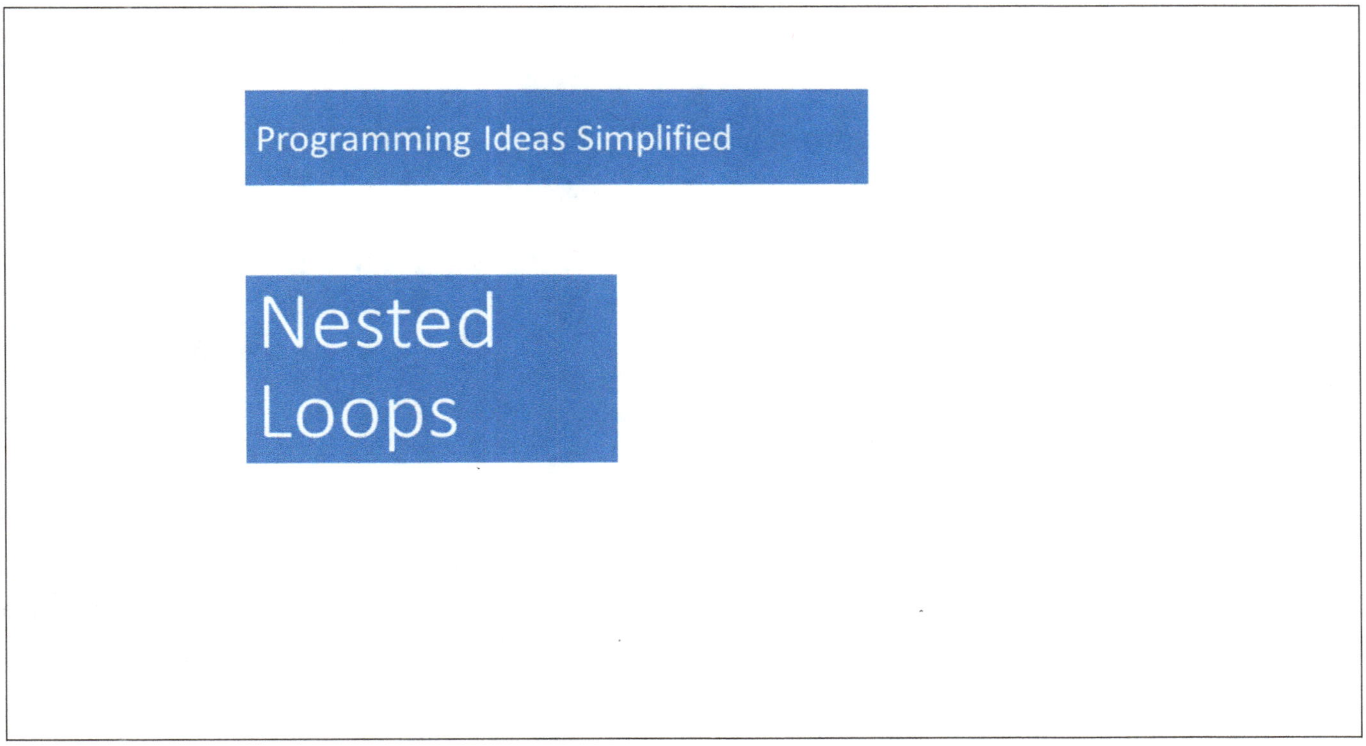
Programming Ideas Simplified
Nested Loops

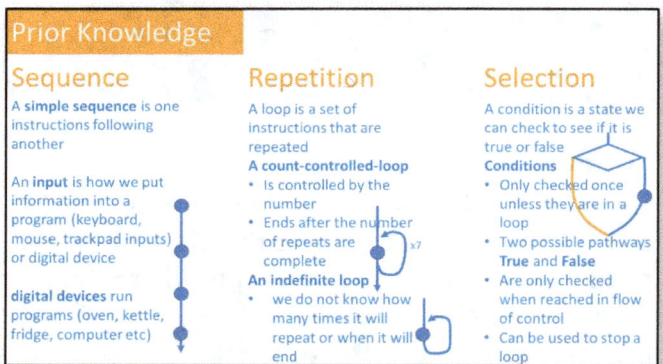

Remind pupils what has been learnt in past years and say they can use this understanding when they come to make things independently. It helps to know the names of the modules they did in previous years.

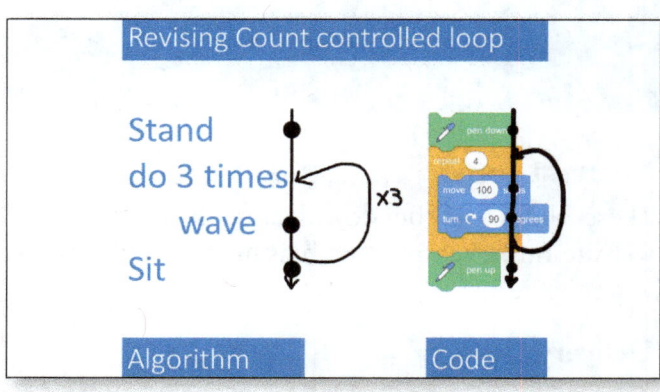

Remind pupils what a count-controlled loop looks like from their work in Year 4.

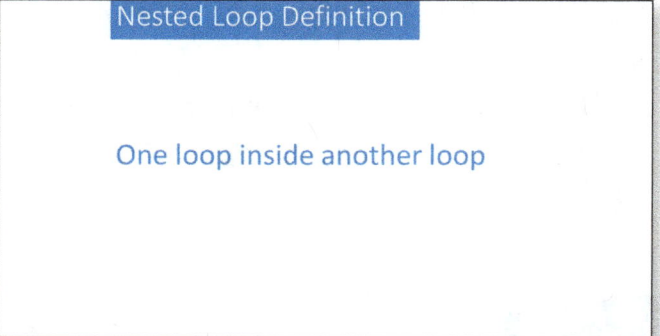

Read this simple definition.

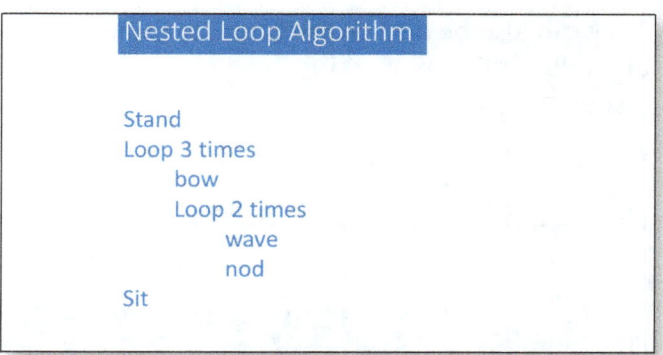

Explain that here we are writing a nested loop algorithm where loop 2 times is inside loop 3 times.

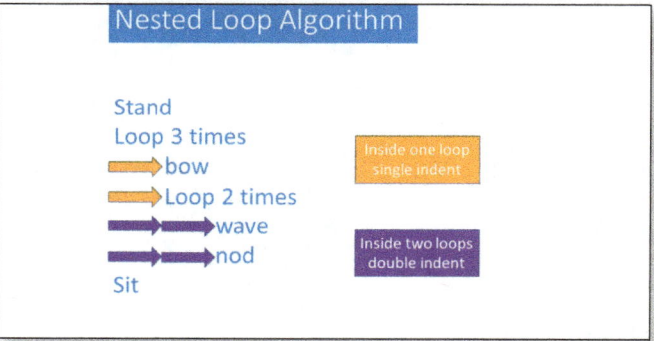

The amount of indents give away which loop is inside and which is outside. In this case, the orange arrows only have one and so are part of the outer loop. There are two purple arrows indents revealing that is part of the inner loop.

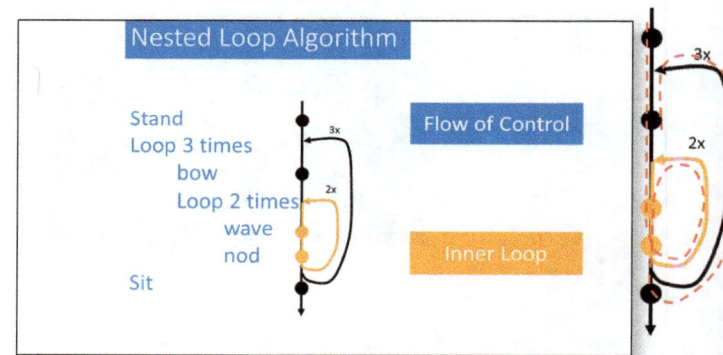

Let us now look at the flow of control. Every one stands which is outside the loop. Then we bow as part of the outer loop then wave and nod and wave and nod through the inner orange loop before back to do the whole thing again three more times before leaving all loops.

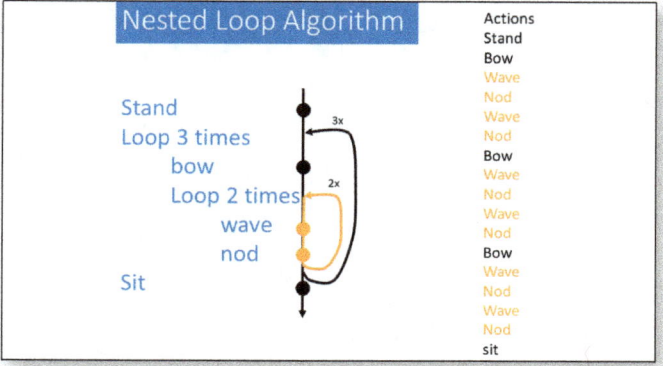

Here is the whole algorithm if changed into a simple sequence. The orange text goes with the inner loop.

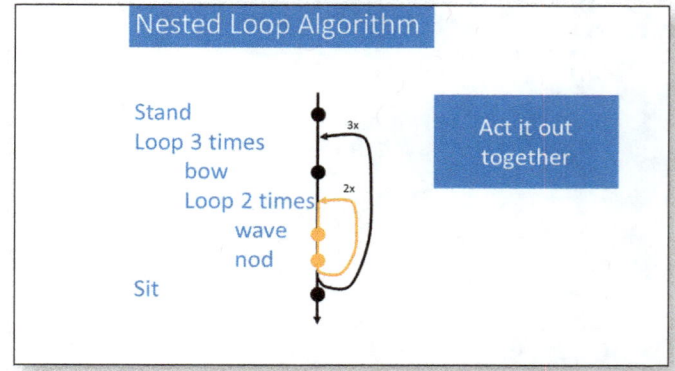

Can you now follow the algorithm to act it out? You can do one with pupils following you, pointing on the board, before doing one themselves.

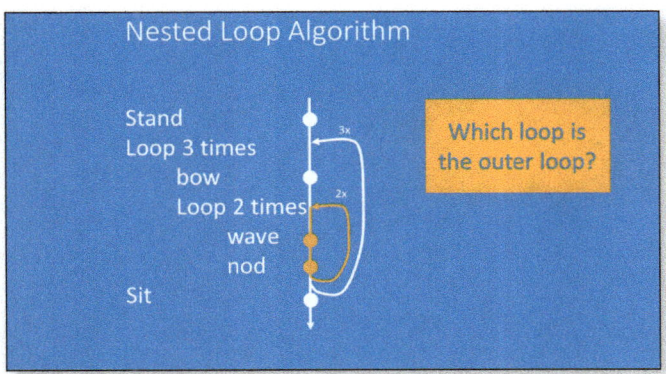

Ask the question

Which loop is the outer loop? 2x or 3x.

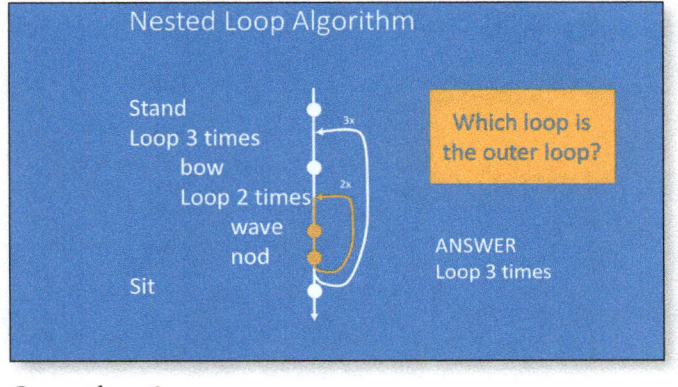

Correct loop 3x.

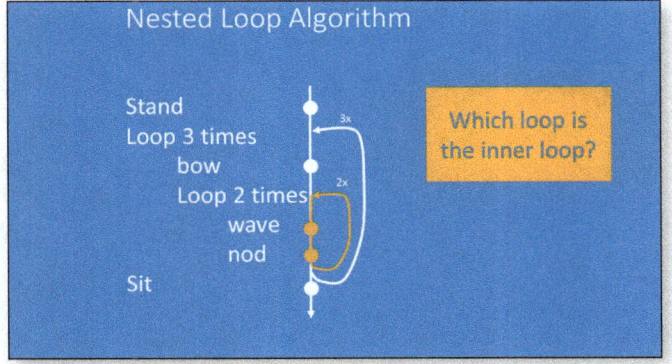

Ask the question

Which loop is the inner loop? 2x or 3x.

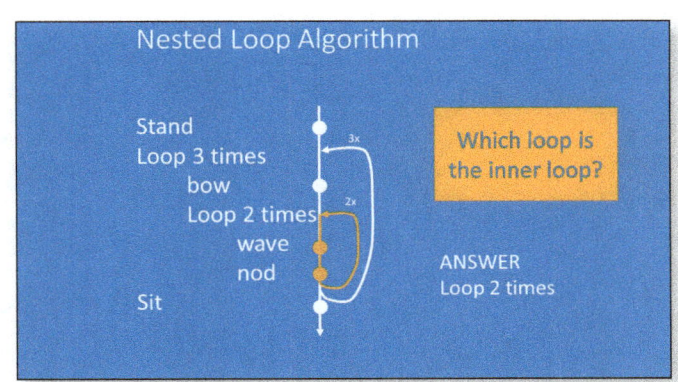

Correct loop 2x.

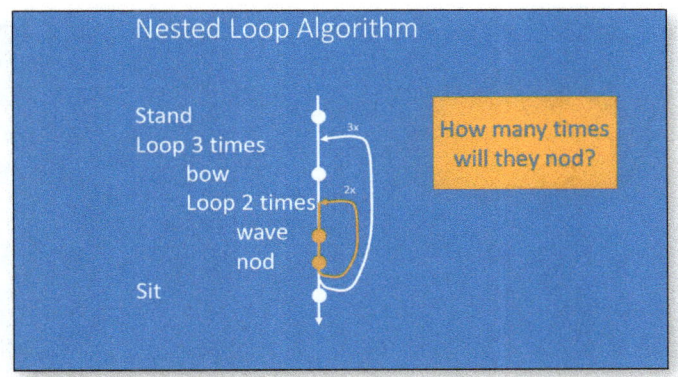

Ask pupils how many loops nod is inside? Answer (2) explain that this means it will multiply both count-controlled loops by each other.

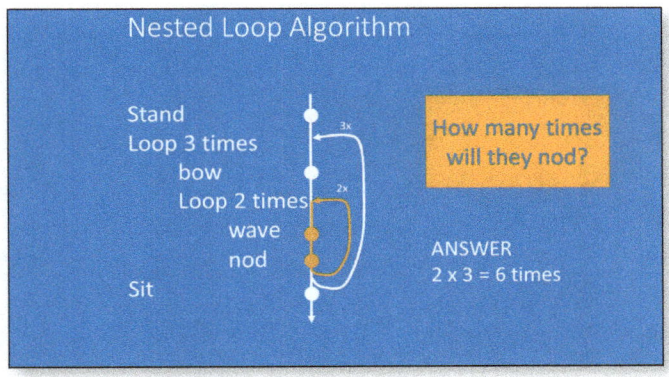

6 times because 2x3=6.

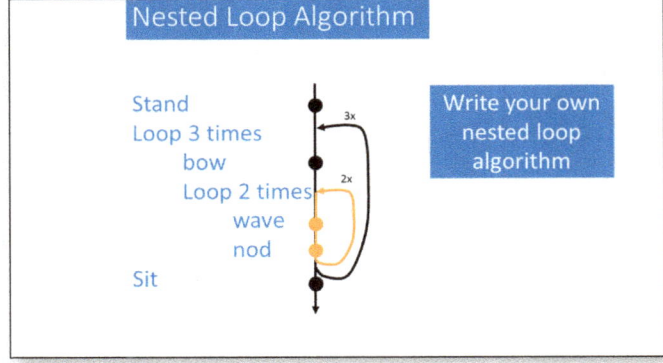

Give pupils a chance to write their own algorithm and read them out to the class.

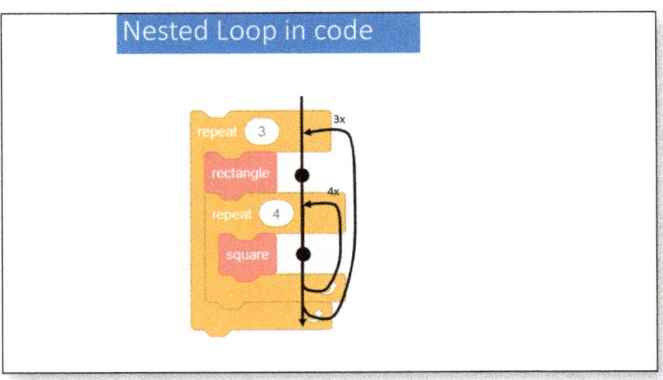

Have a look at a nested loop in code. Is it easier to see the loops in code?

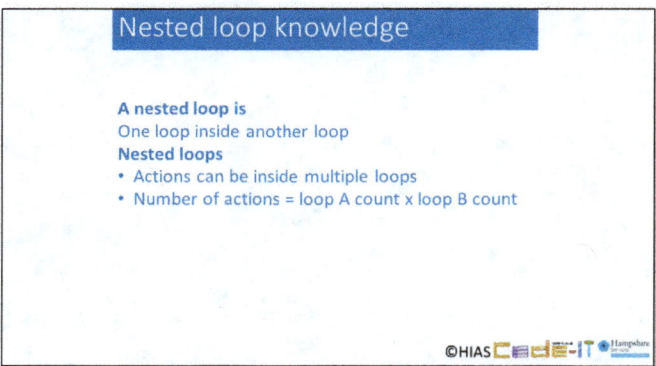

Read the essential knowledge.

Introducing Variables

These slides can be downloaded from the HIAS website https://computing.hias.hants.gov.uk/course/view.php?id=51.

Delivery

They are designed to be delivered to the whole class before pupils move on to using a variable module such as

Variable Fun

Ada Lovelace

Predict the Score

They can also be delivered to a small group or pairs of pupils if they are working independently through resources.

Format

Slides are provided in PDF and PowerPoint formats, and teachers who purchased the book are authorized to adapt the resources within their school or on closed learning platforms such as Seesaw, Google Classroom or Teams, as long as they are not shared outside the school community.

Hints

Extra hints and tips on usage are provided alongside each slide on the following pages.

Resources

Pupils will need whiteboards and pens or paper and pencils.

Knowledge Summary

There is a sheet that summarizes the knowledge gained through these slides and provides a space for pupils to write their own algorithm and flow of control. It can be found on page 11.

Programming Concepts Simplified

Variables

You will need pen and paper or pen and whiteboard

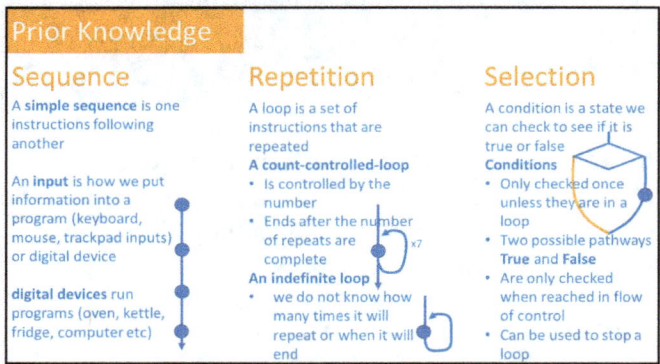

Briefly remind pupils about previous programming concepts.

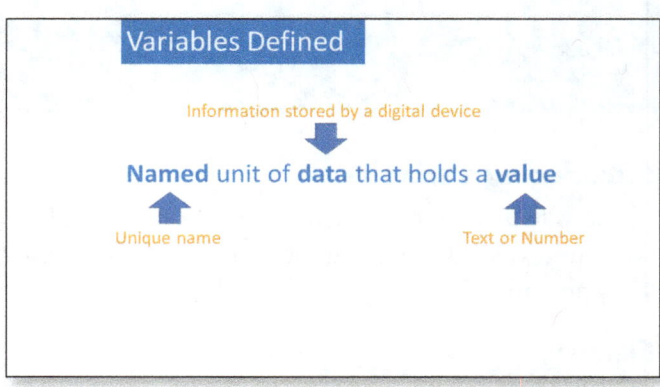

Defining what a variable is before we unpick it in the following slides. Note name, value, data; these three things are very important.

Variables are like whiteboards: we can write on a whiteboard and we can write on a variable.

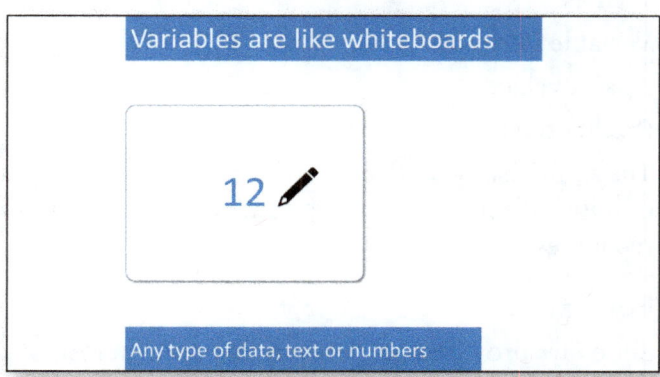

Variables are like whiteboards because we can write text or numbers onto both of them.

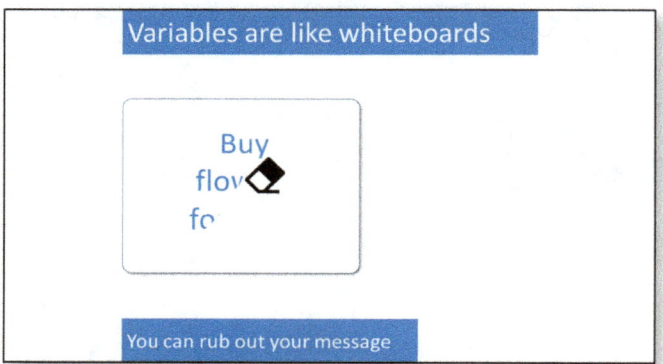

Variables are like whiteboards because we can rub out information on a whiteboard and we can rub out information on a variable.

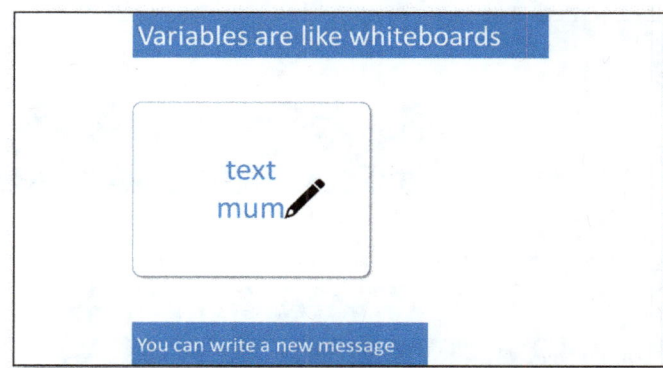

Variables are like whiteboards because once we have rubbed out a message we can write a new message on a whiteboard and we can write a new message on a variable.

To summarize, we can write, rub out and write new information on a whiteboard and a variable.

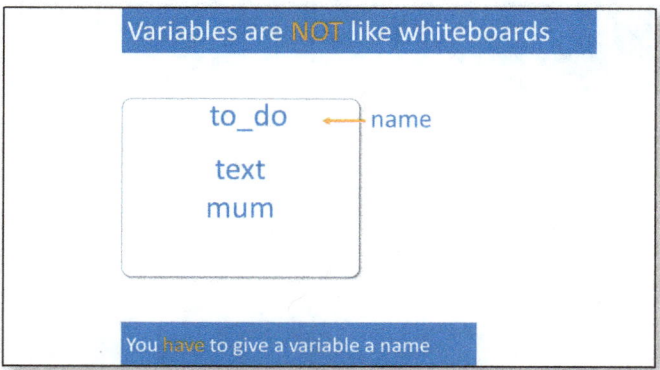

But there is a difference. You don't have to name a whiteboard, but you do have to name a variable.

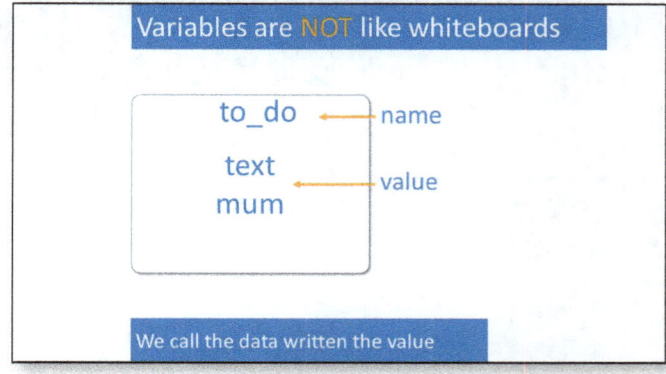

We call the data written on a variable the value. So every variable has both a name and a value.

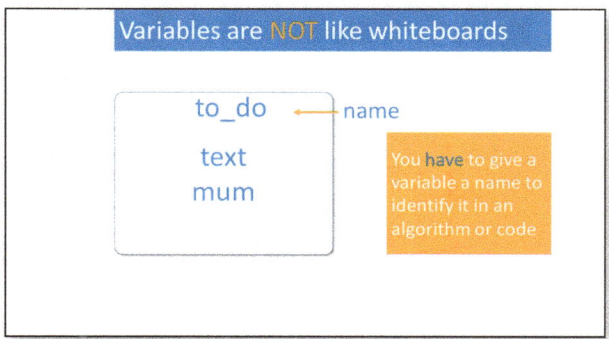

Each variable name has to be unique and it should start with a lowercase letter and be only one word. If you don't give a variable a name, the algorithm or program cannot find it or any value assigned. You can use multiple words in Scratch, but in most other programming languages you can only use one word.

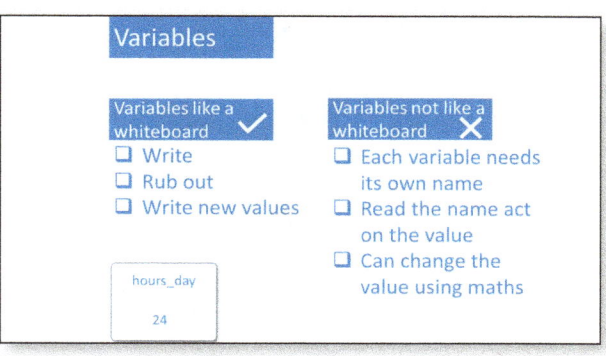

To summarize, we can write, rub out and write new information on a whiteboard and a variable, but only a variable needs a name. Only a variable reads the name but acts on the value. Only a variable can be changed automatically by maths. We will get to these things later.

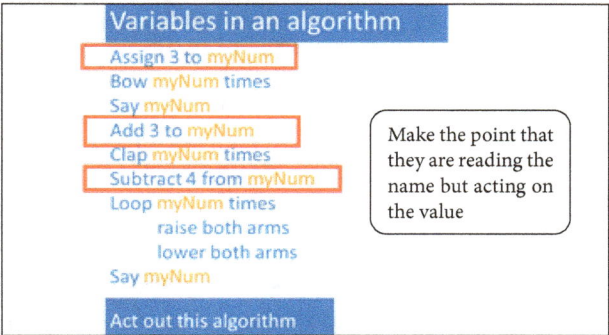

You can go though this first with the whole class writing the variable name and value on a small whiteboard or give them a chance to try it individually first. If anyone gets it wrong, then go through it step by step and every time you get to myNum point back to the value in the small whiteboard before acting on it. Point out where the value is assigned and then added to and subtracted from as outlined in red.

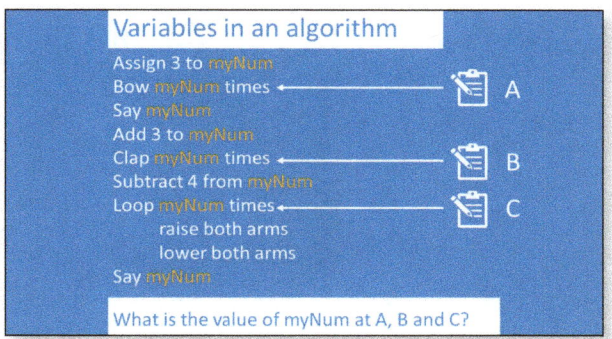

Can they write on their whiteboards A B and C and then say what the value is at each point.

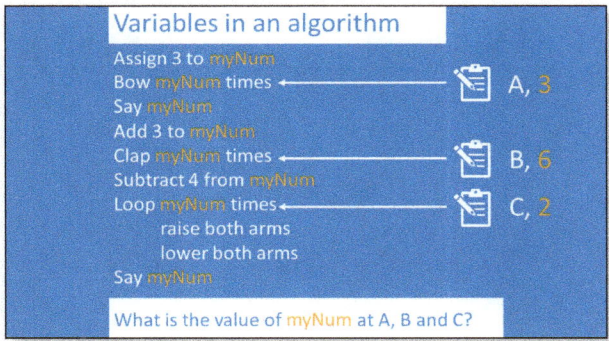

This is the answer to the last slide. Make sure pupils know that these numbers are affected by the addition and subtraction to the variable.

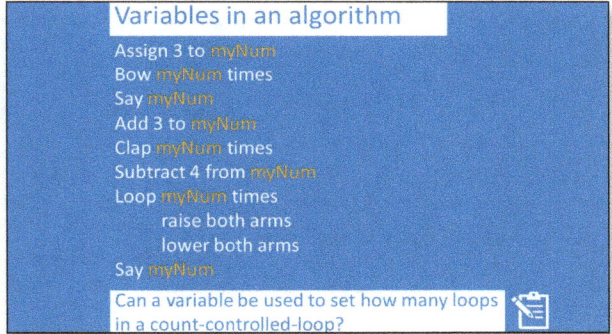

Answers on a whiteboard.

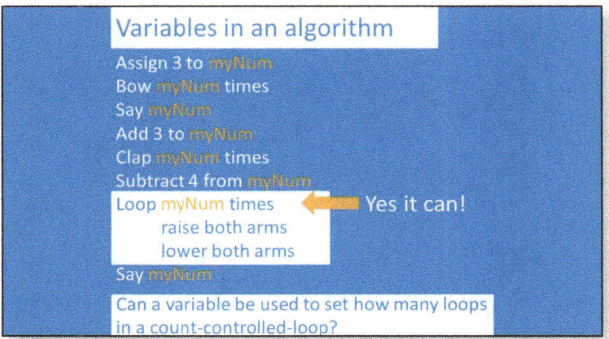

A variable can replace any number or textual value, although we are mainly focusing on number values in this module.

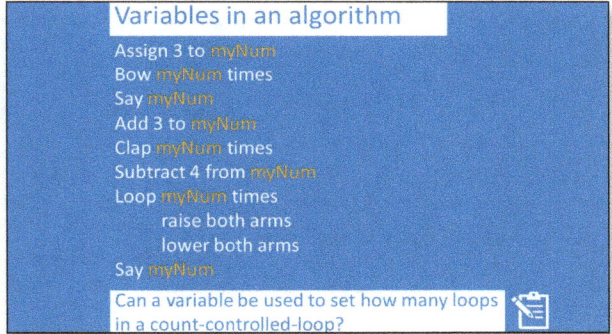

Go through the four things you want them to do. The bullet points on the right. If they are not sure they can adapt your example.

23

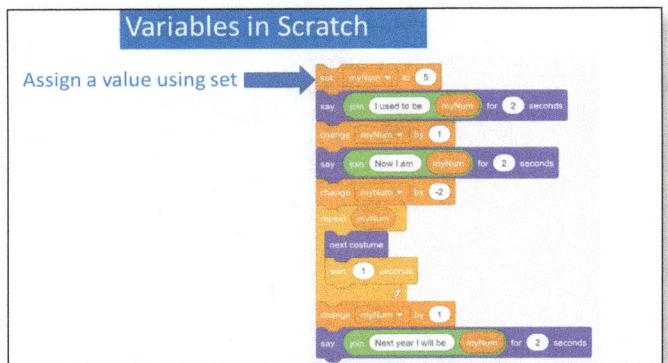

Scratch uses the words set to assign a value to a variable.

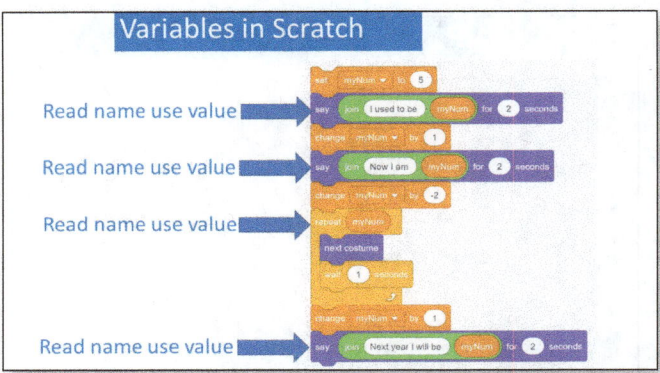

Places Scratch reads the name but uses the value.

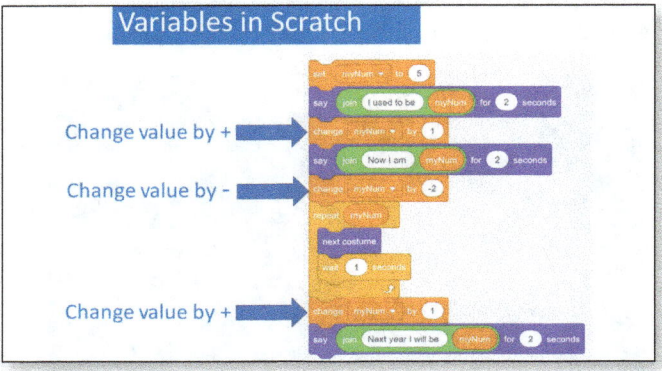

Scratch uses change value to add or subtract from the previous assigned value.

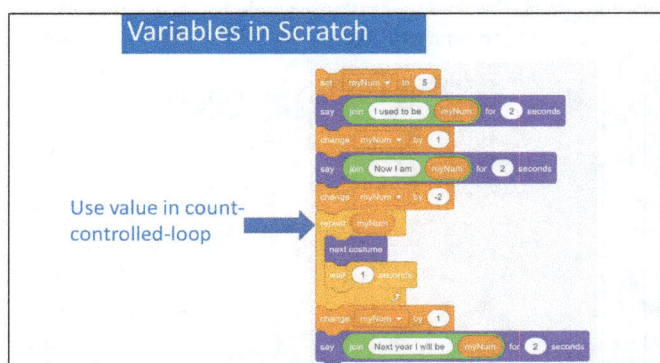

Here the numerical value is used in a count-controlled loop.

It can really help if you then show pupils where to create a variable and demonstrate making one.

To make a variable

- Variable
- Make a variable
- For all sprites

before moving on with the next stage of PRIMM.

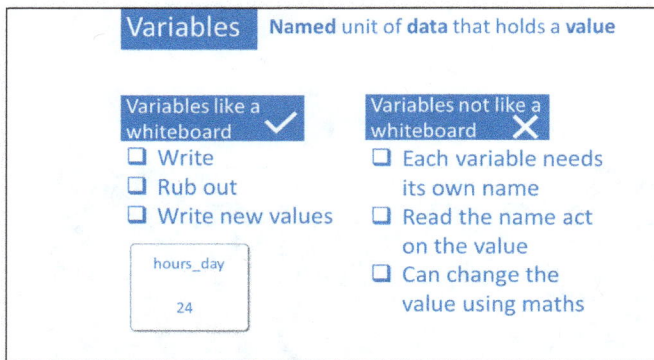

Read this summary of key knowledge.

Introducing Placeholder Variables

These slides can be downloaded from the HIAS website https://computing.hias.hants.gov.uk/course/view.php?id=51.

Delivery

They are designed to be delivered to the whole class before pupils move on to using a placeholder variable module such as

Placeholder variables.

They can also be delivered to a small group or pairs of pupils if they are working independently through resources.

Format

Slides are provided in PDF and PowerPoint formats, and teachers who purchased the book are authorized to adapt the resources within their school or on closed learning platforms such as Seesaw, Google Classroom or Teams, as long as they are not shared outside the school community.

Hints

Extra hints and tips on usage are provided alongside each slide on the following pages.

Resources

Pupils will need whiteboards and pens or paper and pencils.

Knowledge Summary

There is a sheet that summarises the knowledge gained through these slides and provides a space for pupils to write their own algorithm and flow of control. It can be found on page 11.

Programming Concepts Simplified

Placeholder Variables

You will need pen and paper or pen and whiteboard

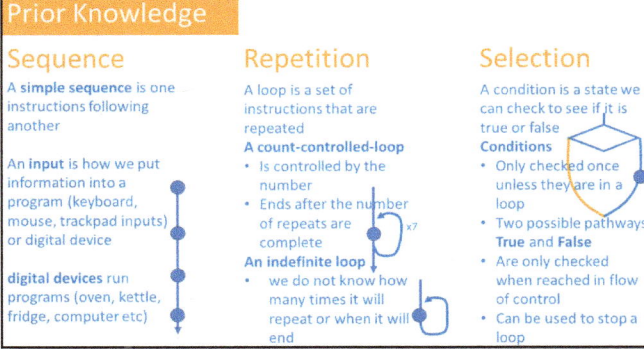

The first slide revises prior knowledge and reminds pupils about the flow of control.

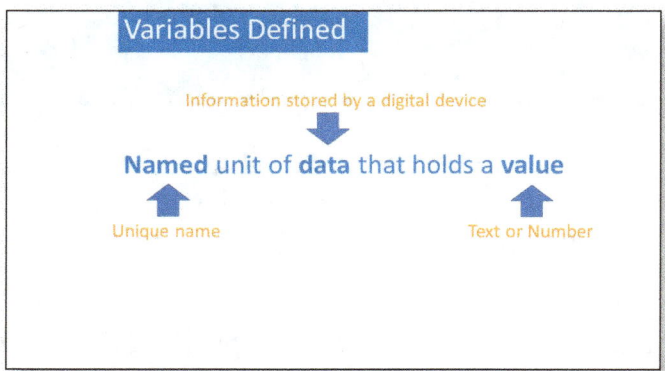

Defining what a variable is before we unpick it it in the following slides. Note name, value, data; these three things are very important.

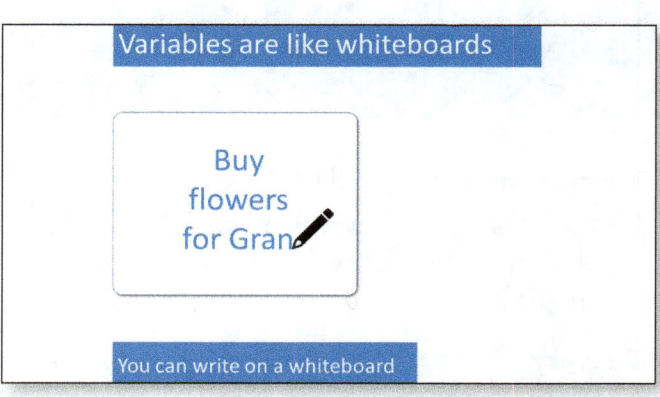

Variables are like whiteboards: we can write on a whiteboard and we can write on a variable.

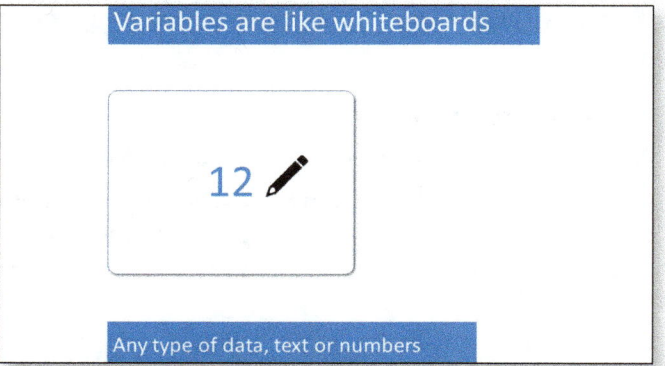

Variables are like whiteboards because we can write text, or numbers onto both of them.

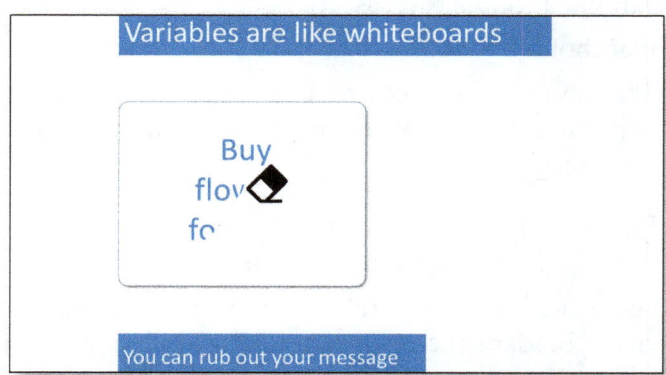

Variables are like whiteboards because we can rub out information on a whiteboard and we can rub out information on a variable.

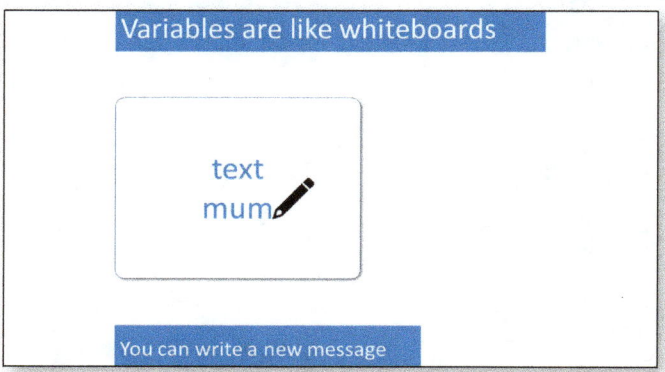

Variables are like whiteboards because once we have rubbed out a message we can write a new message on a whiteboard and we can write a new message on a variable.

To summarize, we can write, rub out and write new information on a whiteboard and a variable.

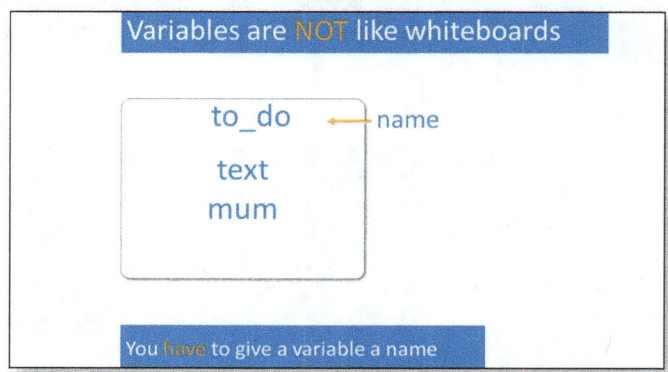

But there is a difference. You don't have to name a whiteboard but you do have to name a variable.

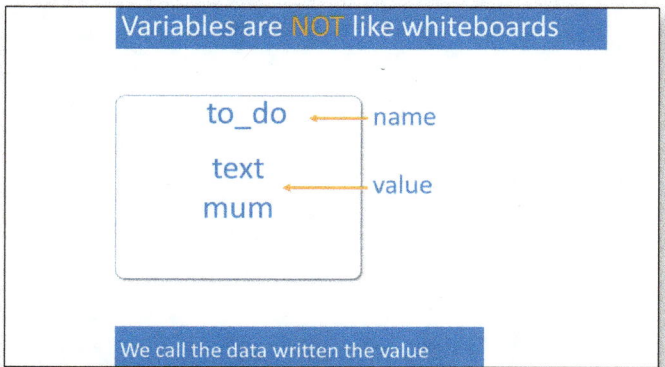

We call the data written on a variable the value. So every variable has both a name and a value.

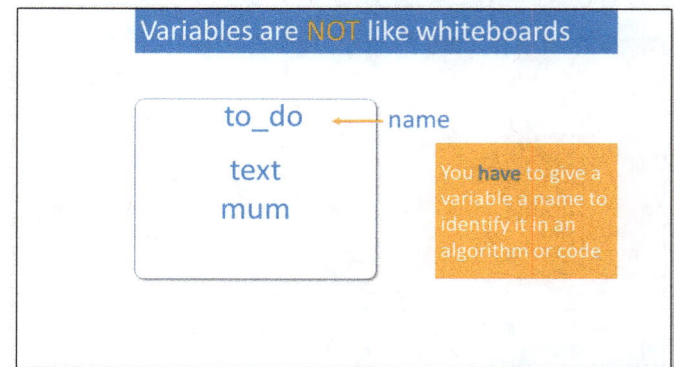

Each variable name has to be unique and it should start with a lower-case letter and be only one word. If you don't give a variable a name, the algorithm or program cannot find it or any value assigned.

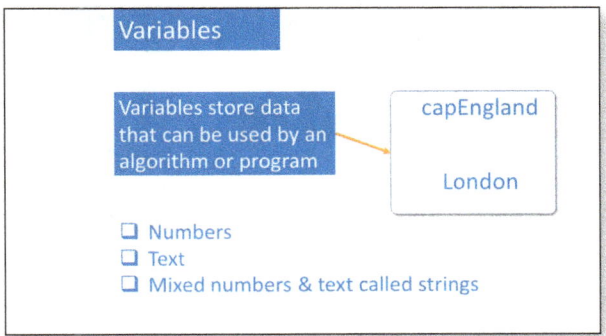

To summarize, we can write, rub out and write new information on a whiteboard and a variable, but only a variable needs a name.

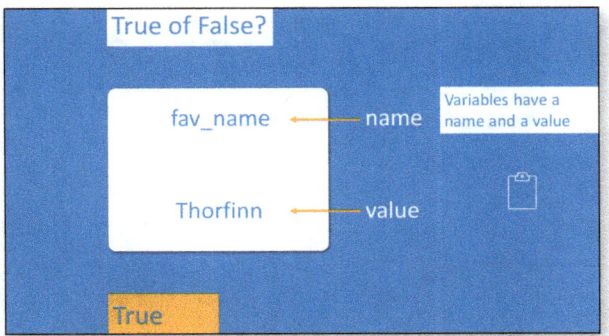

Well done! True is correct.

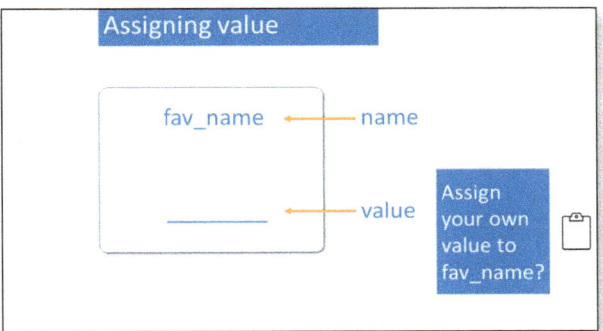

It is your turn now. Write the variable name fav_name and then assign your own value. If you don't have a favourite name, make one up for this exercise.

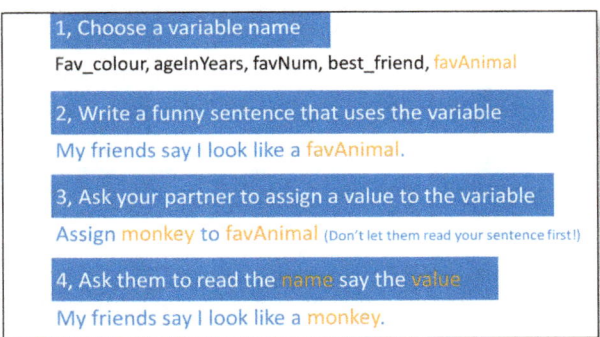

Do this step by step allowing pupils enough time to complete a step before moving on.

1, Choose a variable name and write it down. 2, Write a funny sentence that uses your chosen variable. (Do NOT show your sentence to your partner.) 3, Share what your variable name is and ask your partner to assign a value. 4, Ask them to read the name but say their own value in the sentence.

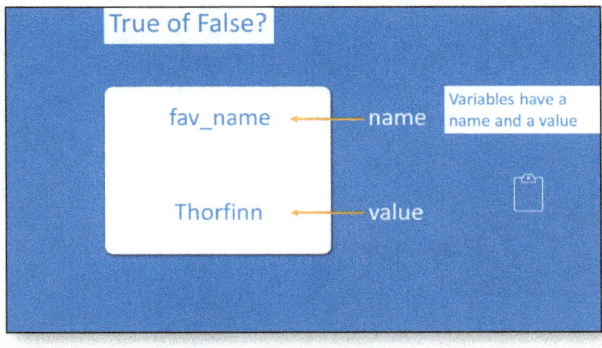

Let us check your understanding. Variables have a name and a value? True or false? Write your answer on a whiteboard.

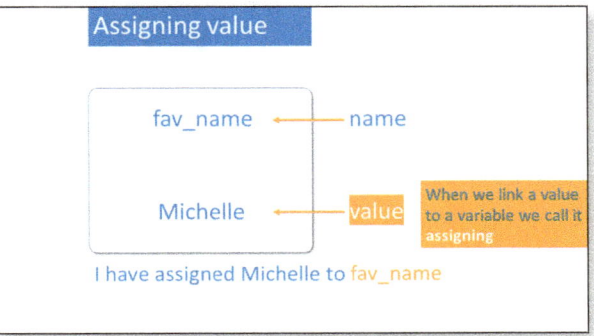

When we link a value to a variable we call this assigning a value. Here I have assigned Michelle to the variable fav_name.

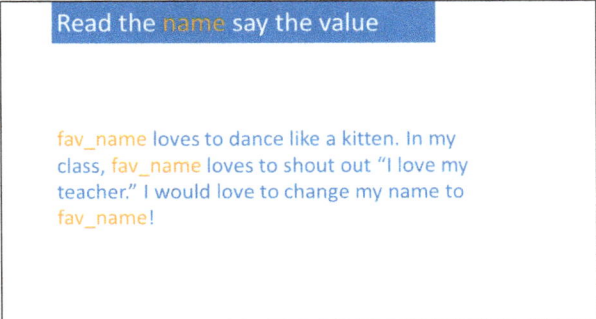

When I read this text every time I get to the fav_name variable I read the name but say the value. So it reads: Michelle loves to dance like a kitten in my class. Michelle loves to shout out. I love my teacher. I would love to change my name to Michelle!

Now read this to your partner, but read your fav_name value not mine.

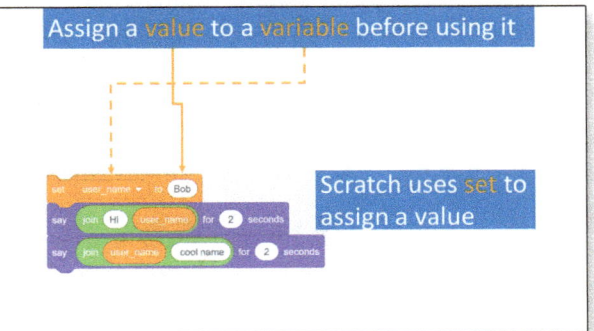

Now let us look at how Scratch uses variables.

The SET block allows us to assign a value. Look at the arrows to see which part of the block is the name and which part is the value. You will need this information soon.

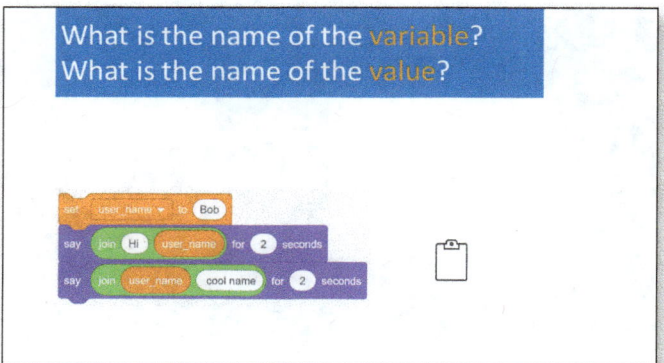

Write down the name of the variable and the value of the variable on your whiteboards.

What is the name of the variable?
What is the name of the value?

Name is user_name

Value is Bob

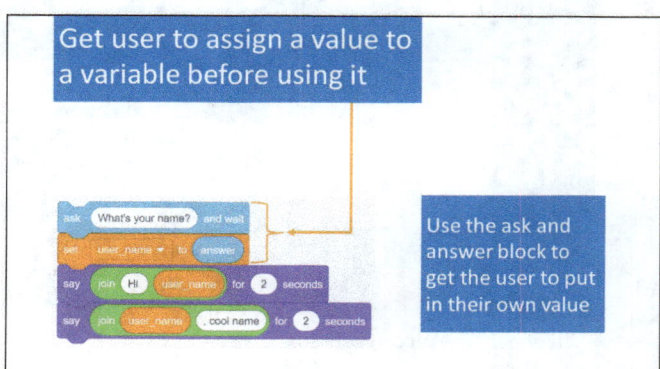

Well done, user_name is the name of the variable and the value is Bob.

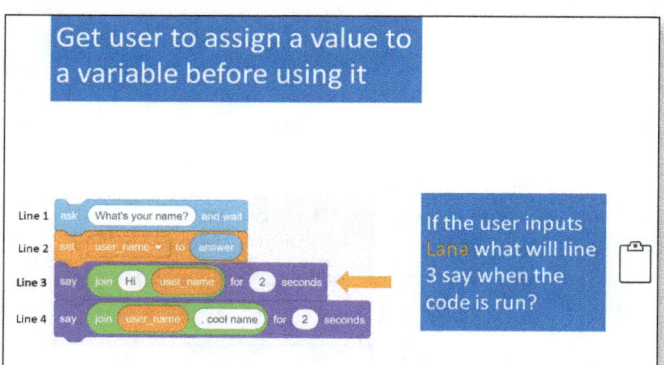

Can you see how Bob is assigned to the variable on the first row. Then we read the name of the variable on the second row, but Scratch shows the value not the name. Just like we did with our funny sentence algorithms just now.

Get user to assign a value to a variable before using it

Use the ask and answer block to get the user to put in their own value

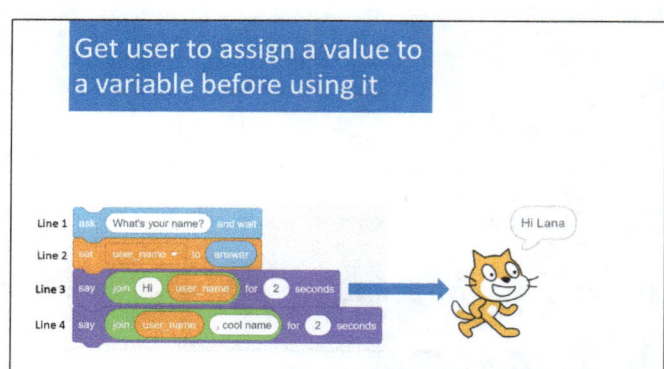

This is even better. We can get the user to assign a value to the variable through the ask and answer input blocks. So on line one, whatever the user typed into the input box is assigned to answer. On line two, the value of answer is assigned to our variable called user_name. Now whenever we use user_name the value assigned by the user will be used.

Get user to assign a value to a variable before using it

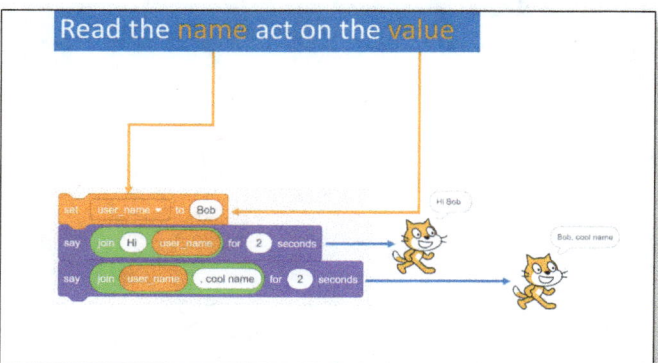

If the user inputs Lana what will line 3 say when the code is run?

If the user inputs Lana, what will line three say when the program is run? Answers on your whiteboards.

Get user to assign a value to a variable before using it

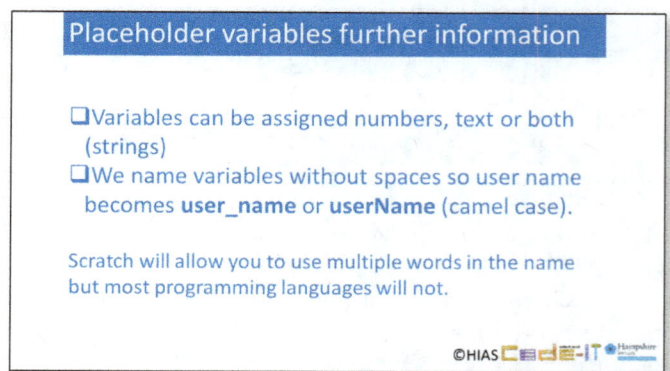

Well done, however, you only get the mark if you wrote Hi Lana, as the text and variable value are combined.

Placeholder variables key information

☐ Variables store data
☐ Variables have a name and a value
☐ Assign a value before using a variable
☐ Read the name act on the value
☐ You can get the user to assign a value to a variable

Read this summary.

Placeholder variables further information

☐ Variables can be assigned numbers, text or both (strings)
☐ We name variables without spaces so user name becomes **user_name** or **userName** (camel case).

Scratch will allow you to use multiple words in the name but most programming languages will not.

©HIAS Code-iT

Read this summary. Whatever project you are doing, I recommend that you demonstrate how to make a variable in Scratch.

PROGRAMMING MODULE THAT USES SIMPLE PROCEDURES

CHAPTER 5 — Basic Procedures

Overview

Pupilx explore how procedures can be used to create fabulous drawing patterns, before creating their own.

To do before the session

1. Look at the grid below and decide which optional and SEN activities you are going to include and exclude.
2. Print pupil worksheets for each activity chosen and staple into a booklet, one for each pupil.
3. Print marksheets for activities chosen to be placed where pupils can access them.
4. Download the code needed and place in a templates folder on your school network or add to a Scratch Studio or link on your learning platform.
5. Download the slides that go with the concept introduction.
6. Study the notes that go with the slides.
7. Examine the teacher help notes that are provided alongside every activity.

To do at the start of the session

If you have not introduced **simple procedures** with this class before, do this first using the resources on page 15 as a whole class activity.

To do after the concept has been introduced

Each activity has whole class notes to help you explain what is needed if it is the first time pupils have carried out this type of activity. There are also core instructions underneath in case you are sticking to the core activities only.

How this module fits into a programming progression

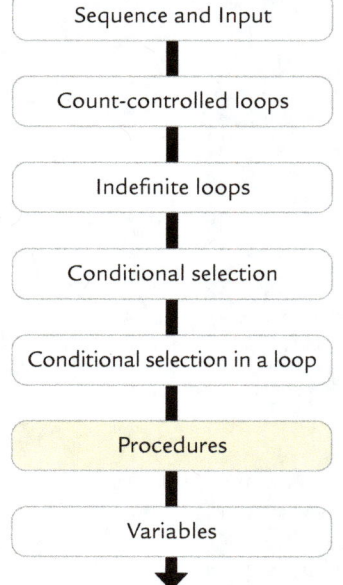

Sequence and Input

Count-controlled loops

Indefinite loops

Conditional selection

Conditional selection in a loop

Procedures

Variables

Vocabulary

Procedure, task, name, call a procedure

Resource Name	Core Optional SEN	Teacher	Pupil Grouping	How Assessed	SCRATCH ACCESS
CONCEPT Simple procedures	CORE	Leads Session	Solo whole class activity	Formative	NO
PARSONS	OPTIONAL SEN OPTIONAL ALL (predict or parsons not both)	Support Poor Readers	Solo or Paired (Teacher choice)	Pupil Marked Marksheet Provided	YES Exploring Basic Procedures Parsons
FLOW	OPTIONAL ALL If you do predict I recommend you do flow first	Can be done as a Whole Class or with a Large Group	Solo or Paired (Teacher Choice)	No Marked Outcome	NO
PREDICT	OPTIONAL ALL (predict or parsons not both)	Support Poor Readers	Paired	Pupil Marked Marksheet Provided	NO
INVESTIGATE	CORE	Support Poor Readers	Paired	Pupil Marked Marksheet Provided	YES Exploring Basic Procedures
CHANGE	CORE	Support Poor Readers	Paired	Pupil Marked Marksheet Provided	YES Exploring Basic Procedures
CREATE	CORE	Assesses Pupil Work and Checks Pupil Self-Assessment	Solo	Pupil Assessed & Teacher Assessed	YES Exploring Basic Procedures

Core activities general instructions

1. Group pupils in roughly same ability pairs. For **investigate** and **change** worksheets, pupils will work in pairs, for **create** they will work separately.

2. Give out the pupil booklets and explain that pupils need to follow the instructions on the sheets to explore how **basic procedures** work.

3. Explain that each pupil will record separately while working alongside their partner and keeping to the same pace as their partner.

4. Demonstrate where they can find the template code and explain that pupils will share one device for investigate and change.

5. Explain that during each question only one person should touch the shared device and they should swap who that person is when there is a new questions.

6. Encourage them to discuss their answers with their partner. If they disagree with their partner, they can record a different answer in their own booklet.

7. Show pupils where it says they should mark their work on the sheet and where the answer sheets are in the classroom.

8. Remind pupils to return marksheets after marking, because there are not enough for every pair to have their own.

Key Programming Knowledge
A procedure is a small section of a program that performs a specific task.

Simple Procedures
Have a name
Are called or run by the name
Can be run many times in a programme
Found in My Blocks in Scratch
In Scratch has define first

Naming
Always name a procedure after the task that it does
Avoid naming procedures with spaces
Avoid using the same name as a variable

Resources

Exploring basic procedures https://scratch.mit.edu/projects/312212285/

Parsons Exploring basic procedures https://scratch.mit.edu/projects/623333620/

	On the sheet, if it says no Scratch, they must work only on the sheet.
	If it says Scratch with a green tick, they can use one device between the pair.
	If it says work with a partner, they must work at the same speed as their partner.
	If it says work on their own, they must do this using a separate device each working alone.

English Computing National Curriculum Programs of Study

Pupils should be taught to:

- **design, write and debug programs that accomplish specific goals**, including controlling or simulating physical systems; solve problems by decomposing them into smaller parts.

- **use sequence,** selection and **repetition in programs;** work with variables **and various forms of input and output**

- **use logical reasoning to explain how some simple algorithms work and to detect and correct errors in algorithms and programs**

Scottish Curriculum for Excellence Technologies
I understand the instructions of a visual programming language and can predict the outcome of a program written using the language. TCH 1-14a

I can explain core programming language concepts in appropriate technical language TCH 2-14a

I can demonstrate a range of basic problem solving skills by building simple programs to carry out a given task, using an appropriate language. TCH 1-15a

I can create, develop and evaluate computing solutions in response to a design challenge. TCH 2-15a

Welsh National Curriculum Relevant Strands
Progression Step 3.

- I can use conditional statements to add control and decision-making to algorithms.

- I can explain and debug algorithms.

BASIC PROCEDURES PARSONS

Start Scratch and load Parsons exploring basic procedures

Work with a partner

Basic Procedures

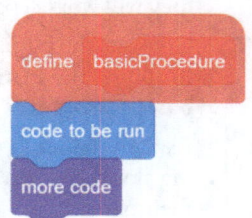

Use the algorithm below to help you connect the Scratch blocks in the correct places in the Parsons exploring basic procedures.

Main Program

Start

Point right

go to x –130 y 0

Clear all old lines

square procedure

Move forward 60

square procedure

Move forward 80

Do 5 times

    Right 72 degrees

    eqi_triangle procedure

    Pause 1/2 second

Procedures

define eqi_triangle	define square
Start drawing pen down	Start drawing pen down
loop 3	loop 4
move 50 forward	move 30 forward
right 120 degrees	right 90 degrees
stop drawing pen up	stop drawing pen up

Now mark your work using the Parsons marksheet

SUPPORTING PARSONS

Whole class advice

Load Parsons exploring basic procedures code and then use the algorithm on this page to build the code. When you have completed it, run the code and check your answer with the marking sheet.

Send advice

Parsons problems can be made less complex by connecting more blocks in the example Scratch code and saving that version as a new template.

Understanding programming

You can find out more about Parsons problems in the teacher book that accompanies this series.

Individual advice

Point out that the code inside a loop is indented in the planning algorithm and in the code. This can help some pupils connect those aspects in both.

Use the algorithm below to help you connect the Scratch blocks in the correct places in the Parsons exploring basic procedures

Notes on the activity

This allow pupils to build part of the code first before investigating, modifying and creating code of their own. The algorithm is written in language similar but also different to the code. This helps pupils by enabling them to see an example of planning which will help them when they come to plan their own project. On its own, it is not enough deep thinking about the code to enable agency, but as a starter or SEN activity it is useful to see how code can be built.

Able advice

Parsons problems can be made more complex by separating more blocks in the example Scratch code and saving that version as a new template.

Procedures

define eqi_triangle	define square
Start drawing pen down	Start drawing pen down
loop 3	loop 4
move 50 forward	move 30 forward
right 120 degrees	right 90 degrees
stop drawing pen up	stop drawing pen up

Main Program
Start
Point right
go to x –130 y 0
Clear all old lines
square procedure
Move forward 60
square procedure
Move forward 80
Do 5 times
   Right 72 degrees
   eqi_triangle procedure
   Pause 1/2 second

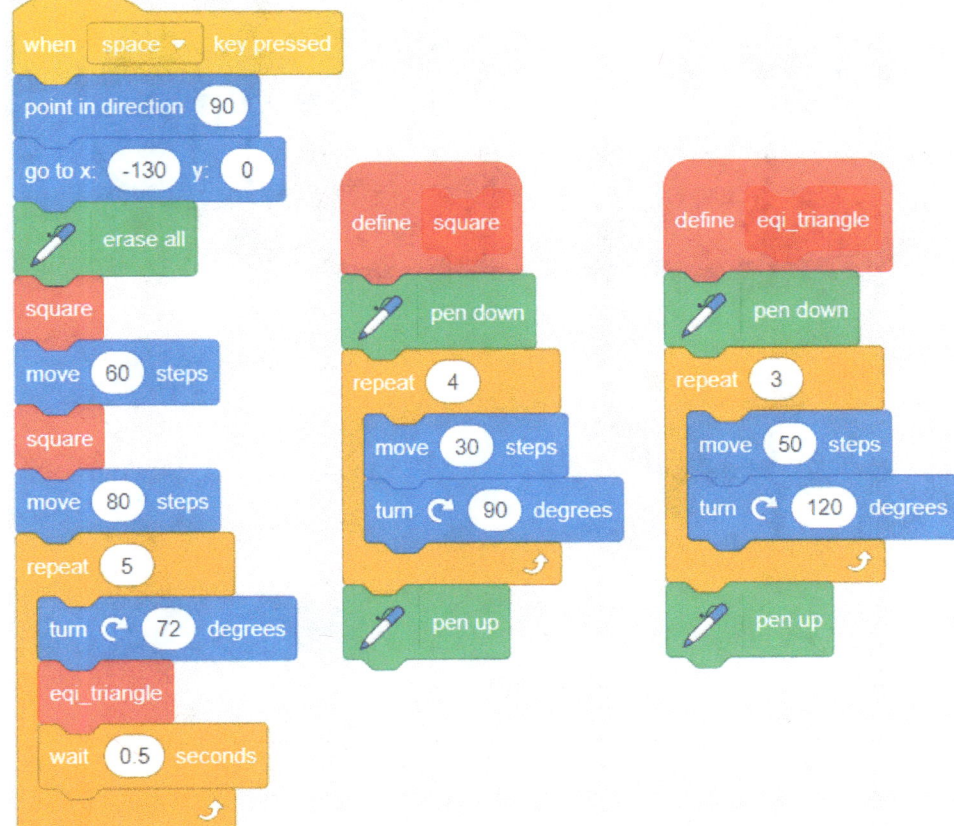

BASIC PROCEDURES

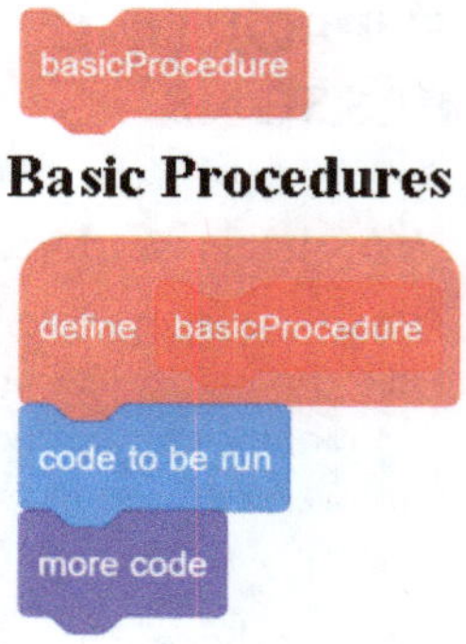

FLOW

Read the code carefully with your partner and follow the order the code is run. Make sure you jump over to the procedure when it is started in the main programme.

Work with a partner

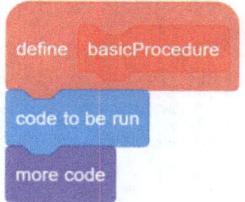
Basic Procedures

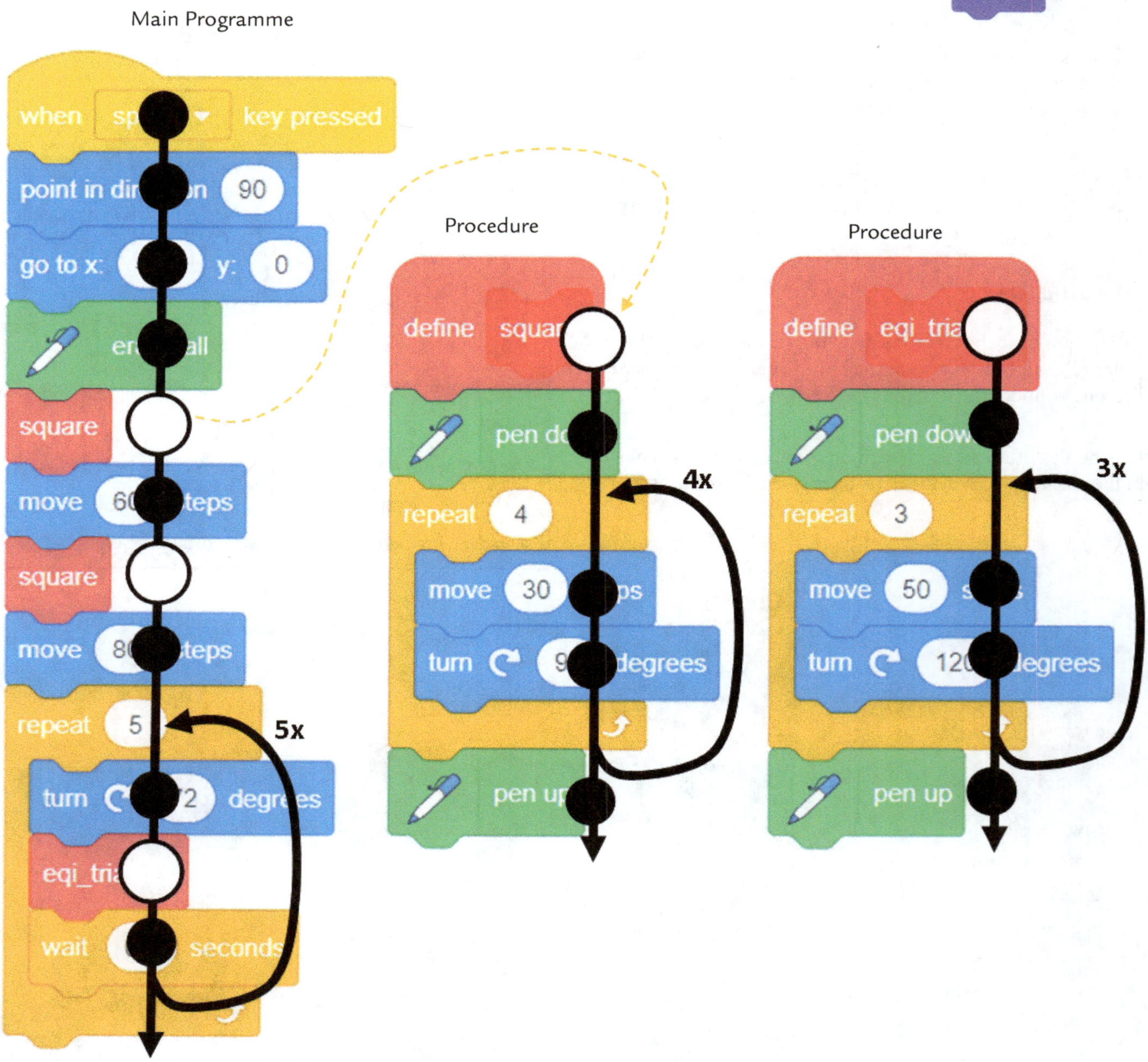

Main Programme

when space key pressed
point in direction 90
go to x: y: 0
erase all
square
move 60 steps
square
move 80 steps
repeat 5   **5x**
turn 72 degrees
eqi_tria
wait seconds

Procedure

define squar
pen down
repeat 4   **4x**
move 30 steps
turn 90 degrees
pen up

Procedure

define eqi_tria
pen down
repeat 3   **3x**
move 50 steps
turn 120 degrees
pen up

photocopiable page

SUPPORTING FLOW

Read the code carefully with your partner and follow the order the code is run. Make sure you jump over to the procedure when it is started in the main programme.

Whole class instructions

Look at this code carefully. Trace the flow of the code, making sure that when you get to one of the empty circles you make sure you find and go through the flow of control for the procedure before coming back to the main programme. The dashed orange line shows you how for the first one.

Notes on the activity

This activity builds on the concept introduction and is a great activity to do before predicting what the code does. There is no marked outcome, so make sure pupils work through it carefully. It can be done as a whole class.

Send advice

Some pupils will really benefit from going through this in a small group with you.

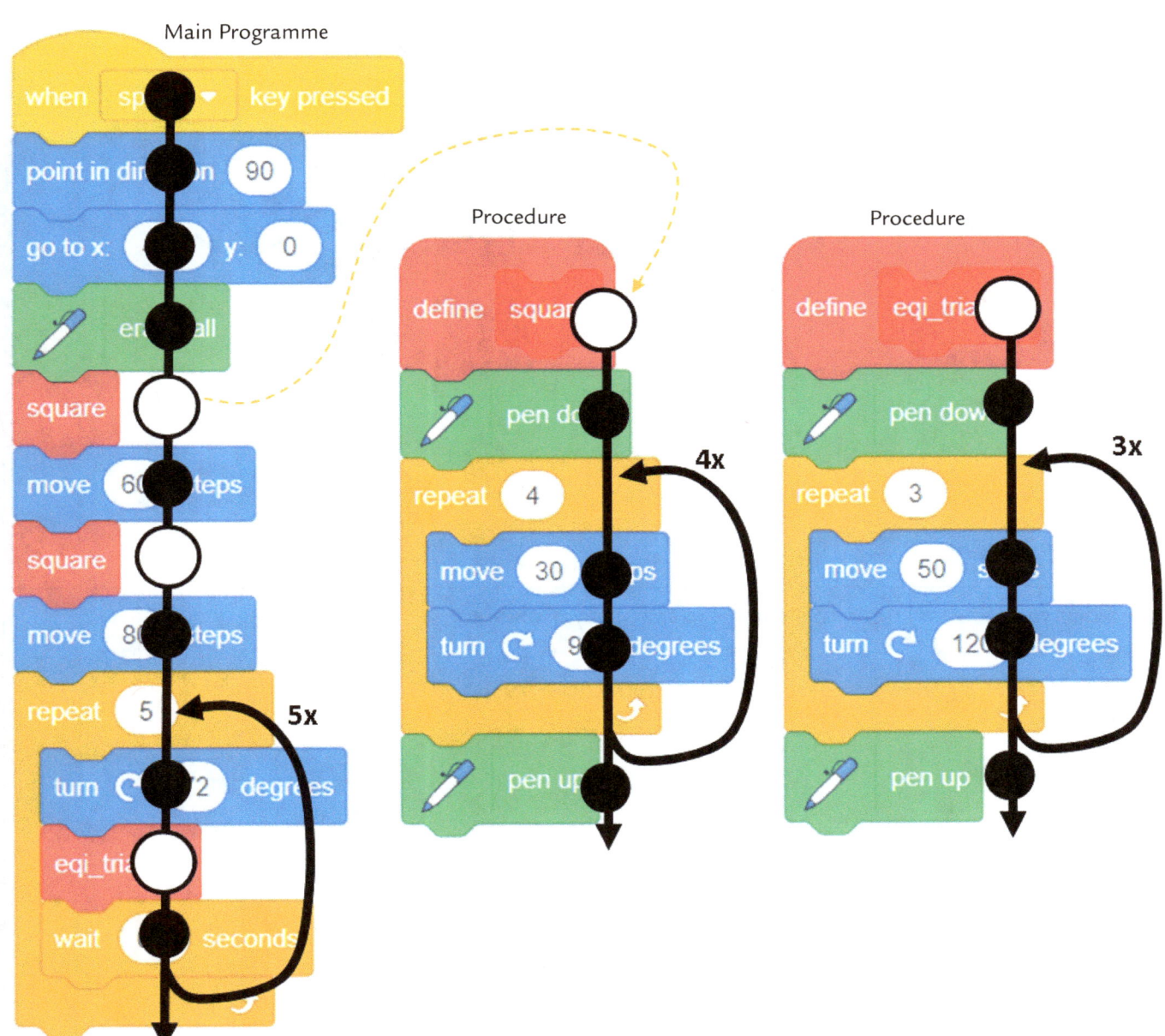

BASIC PROCEDURES

Work with a partner

Basic Procedures

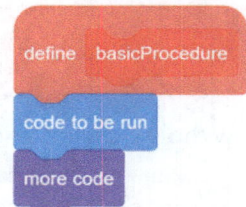

PREDICT

Read the code carefully with your partner and then draw what you think it will create in the box provided.

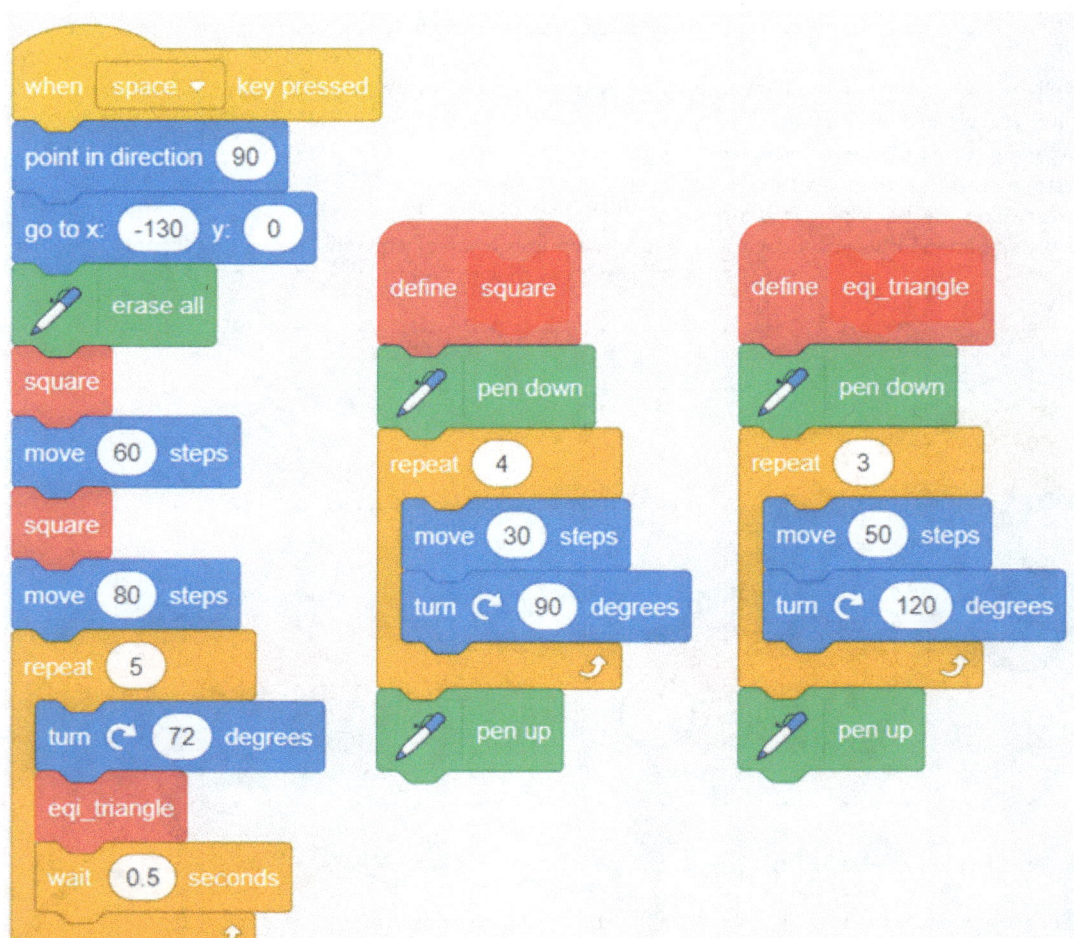

I predict the code will draw this when the space key is pressed

HINT How many eqi_triangles will be drawn?

Now mark your work using the predict marksheet

photocopiable page

SUPPORTING
PREDICT

Read the code carefully with your partner and then draw what you think it will create in the box provided.

Notes on the activity

This optional activity helps pupils to think about the bigger purpose of the program before they start looking at parts of it in later sections.

Whole class advice

Make sure you work with your partner on this sheet. Take it in turns to read a section and tell your partner what you think it does. Then draw what you think the code will do in the box at the bottom. If you want to use a ruler that is fine.

Send advice

It can help to act out this code on the playground with a piece of chalk or on a piece of paper with a pencil. Point in direction 90 is point right.

Individual advice

Decompose the code into three sections start with square code what do you think it will draw?

The eqi_triangle what do you think it will draw?

Now look at the main code and go through step by step, drawing what happens as you go.

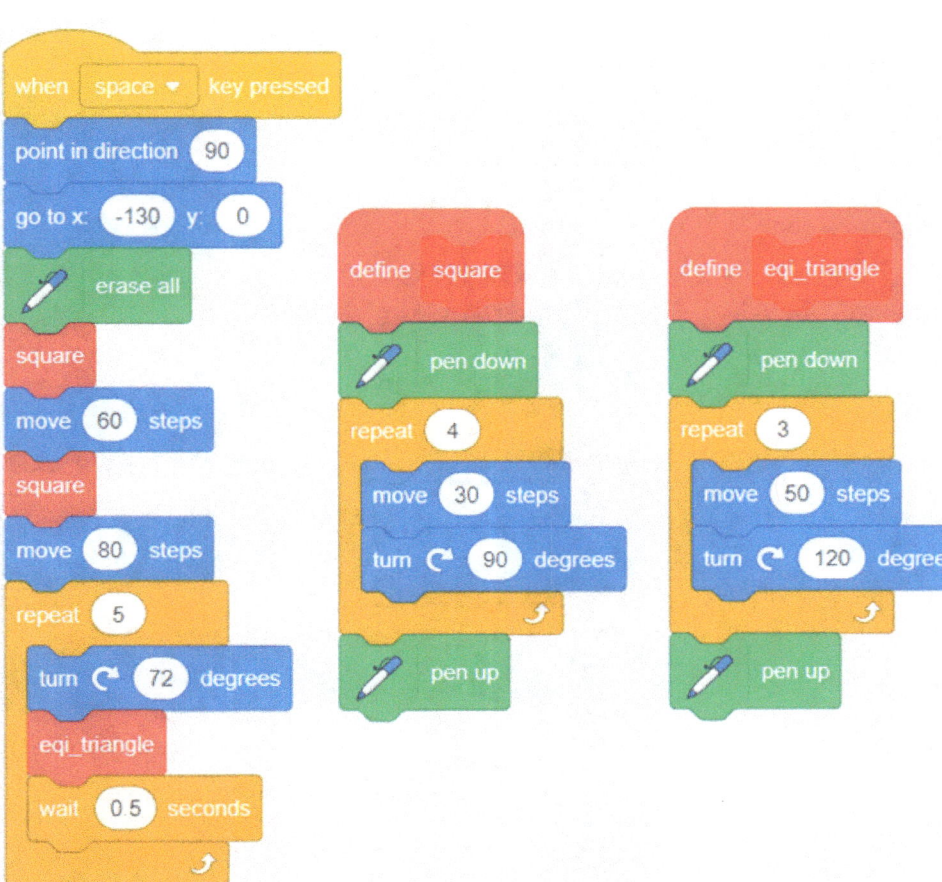

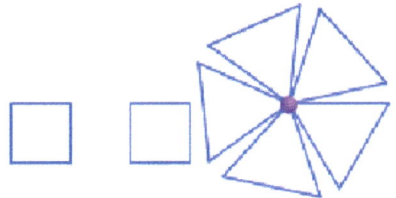

Two squares (extra 1 mark)

Two squares in a line (1 extra mark)

A single triangle (1 extra mark)

Five triangles (1 extra mark)

Five triangles in a spiral around a central point (1 extra mark)

If you got all of these you would score 5 marks

BASIC PROCEDURES
INVESTIGATE

Work with a partner

Basic Procedures

Work with a partner. Open Scratch and load exploring basic procedures.

Run the program as many times as you want.
Work with a partner to answer these questions.

1. How many times in the main program *(starts when space key is pressed)* is the **square** procedure run?

2. When the square procedure is run. How many times will it move 30 forward?

3. How many times in the main program is the **eqi_triangle** procedure run?

4. What shapes do the two procedures draw?

   _____   _____

5. Which shape has the longest perimeter?

6. Connect the black lines on the diagram to show which procedure blocks in the main program call which procedures.

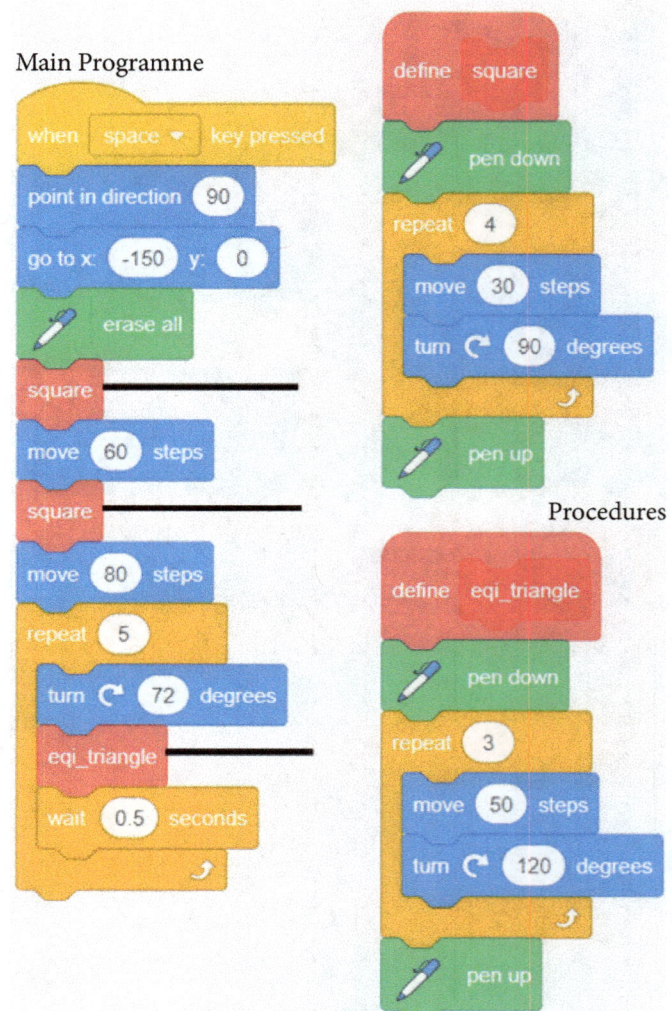

7. Which blocks are initialisation in the main program? *HINT Initialisation makes sure the code always runs the same way every time it is run by removing the effects of being run the last time and sending the sprite back to the same starting place.*

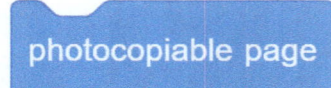

photocopiable page

Now mark your work using the investigate marksheet

SUPPORT INVESTIGATE

Run the program as many times as you want.
Work with a partner to answer these questions.

1. How many times in the main program *(starts when space key is pressed)* is the **square** procedure run?

   2 (1 mark)

2. When the square procedure is run. How many times will it move 30 forward?

   4 (1 mark)

3. How many times in the main program is the **eqi_triangle** procedure run?

   5 (1 mark) as it is in a count-controlled-loop

4. What shapes do the two procedures draw?

   Square and Triangle (1 mark)

5. Which shape has the longest perimeter?

   Triangle (1 mark)

6. Connect the black lines on the diagram to show which procedure blocks call which procedures.

   All three arrows pointing to the correct procedures (1 mark)

7. Which blocks are initialisation in the main program? *HINT Initialisation makes sure the code always runs the same way every time it is run by removing the effects of being run the last time and sending the sprite back to the same starting place.*

   Point in direct 90, go to x –150 y 0, erase all (1 mark if you have two or more of these).

   Now mark your work using the investigate marksheet

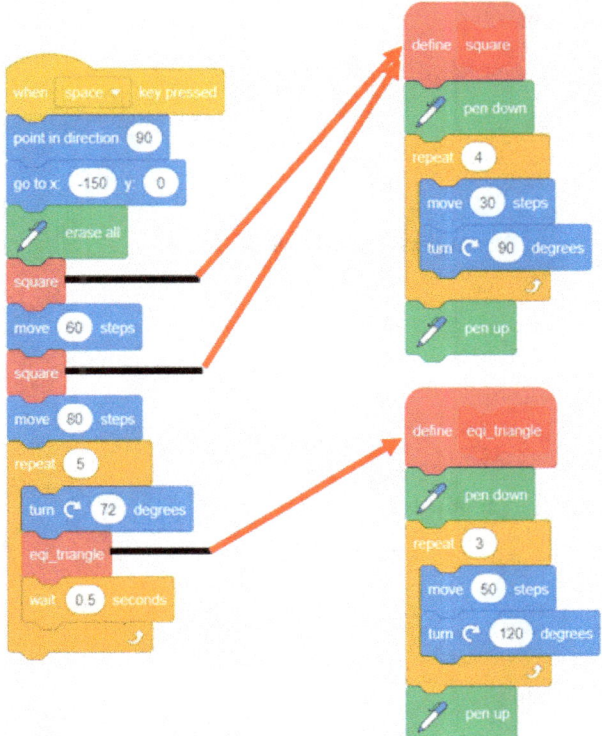

Q1 How many square procedure starting blocks are there?

Q2 Revision from Y4 on count-controlled-loop. HINT Loop

Q3 Revision from Y4 on count-controlled-loop. HINT Loop

Q4 Run program to see.

Q5 HINT Move steps.

SEND Q5 Remind what perimeter is.

SEND Q6 Do one as an example.

Q7 Read the hint a part at a time and ask pupils if there is any code that does that job.

SEND Q7 Initialisation code is often at the top of the code section before drawing code is run.

Notes on the activity

Investigating the code encourages pupils to think deeply about how it works. Check that every pupil is filling in and marking the questions individually but at the pace of the slowest in the pair. Sometimes a pair decides not to mark to speed up their efforts. Marking gives valuable information, so I recommend sending them back to mark their work. A class instruction to come and talk to you if they have over half of the questions wrong or they do not understand the answer after they have marked it helps to check progress is being made correctly. There is real value in collecting these scores to build up a summative picture of pupil progress.

Whole class advice

Work in pairs, one device between the pair. Take it in turns every question to swap who runs code. You must work at the same pace as your partner and not move on to the next question until you have both written your answer down. If you disagree, write a different answer. You must mark your work before moving on to the next section.

Send advice

Support pairs of pupils who are poor readers by reading questions, reading code samples and covering up questions until they get to them.

BASIC PROCEDURES
CHANGE

Work with a partner

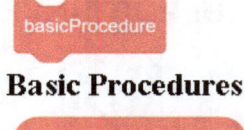
Basic Procedures
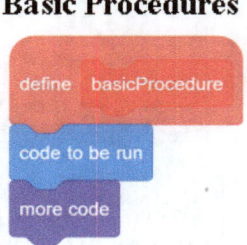

Work with a partner. Open Scratch and load
exploring basic procedures

Make changes to the code to answer these questions

1. What happens when you remove the two **pen up** blocks from the procedures? *Put them back again afterwards.*

2. What would you change to **increase the distances** between the squares?

3. What would you change to make all the squares **larger**?

4. What would you change to make all the triangles **smaller**?

5. What changes would you need to draw **six equally spaced triangles** instead of 5? *HINT 5 × 72degrees = 360, 6 × 60degrees = 360.*

6. What would you change to make the squares **only draw three sides**?

photocopiable page

Now mark your work using the change marksheet

SUPPORTING CHANGE

Whole class advice

Work in pairs, one device between the pair. Take it in turns every question to swap who runs code. You must work at the same pace as your partner and not move on to the next question until you have both written your answer down. If you disagree, write a different answer. You must mark your work before moving on to the next section.

Notes on the activity

Changing or modifying code is a core part of this module, so I suggest you do not leave it out. It is an important step towards creation of their own code. Parts they have modified they will feel more ownership of. Recording marks will help with assessment.

Send advice

Support pairs of pupils who are poor readers by reading questions, reading code samples and covering up questions until they get to them.

Make changes to the code to answer these questions

1. What happens when you remove the two **pen up** blocks from the procedures? *Put them back again afterwards.*

   It draws lines between the shapes (1 mark)

   Q1 Have pupils actually removed the blocks?

2. What would you change to **increase the distances** between the squares?

   Either add an extra move block between the code that starts the square procedures OR change move 60 steps to a higher number (1 mark)

   Q2 What block creates the current distance between both squares? Answer: Move 60 steps.

3. What would you change to make all the squares **larger**?

   Increase steps in move 30 block in the square procedure (1 mark)

   Q3 What code block sets the length of the side of the square? Answer: Move 30 steps. Point to square procedure as you say this.

4. What would you change to make all the triangles **smaller**?

   Decrease steps in move 50 block in the eqi_triangle procedure (1 mark)

   Q4 What code block sets the length of the side of the triangle? Answer: Move 50 steps. Point to equ_triangle procedures as you say this.

5. What changes would you need to draw **six equally spaced triangles** instead of 5? *HINT 5 × 72degrees = 360, 6 × 60degrees = 360.*

   Change repeat 5 to repeat 6 (1mark)

   Change turn 72 degrees to turn 60 degrees (1 mark)

   Q5 Which hint is linked to the current code and how is it linked?

   5=number of repeats

   72= degrees turned

   Now how can you use the new hint info?

6. What would you change to make the squares **only draw three sides**?

   Change repeat 4 to repeat 3 in the square procedure (1 mark)

   Q6 What makes the code draw four sides at the moment? Answer: Repeat 4. Point to square procedure as you say this.

BASIC PROCEDURES
CREATE

Work on your own

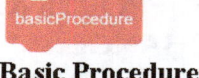
Basic Procedures

Complete task 1 and task 2 and then choose one or more options to do.
You MUST create this **inside** your own copy of **exploring basic procedures.**
Delete the main programme but keep the square and epi_triangle procedures.

Task 1 Use the shape information below to make at least two other regular 2D shape procedures.

Shape	Pentagon	Hexagon	Heptagon	Octagon	Nonagon
Number of sides	5	6	7	8	9
Angle needed	72	60	51.4	45	40

Task 2 Now use your new procedure blocks and the old ones to to make a new main program that creates a pattern.

Now choose one or more options from below

Option 1

Can you create squared or triangular paper using the smallest number of main program commands? (You can use as many procedures as you like).

Option 2

Can you fill the screen with randomly drawn shapes using procedure run by a main program?

Option 3

Draw a picture of an object using shape procedures.

Teacher and Pupil Assessment

Circle one column on each row to show what you think you have achieved

	Not created or used a basic procedure called by a main program	Created basic procedures called by a main program	Created basic procedures called by a main program that has a loop
Basic Procedures	0 marks	1 mark	2 marks
		Not used previous programming concepts for real purpose	Used previous programming concepts for real purpose
Used previous programming concept such as loop or condition correctly		0 marks	1 mark

SUPPORTING CREATE

Complete Task 1 and Task 2 and then choose one or more options to do.
You MUST create this inside your own copy of exploring basic procedures.

Task 1 Use the shape information below to make at least two other regular 2D shape procedures.

Task 2 Now use your new procedure blocks and the old ones to to make a new main program that creates a pattern.

Shape	Pentagon	Hexagon	Heptagon	Octagon	Nonagon
Number of sides	5	6	7	8	9
Angle needed	72	60	51.4	45	40

Option 1

Can you create squared or triangular paper using the smallest number of main program commands? (You can use as many procedures as you like).

Option 2

Can you fill the screen with randomly drawn shapes using procedure run by a main program?

Option 3

Draw a picture of an object using shape procedures.

> **Option 1** Often when pupils make repeated patterns they allow code to overlap on the same place rather than adjust the numbers of loops or the angles. Saying I like this but how would you keep the same pattern without it drawing over and over again in same spot (point to where it has).

Teacher and Pupil Assessment

Circle one column on each row to show what you think you have achieved

	Not created or used a basic procedure called by a main program	Created basic procedures called by a main program	Created basic procedures called by a main program that has a loop
Basic Procedures	0 marks	1 mark	2 marks
		Not used previous programming concepts for real purpose	Used previous programming concepts for real purpose
Used previous programming concept such as loop or condition correctly	0 marks	1 mark	

Notes on the activity

The make part of a project is really important, and teachers should always make sure that pupils have time to make their own project, even if that means reducing the time spent on other stages for pupils who work slowly. It helps if pupils work on their own for this while supporting their partner.

Whole class advice

Work on your own, one device each. You can discuss the work with your former partner, but you are responsible for creating your own projects. Save your work regularly. Read the instructions carefully. Assess your own work by circling where you think you are in the assessment grid at the bottom of the page.

Send advice

Better to concentrate on extending Task 1 and 2 without covering options.

Task 1 Make sure pupils use a copy of the original program rather than making a new blank program, as a lot of time can be wasted recreating existing code.

Task 2 Lots of programming involves adapting existing code rather than creating code from nothing.

Task 1 & 2 You may want to check Tasks 1 and 2 are completed properly before pupils are allowed to go onto the options. Have they created new procedures with define at the top of the code? Have these procedures been started using code in the main program?

Option 1 You will probably have some squared maths paper in the class as an example to show pupils.

Option 2 Point out pick random command in green operator blocks.

Assessment Examples

There are some assessment examples on the next page.

ASSESSMENT EXAMPLES

	Not created or used a basic procedure in a main program	Used basic procedures in a main program	Used basic procedures in a main program that has loops
Basic Procedures	0 marks	1 mark	2 marks

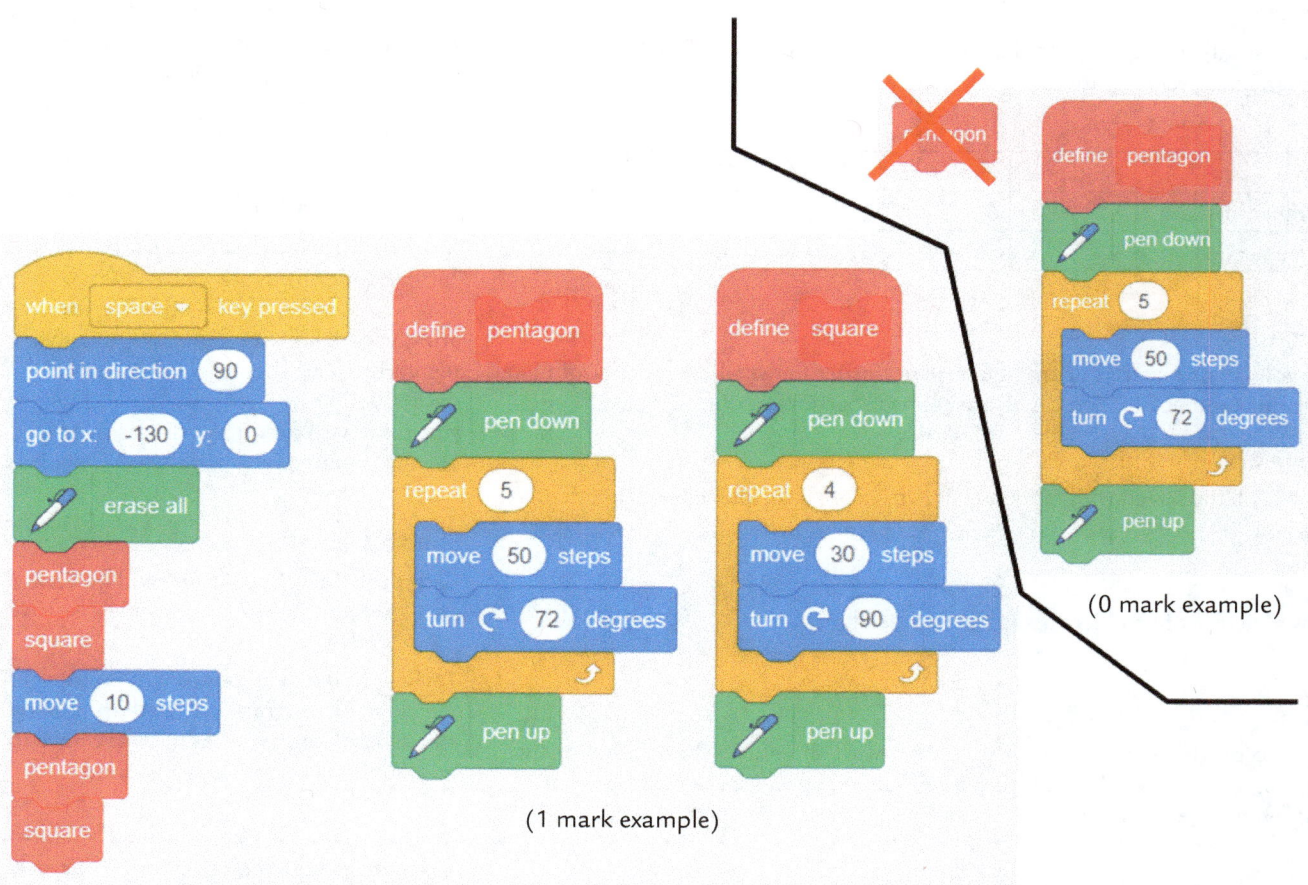

(0 mark example)

(1 mark example)

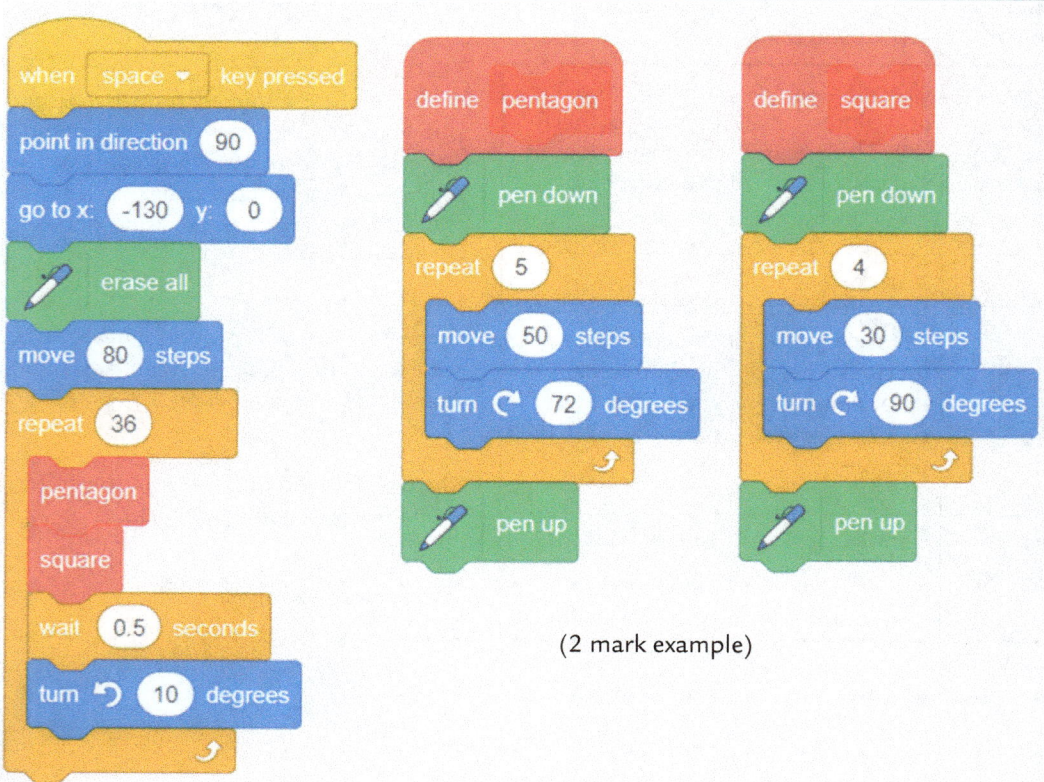

(2 mark example)

PARSONS MARKSHEET

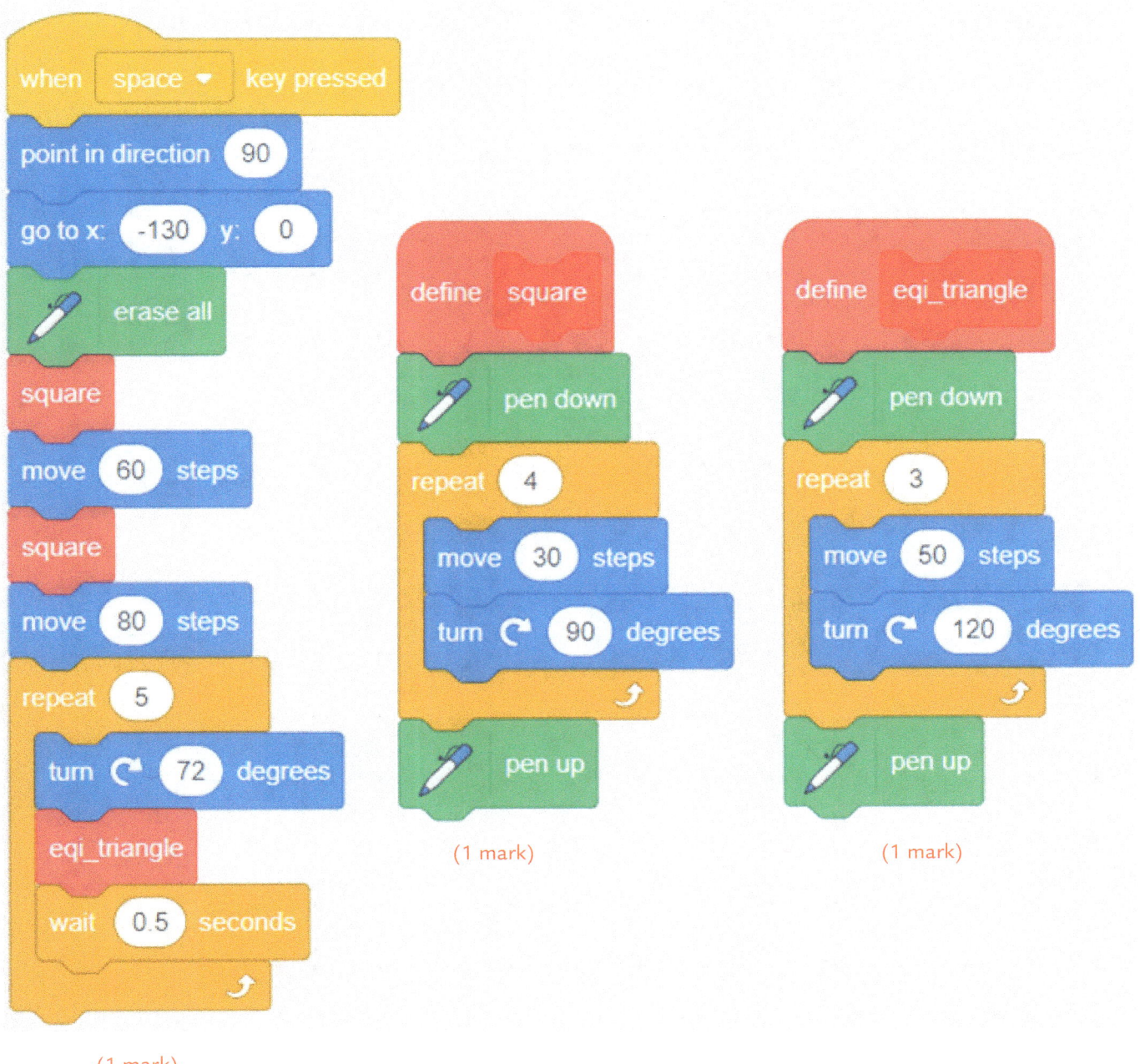

when space ▼ **key pressed**

point in direction 90

go to x: -130 **y:** 0

🖊 **erase all**

square

move 60 **steps**

square

move 80 **steps**

repeat 5
  turn ↻ 72 **degrees**
  eqi_triangle
  wait 0.5 **seconds**

(1 mark)

define square

🖊 **pen down**

repeat 4
  move 30 **steps**
  turn ↻ 90 **degrees**

🖊 **pen up**

(1 mark)

define eqi_triangle

🖊 **pen down**

repeat 3
  move 50 **steps**
  turn ↻ 120 **degrees**

🖊 **pen up**

(1 mark)

PREDICT MARKSHEET

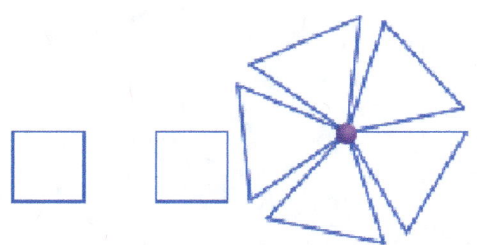

Two squares (extra 1 mark)

Two squares in a line (1 extra mark)

A single triangle (1 extra mark)

Five triangles (1 extra mark)

Five triangles in a spiral around a central point (1 extra mark)

If you got all of these you would score 5 marks

INVESTIGATE MARKSHEET

Run the program as many times as you want.
Work with a partner to answer these questions.

1. How many times in the main program *(starts when space key is pressed)* is the **square** procedure run?
    2 (1 mark)

2. When the square procedure is run. How many times will it move 30 forward?
    4 (1 mark)

3. How many times in the main program is the **eqi_triangle** procedure run?
    5 (1 mark) as it is in a count-controlled-loop

4. What shapes do the two procedures draw?
    Square and triangle (1 mark)

5. Which shape has the longest perimeter?
    Triangle (1 mark)

6. Connect the black lines on the diagram to show which procedure blocks call which procedures
    All three arrows pointing to the correct procedures (1 mark)

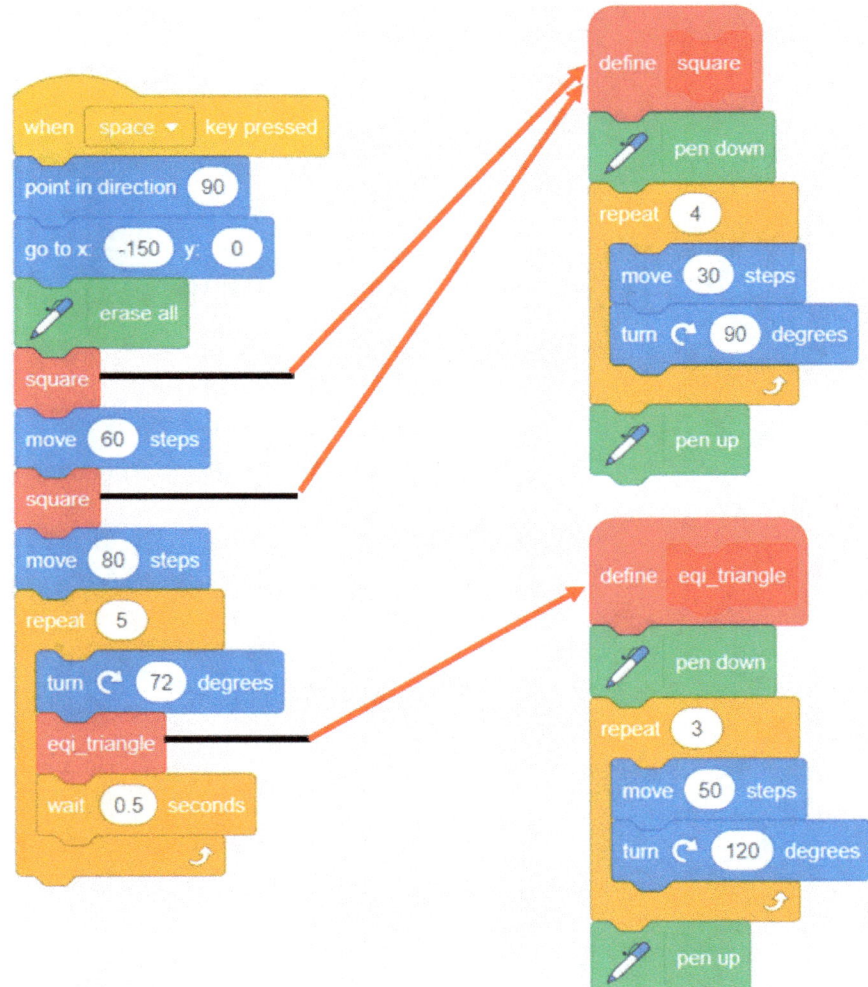

7. Which blocks are initialisation in the main program? *HINT Initialisation makes sure the code always runs the same way every time it is run by removing the effects of being run the last time and sending the sprite back to the same starting place.*
    Point in direction 90, go to x −150 y 0, erase all (1 mark if you have two or more of these)

CHANGE MARKSHEET

Make changes to the code to answer these questions.

1. What happens when you remove the two **pen up** blocks from the procedures? *Put them back again afterwards.*

    It draws lines between the shapes (1 mark)

2. What would you change to **increase the distances** between the squares?

    Either add an extra move block between the code that starts the square procedures OR change move 60 steps to a higher number (1 mark)

3. What would you change to make all the squares **larger?**

    Increase steps in move 30 block in the square procedure (1 mark)

4. What would you change to make all the triangles **smaller?**

    Decrease steps in move 50 block in the eqi_triangle procedure (1 mark)

5. What changes would you need to draw **six equally spaced triangles** instead of 5? *HINT 5 x 72 degrees = 360, 6 x 60degrees = 360.*

    Change repeat 5 to repeat 6 (1 mark)

    Change turn 72 degrees to turn 60 degrees (1 mark)

6. What would you change to make the squares **only draw three sides?**

    Change repeat 4 to repeat 3 in the square procedure (1 mark)

PROGRAMMING MODULE THAT USES SIMPLE PROCEDURES AND NESTED LOOPS

> **Overview**
> Pupils explore how nested loops with procedures can be used to create drawing patterns before creating their own.

To do before the session

1. Look at the grid below and decide which optional and SEN activities you are going to include and exclude.
2. Print pupil worksheets for each activity chosen and staple into a booklet one for each pupil.
3. Print marksheets for activities chosen to be placed where pupils can access them.
4. Download the code needed and place in a templates folder on your school network or add to a Scratch Studio or link on your learning platform.
5. Download the slides that go with the concept introduction.
6. Study the notes that go with the slides.
7. Examine the teacher help notes that are provided alongside every activity.

To do at the start of the session

If you have not introduced **nested loops** with this class before do this first using the resources in Chapter 2 as a whole class activity.

To do after the concept has been introduced

To do after the concept has been introduced Each activity has whole class notes to help you explain what is needed if it is the first time pupils have carried out this type of activity. There are also core instruction underneath in case you are sticking to the core activities only.

How this module fits into a programming progression

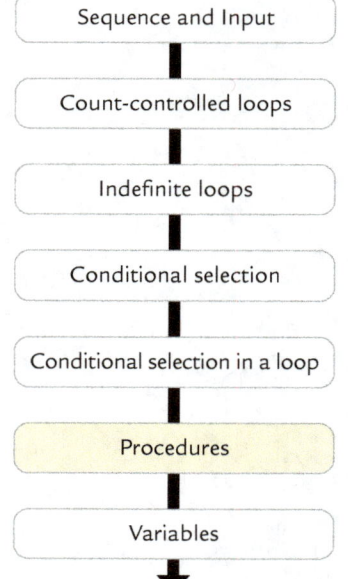

Sequence and Input

Count-controlled loops

Indefinite loops

Conditional selection

Conditional selection in a loop

Procedures

Variables

> **Vocabulary**
> Procedure, task, name, call a procedure

Resource Name	Core Optional SEN	Teacher	Pupil Grouping	How Assessed	SCRATCH ACCESS
CONCEPT Nested Loops	CORE	Leads Session	Solo whole class activity	Formative	NO
PARSONS	OPTIONAL SEN OPTIONAL ALL (predict or parsons not both)	Support Poor Readers	Solo or Paired (Teacher choice)	Pupil Marked Marksheet Provided	YES PARSONS NESTED LOOPS WITH PROCEDURES
FLOW	OPTIONAL ALL If you do predict I recommend you do flow first	Can be done as a Whole Class or with a Large Group	Solo or Paired (Teacher Choice)	No Marked Outcome	NO
PREDICT	OPTIONAL ALL (predict or parsons not both)	Support Poor Readers	Paired	Pupil Marked Marksheet Provided	NO
INVESTIGATE	CORE	Support Poor Readers	Paired	Pupil Marked Marksheet Provided	YES NESTED LOOPS WITH PROCEDURES
CHANGE	CORE	Support Poor Readers	Paired	Pupil Marked Marksheet Provided	YES NESTED LOOPS WITH PROCEDURES
CREATE	CORE	Assesses Pupil Work and Checks Pupil Self-Assessment	Solo	Pupil Assessed & Teacher Assessed	YES NESTED LOOPS WITH PROCEDURES

Core activities general instructions

1. Group pupils in roughly same ability pairs. For **investigate** and **change** worksheets, pupils will work in pairs, for **create** they will work separately.

2. Give out the pupil booklets and explain that pupils need to follow the instructions on the sheets to explore how **basic procedures** work.

3. Explain that each pupil will record separately whilst working alongside their partner and keeping to the same pace as their partner.

4. Demonstrate where they can find the template code and explain that pupils will share one device for investigate and change.

5. Explain that during each question only one person should touch the shared device and they should swap who that person is when there is a new question.

6. Encourage them to discuss their answers with their partner. If they disagree with their partner, they can record a different answer in their own booklet.

7. Show pupils where it says they should mark their work on the sheet and where the answer sheets are in the classroom.

8. Remind pupils to return marksheets after marking, because there are not enough for every pair to have their own.

Key Programming Knowledge

A procedure is a small section of a program that performs a specific task.
A nested loop is one loop inside another loop

Nested Loops

Are cumulative in that you multiply the inner by the outer to see how many times actions are looped in the inner loop

---

Resources

Exploring nested loops with procedures: https://scratch.mit.edu/projects/313046398/
Parsons exploring nested loops with procedures`; https://scratch.mit.edu/projects/623838513/

	On the sheet, if it says no Scratch, they must work only on the sheet.
	If it says Scratch with a green tick, they can use one device between the pair.
	If it says work with a partner, they must work at the same speed as their partner.
	If it says work on their own, they must do this using a separate device each working alone.

English Computing National Curriculum Programs of Study

Pupils should be taught to:

- **design, write and debug programs that accomplish specific goals,** including controlling or simulating physical systems; solve problems by decomposing them into smaller parts

- **use sequence,** selection and **repetition in programs;** work with variables **and various forms of input and output**

- **use logical reasoning to explain how some simple algorithms work and to detect and correct errors in algorithms and programs**

Scottish Curriculum for Excellence Technologies

I understand the instructions of a visual programming language and can predict the outcome of a program written using the language. TCH 1-14a

I can explain core programming language concepts in appropriate technical language TCH 2-14a

I can demonstrate a range of basic problem solving skills by building simple programs to carry out a given task, using an appropriate language. TCH 1-15a

I can create, develop and evaluate computing solutions in response to a design challenge. TCH 2-15a

Welsh National Curriculum Relevant Strands

Progression Step 3.

- I can use conditional statements to add control and decision-making to algorithms.

- I can explain and debug algorithms.

NESTED LOOPS WITH PROCEDURES PARSONS

Work with a partner

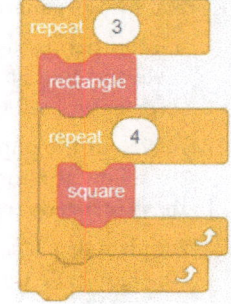

Nested Loops

Start Scratch and Load
PARSONS EXPLORING NESTED LOOPS
WITH PROCEDURES

Use the algorithm below to help you connect the Scratch blocks in the correct places in the PARSONS EXPLORING NESTED LOOPS WITH PROCEDURES

Main Programme	Procedure	Procedure
Green flag start	Define rectangle	Define square
Point right	Pen down start drawing	Pen down start drawing
Go to centre (x 0 y 0)	Do 2 times	Do 4 times
Rub out old lines	50 steps	20 steps
Loop 4 times	Right 90 degrees	Right 90 degrees
Right 90 degrees	Pause 0.2 seconds	Pause 0.2 seconds
Run Rectangle procedure	20 steps	Pen up to stop drawing
80 steps	Right 90 degrees	
Loop 3 times	Pause 0.2 seconds	
Run square procedure	Pen up to stop drawing	
Right 120 degrees		
-80 steps		

Now mark your work using the Parsons marksheet

SUPPORTING PARSONS

Whole class advice

Load Parsons exploring nested loops with procedures code and then use the algorithm on this page to build the code. When you have completed it, run the code and check your answer with the marking sheet.

Understanding programming

You can find out more about Parsons problems in the teacher book, Chapter 19.

Use the algorithm below to help you connect the Scratch blocks in the correct places in the Parsons exploring basic procedures.

Notes on the activity

This allows pupils to build the code first before investigating, modifying and creating code of their own. The algorithm is written in language similar but also different to the code. This helps pupils by enabling them to see an example of planning which will help them when they come to plan their own project. On its own it is not enough deep thinking about the code to enable agency, but as a starter or SEN activity it is useful to see how code can be built.

Send advice

Parsons problems can be made less complex by connecting more blocks in the example Scratch code and saving that version as a new template.

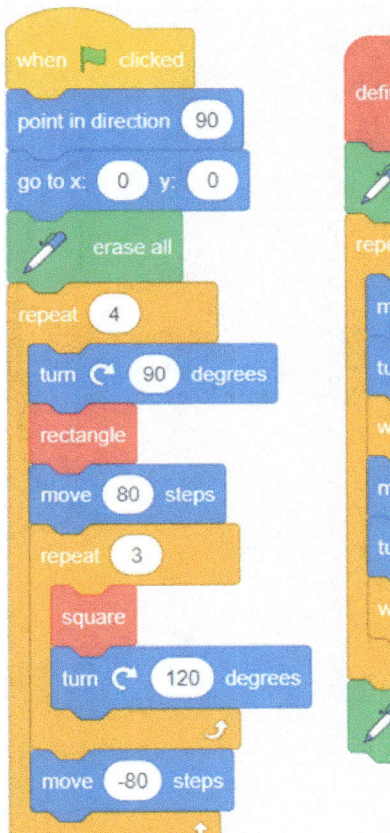

Main Programme

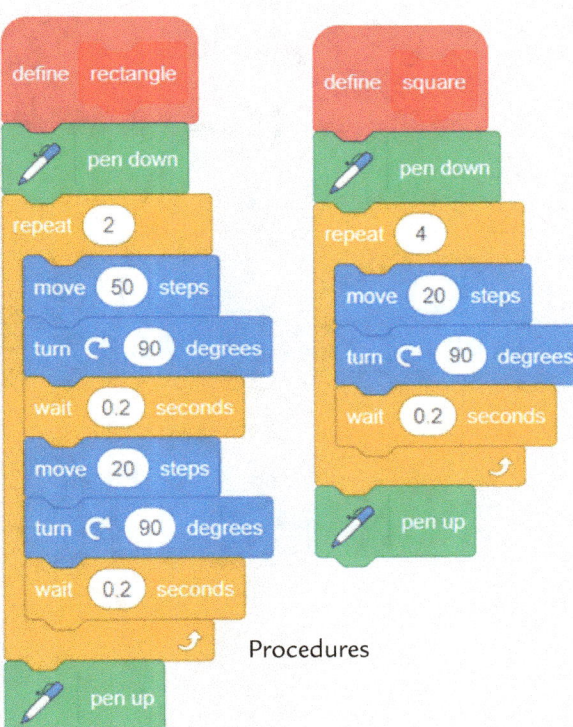

Procedures

Individual advice

It is easier to build the procedures before building the main programme last.

Individual advice

Pointing out that the code inside a loop is indented in the planning algorithm and code inside a loop in a loop is indented twice can help some pupils.

Individual advice

Last line is single indent only; this can catch some pupils out.

Main Programme	Procedure	Procedure
Green flag start	Define rectangle	Define square
Point right	Pen down start drawing	Pen down start drawing
Go to centre (x 0 y 0)	Do 2 times	Do 4 times
Rub out old lines	50 steps	20 steps
Loop 4 times	Right 90 degrees	Right 90 degrees
Right 90 degrees	Pause 0.2 seconds	Pause 0.2 seconds
Run Rectangle procedure	20 steps	Pen up to stop drawing
80 steps	Right 90 degrees	
Loop 3 times	Pause 0.2 seconds	
Run square procedure	Pen up to stop drawing	
Right 120 degrees		
-80 steps		

NESTED LOOPS WITH PROCEDURES

FLOW

Read the code carefully with your partner and follow the order the code is run with your finger in the **main programme**. When you get to a block that runs rectangle and square just say drawing a rectangle or drawing a square. DO NOT TRACE THE CODE IN THE PROCEDURES; it gets too complex.

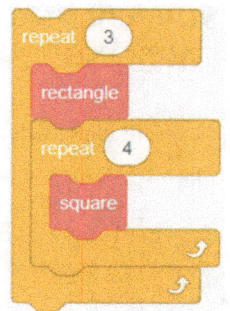

Nested Loops

Main Programme

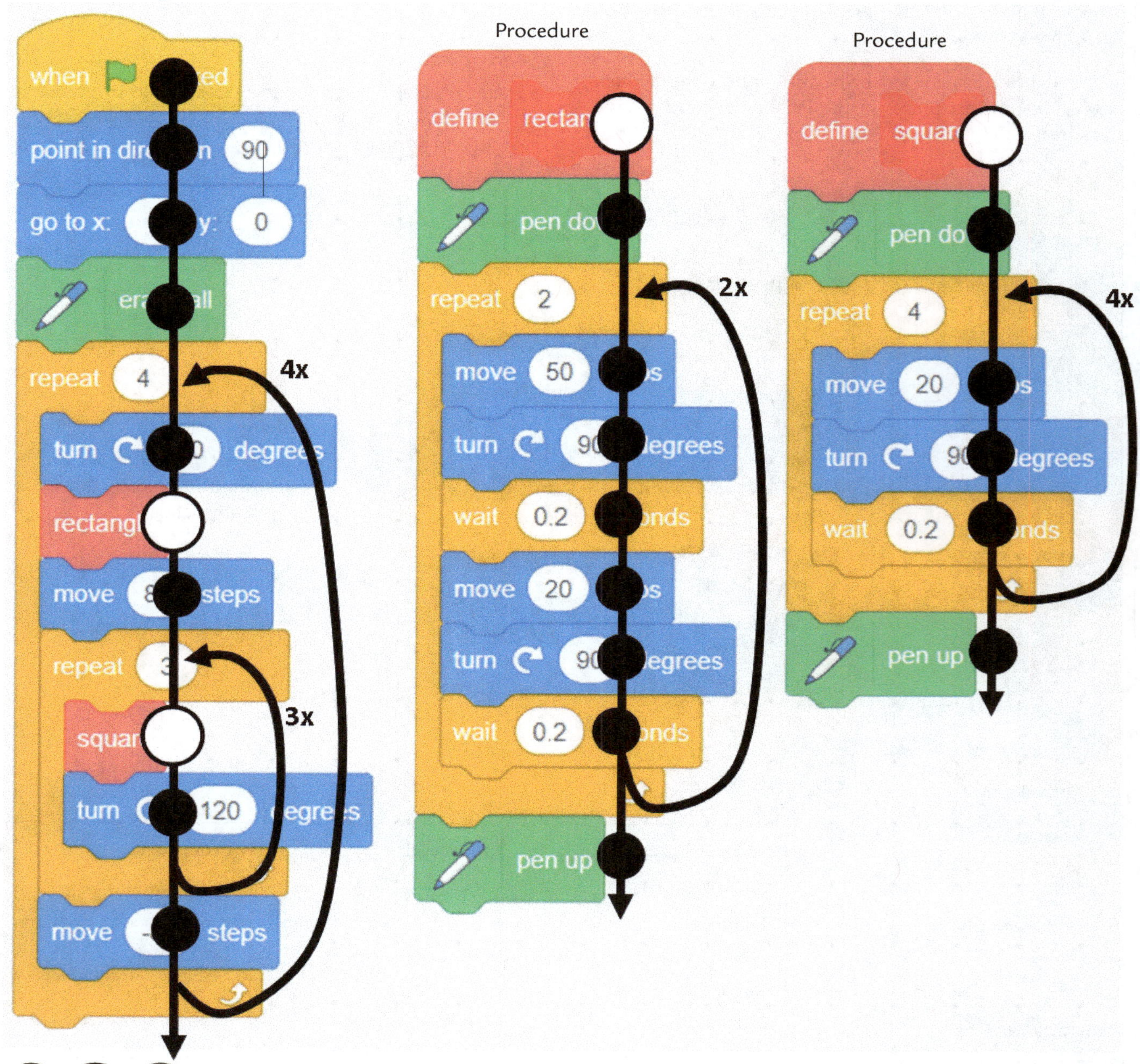

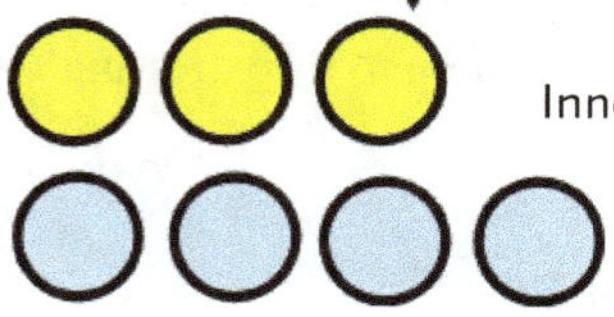

Procedure

Procedure

○ ○ ○   Inner loop

○ ○ ○ ○   Outer loop

photocopiable page

SUPPORTING FLOW

Read the code carefully with your partner and follow the order the code is run with your finger in the main programme. When you get to a block that runs rectangle and square just say drawing a rectangle or drawing a square. DO NOT TRACE THE CODE IN THE PROCEDURES; it gets too complex.

Notes on the activity

This activity builds on the concept introduction and is a great activity to do before predicting what the code does. There is no marked outcome, so make sure pupils work through it carefully. It can be done as a whole class.

Whole class instructions

Look at this code carefully. Trace the flow of the code, making sure that when you get to one of the empty circles you make sure you find and go through the flow of control for the procedure before coming back to the main programme.

Programmimg knowledge

One of the reasons for using procedures is to reduce complexity by replacing a complex task with a single command.

Send advice

Some pupils will really benefit from going through this in a group with you.

Main Programme

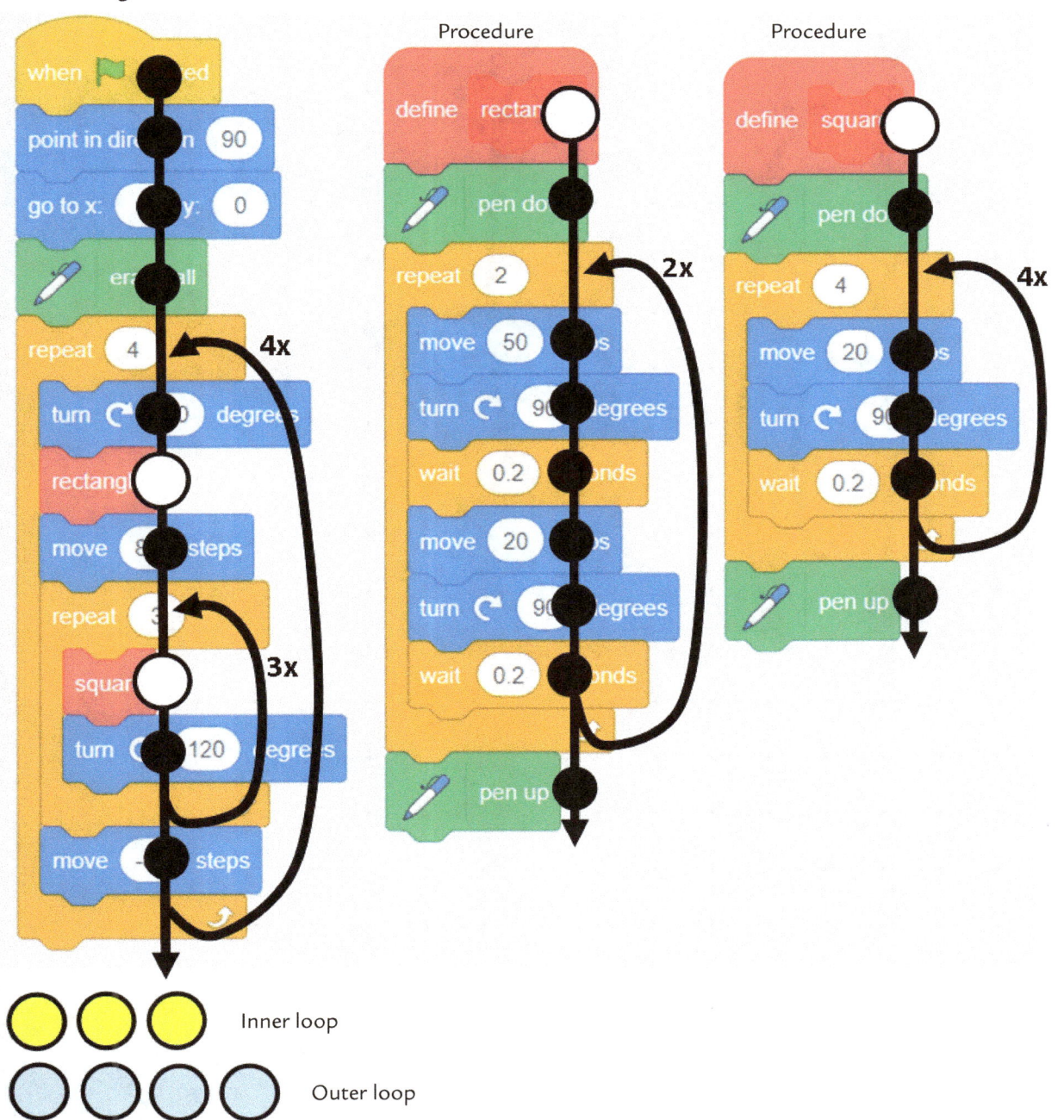

Inner loop

Outer loop

NESTED LOOPS WITH PROCEDURES

PREDICT

Read the code carefully with your partner and then draw
what you think it will create in the box provided

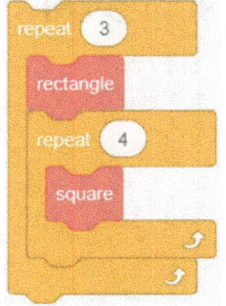

Nested Loops

Main Programme

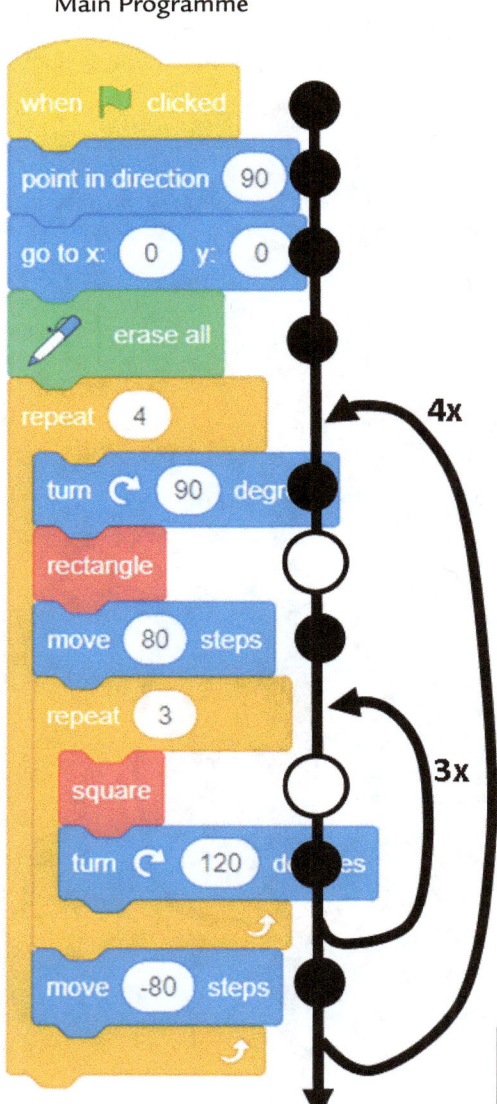

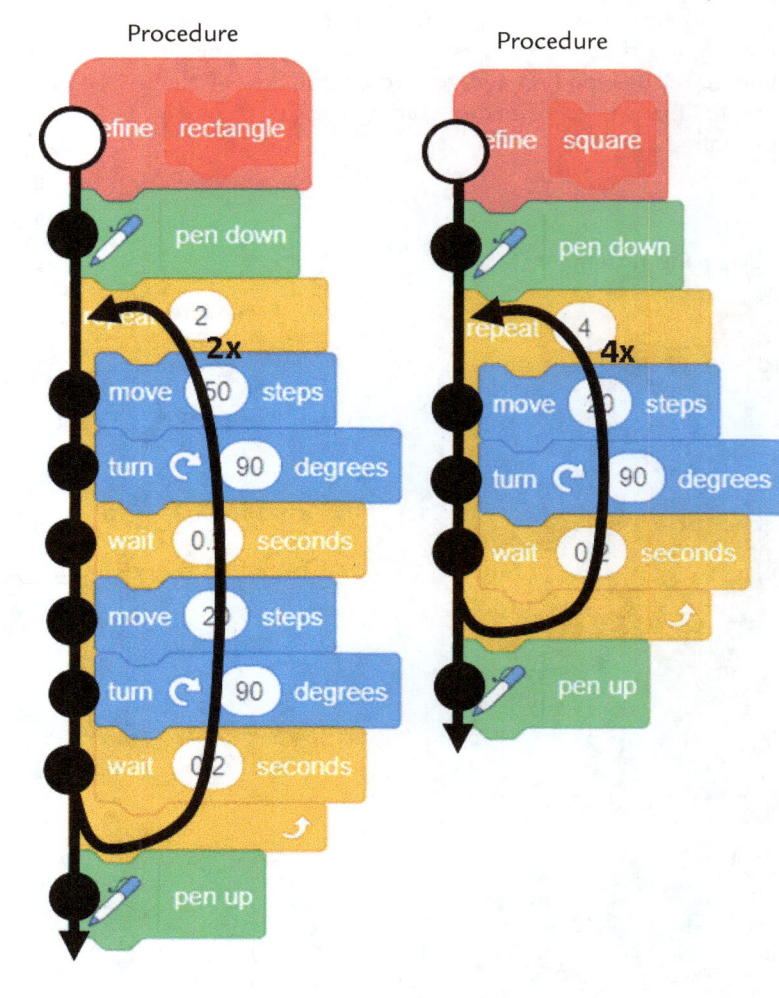

Procedure

Procedure

I predict the code will draw this when the green flag is pressed

Now mark your work using the predict marksheet

photocopiable page

SUPPORTING PREDICT

Read the code carefully with your partner and then draw what you think it will create in the box provided

Notes on the activity

This optional activity helps pupils to think about the bigger purpose of the program before they start looking at parts of it in later sections.

Whole class advice

Make sure you work with your partner on this sheet. Take it in turns to read a section and tell your partner what you think it does. Then draw what you think the code will do in the box at the bottom. If you want to use a ruler that is fine.

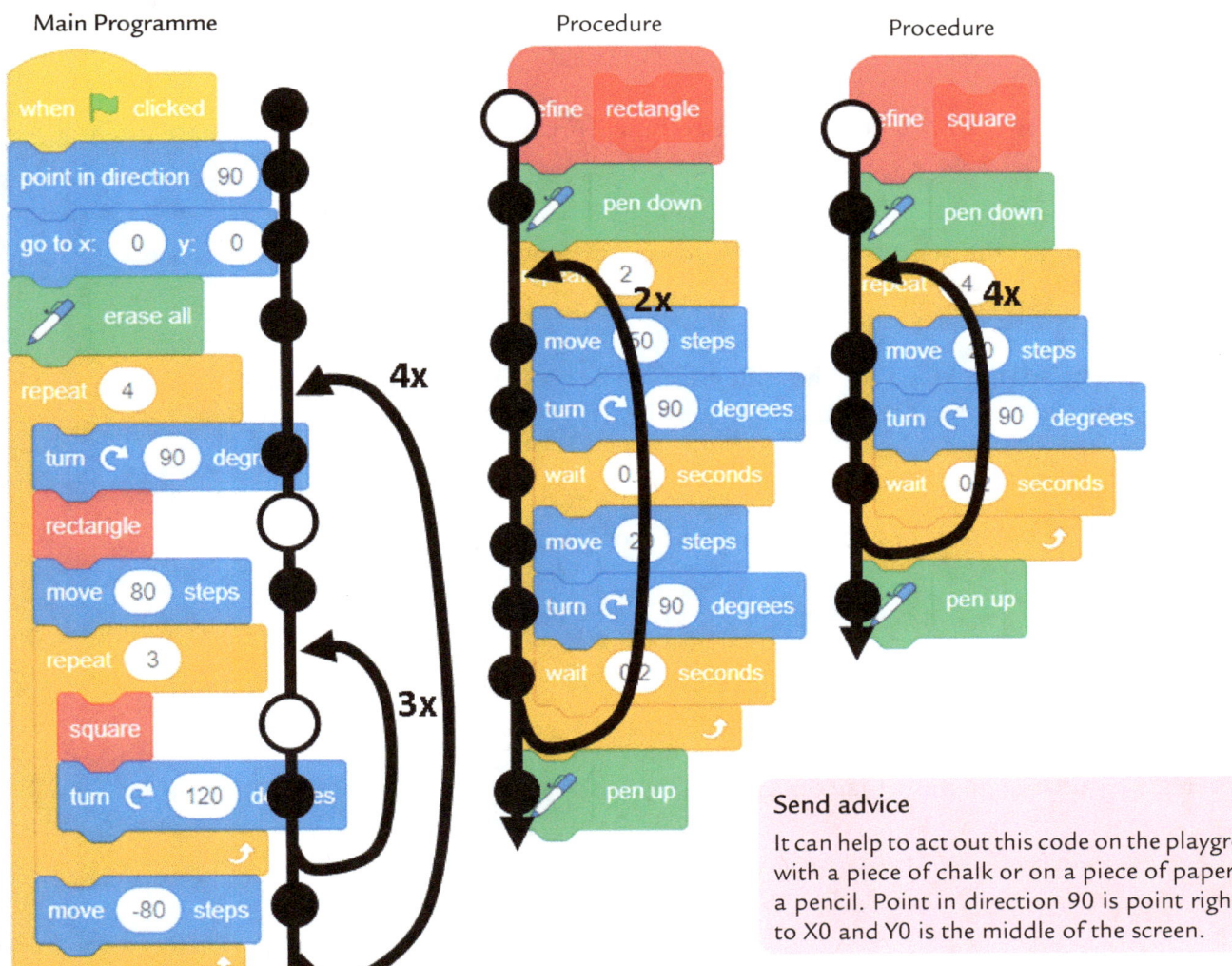

Main Programme

Procedure

Procedure

Send advice

It can help to act out this code on the playground with a piece of chalk or on a piece of paper with a pencil. Point in direction 90 is point right. Go to X0 and Y0 is the middle of the screen.

Individal advice

Decompose the code into three sections. Start with square code. What do you think it will draw?

The rectangle – what do you think it will draw?

Now look at the main code and go through step by step drawing – what happens as you go?

I predict the code will draw this when the green flag is pressed

Now mark your work using the predict marksheet

NESTED LOOPS WITH PROCEDURES
INVESTIGATE

Work with a partner

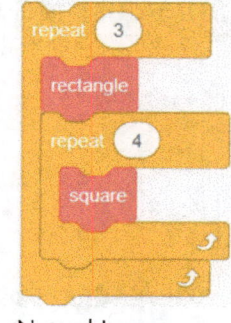

Nested Loops

Work with a partner. Open Scratch and load
exploring nested loops with procedures

Run the program as many times as you want.
Work with a partner to answer these questions.

1. How many times is move –80 steps run?

2. How many times in the main program is the rectangle procedure used?

3. How many times in the main program is the square procedure used?

4. Initialisation means thinking about how the code can be reused by resetting itself back to where it started
   and removing the effects of previous use. List any instructions that might be initialisation.

5. Tick the repeat loop that is nested inside another loop
   ☐ Repeat 2
   ☐ Repeat 3
   ☐ Repeat 4

6. Can a procedure be run more than once?

Now mark your work using the investigate marksheet

SUPPORT INVESTIGATE

Q1 Ask if it is inside a loop? Answer yes repeat 4.

Run the program as many times as you want.
Work with a partner to answer these questions.

1. How many times is move −80 steps run?
    4 (1 mark)

2. How many times in the main program is the rectangle procedure used?
    4 (1 mark)

3. How many times in the main program is the square procedure used?
    12 (1 mark)

4. Initialisation means thinking about how the code can be reused by resetting itself back to where it started and removing the effects of previous use. List any instructions that might be initialisation.
    Point in direction 90, go to X:0 Y:0, erase all
    (1 marks for 2 or more of these)

5. Tick the repeat loop that is nested inside another loop
    ☐ Repeat 2
    ☐ Repeat 3
    ☐ Repeat 4

6. Can a procedure be run more than once?
    Yes (1 mark)

Now mark your work using the investigate marksheet

Notes on the activity

Investigating the code encourages pupils to think deeply about how it works. Check that every pupil is filling in and marking the questions individually but at the pace of the slowest in the pair. Sometimes a pair decides not to mark to speed up their efforts. Marking gives valuable information, so I recommend sending them back to mark their work. A class instruction to come and talk to you if they have over half of the questions wrong or they do not understand the answer after they have marked it helps to check progress is being made correctly. There is real value in collecting these scores to build up a summative picture of pupil progress.

Q2 Ask if it is inside a loop. Answer Yes repeat 4.

Q3 Ask if it is inside a loop and if that loop is nested inside another loop. Answer 3 x 4 = 12.

Q4 Initialisation code is often found at the top of sections of code.

Q4 Are their any blocks that reset? Wipe out? Send back to start?

Q5 Nested means one loop inside another.

Q6 Have they run any square or rectangle procedures (define) more than once?

NESTED LOOPS WITH PROCEDURES CHANGE

Work with a partner

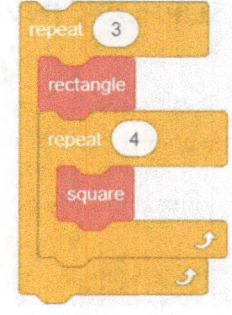

Work with a partner. Open Scratch and load exploring nested loops with procedures

Nested Loops

Make changes to the code to answer these questions

1. How can you make the program run more slowly? What did you change to do this?

2. In the main programme, the outer loop (repeat 4) draws four rectangles at right angles to each other. Change this to draw three rectangles evenly spaced. *HINT 360 divided by 3 = 120 degrees.* What did you change?

3. In the main programme, the inner nested loop (repeat 3) draws 3 squares at the end of each rectangle. Change this to draw five squares evenly spaced. *HINT 360 divided by 5 = 72 degrees.* What did you change?

4. What would you change to make the program draw smaller rectangles without changing the pattern? What did you change?

5. What would you add to make the pattern multicoloured? *HINT Pen commands.* What did you change/add?

Now mark your work using the change marksheet

photocopiable page

SUPPORTING CHANGE

Whole class advice

Work in pairs, one device between the pair. Take it in turns every question to swap who runs code. You must work at the same pace as your partner and not move on to the next question until you have both written your answer down. If you disagree, write a different answer. You must mark your work before moving on to the next section.

Send advice

Support pairs of pupils who are poor readers by reading questions, reading code samples and covering up questions until they get to them.

Notes on the activity

Changing or modifying code is a core part of this module, so I suggest you do not leave it out. It is an important step towards creation of their own code, as parts they have modified they will feel more ownership of. Recording marks will help with assessment.

Make changes to the code to answer these questions

1. How can you make the program run more slowly? What did you change to do this?

   Increase any wait time OR add a wait block anywhere (1 mark)

   Q1 What time-related blocks could you change or add?

2. In the main programme, the outer loop (repeat 4) draws four rectangles at right angles to each other. Change this to draw three rectangles evenly spaced. *HINT 360 divided by 3 = 120 degrees.* What did you change?

   In the main programme change repeat 4 to repeat 3 AND change turn right 90 to turn right 120 (1 mark)

   Q2 Start by pointing out the code mentioned in the question. This is often better done as a question. So where is the repeat 4 the question mentions? Where is the code to start drawing rectangles? Why does it draw four of these?

3. In the main programme, the inner nested loop (repeat 3) draws 3 squares at the end of each rectangle. Change this to draw five squares evenly spaced. *HINT 360 divided by 5 = 72 degrees.* What did you change?

   In the main programme change repeat 3 to repeat 5 AND change turn right 120 to turn right 72 (1 mark)

   Q3 Start by pointing out the code mentioned in the question. This is often better done as a question. So where is the inner nested loop? Where is the code to start drawing squares? Why does it draw three of these?

4. What would you change to make the program draw smaller rectangles without changing the pattern? What did you change?

   In the rectangle procedure change both move steps to smaller numbers or just one (1 mark)

   Q4 Ask what code sets the size of the rectangles at the moment?

5. What would you add to make the pattern multicoloured? *HINT Pen commands.* What did you change/add?

   Either add a change colour by pen block somewhere inside a loop or inside a shape procedure loop or build new code with the same block inside a separate loop. You could also have used separate set pen colour blocks inside another loop with waits in between them (1 mark for any method that works)

   Q5 A bit or reassurance that this question can be completed in many ways will help pupils to experiment. If that doesn't work then point out useful blocks like **set pen colour** and **change pen colour by**.

Now mark your work using the change marksheet

NESTED LOOPS WITH PROCEDURES CREATE

Work on your own

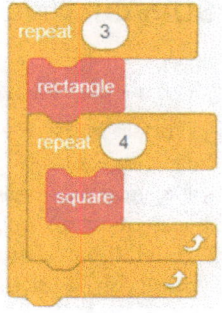

Nested Loops

Work within exploring nested loops with procedures to complete either Task 1 or Task 2

Task 1

Create another nested loop within the inner repeat 3 loop and another procedure called tinysquare to draw a pattern of tiny squares at the end of each square.

Task 2

Change the programme to have three or more levels of nesting to create an evenly spaced pattern

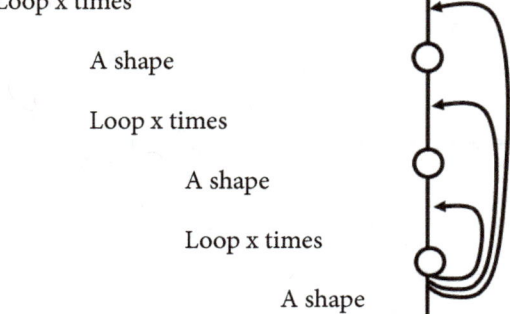

Loop x times

   A shape

   Loop x times

      A shape

      Loop x times

         A shape

Optional task

Write a program where the user inputs the amount of loops the outer nested loop should make and adjusts the spacing to fit the number of shapes

(Useful blocks)

Teacher and Pupil Assessment

Circle one column on each row to show what you think you have achieved

	Not created a nested loop in a main program	Created a nest within a nest	1 mark criteria plus created a program that the user can use to control the number of shapes
Basic Procedures	0 marks	1 mark	2 marks
		Not used previous programming concepts for real purpose	Used previous programming concepts for real purpose
Used previous programming concept such as procedures or conditions correctly	0 marks		1 mark

photocopiable page

SUPPORTING CREATE

Work within exploring nested loops with procedures to complete either Task 1 or Task 2

Task 1

Create another nested loop within the inner repeat 3 loop and another procedure called tinysquare to draw a pattern of tiny squares at the end of each square.

Task 2

Change the programme to have three or more levels of nesting to create an evenly spaced pattern

Loop x times

    A shape

    Loop x times

        A shape

        Loop x times

            A shape

Optional task

Write a program where the user inputs the amount of loops the outer nested loop should make and adjusts the spacing to fit the number of shapes

(Useful blocks)

Notes on the activity

The make part of a project is really important and teachers should always make sure that pupils have time to make their own project, even if that means reducing the time spent on other stages for pupils who work slowly. It helps if pupils work on their own for this whilst supporting their partner.

Whole class advice

Work on your own, one device each. You can discuss the work with your former partner but you are responsible for creating your own projects. Save your work regularly. Read the instructions carefully. Assess your own work by circling where you think you are in the assessment grid at the bottom of the page.

Task 1 & 2 Remind pupils that they will still need to space their new procedures evenly. This loop will need to nest within repeat 3 loop.

Sen support

Task 2 is the easiest project if you add one more level of nesting only, so it may be worth focussing pupils on that first and then doing Task 1 instead of the optional task.

Optional Task The green block divides this enables a pupil to calculate the correct spacing angle as 360 dividing by number of objects in the full circle. See next page for an example.

Optional Task You may want to remind pupils that ask collects data from the user and inputs it into the answer block.

Teacher and Pupil Assessment

Circle one column on each row to show what you think you have achieved

	Not created a nested loop in a main program	Created a nest within a nest	1 mark criteria plus created a program that the user can use to control the number of shapes
Basic Procedures	0 marks	1 mark	2 marks
		Not used previous programming concepts for real purpose	Used previous programming concepts for real purpose
Used previous programming concept such as procedures or conditions correctly		0 marks	1 mark

Assessment

There is more marking and assessment support on the next page.

SUPPORTING CREATE ASSESSMENT

One possible solution for Task 1
See outlined area for new code

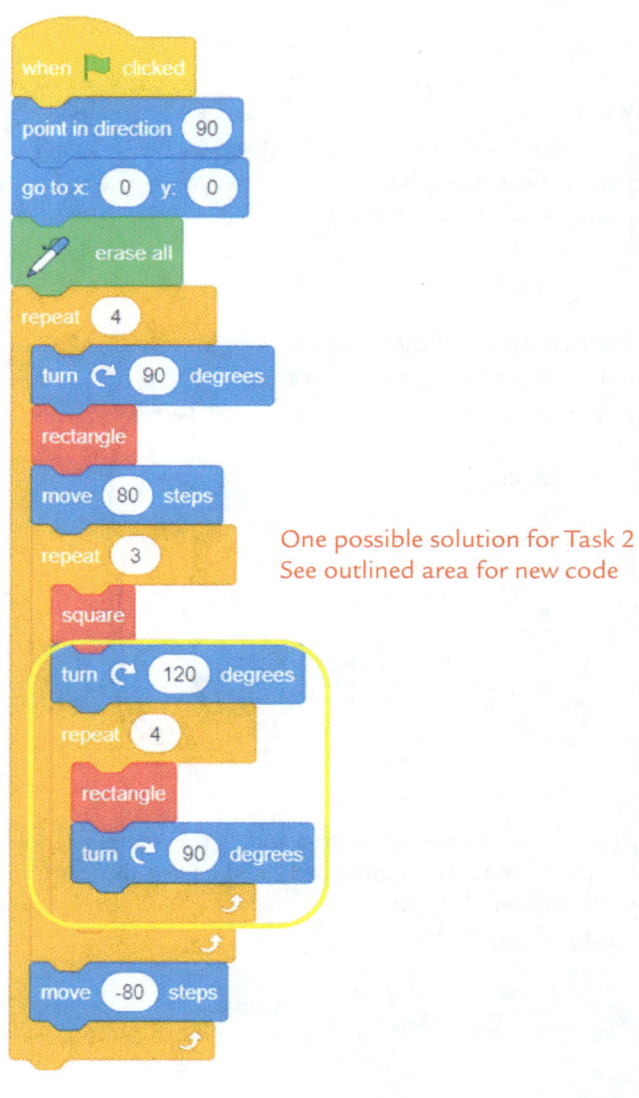

One possible solution for Task 2
See outlined area for new code

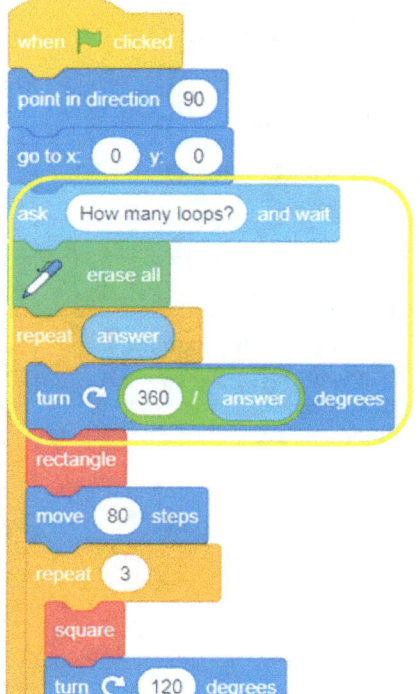

One possible solution for
Optional Task
See outlined area for new code

PARSONS MARKSHEET

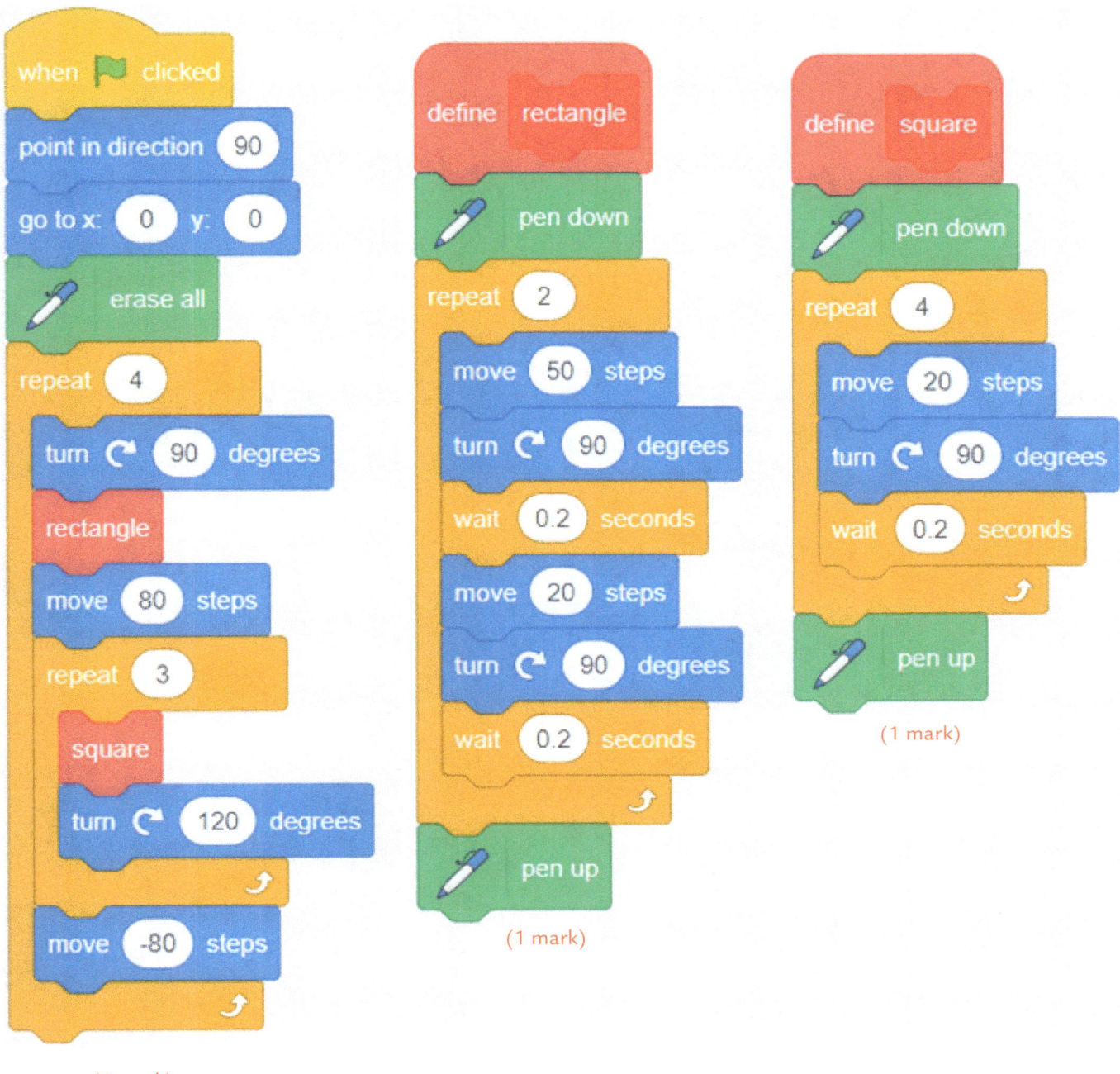

when 🚩 clicked
point in direction 90
go to x: 0 y: 0
erase all
repeat 4
  turn ↻ 90 degrees
  rectangle
  move 80 steps
  repeat 3
    square
    turn ↻ 120 degrees
  move -80 steps

(1 mark)

define rectangle
pen down
repeat 2
  move 50 steps
  turn ↻ 90 degrees
  wait 0.2 seconds
  move 20 steps
  turn ↻ 90 degrees
  wait 0.2 seconds
pen up

(1 mark)

define square
pen down
repeat 4
  move 20 steps
  turn ↻ 90 degrees
  wait 0.2 seconds
pen up

(1 mark)

PREDICT MARKSHEET

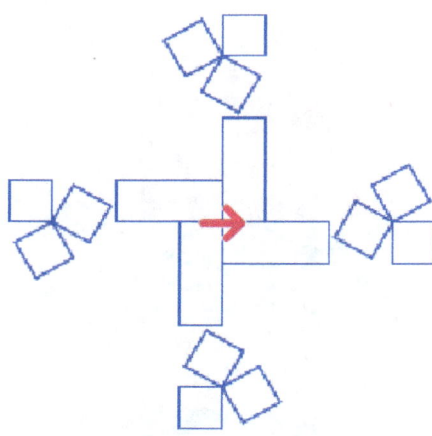

Start at the top add all marks for every line which is correct

Four rectangles (1 mark)

Four rectangles in a cross (1 mark)

A set of three squares (1 mark)

A set of three squares at the end of a rectangle (1 mark)

Four sets of three squares (1 mark)

Four sets of three squares at the end of a rectangle (1mark)

Maximum 6 marks

INVESTIGATE MARKSHEET

Run the program as many times as you want.
Work with a partner to answer these questions.

1. How many times is move –80 steps run?
    4 (1 mark)

2. How many times in the main program is the rectangle procedure used?
    4 (1 mark)

3. How many times in the main program is the square procedure used?
    12 (1 mark)

4. Initialisation means thinking about how the code can be reused by resetting itself back to where it started and removing the effects of previous use. List any instructions that might be initialisation.
    Point in direction 90, go to X:0 Y:0, erase all (1 marks for 2 or more of these)

5. Tick the repeat loop that is nested inside another loop
    ☐ Repeat 2
    ☐ Repeat 3
    ☐ Repeat 4

6. Can a procedure be run more than once?
    Yes (1 mark)

photocopiable page

CHANGE MARKSHEET

Make changes to the code to answer these questions

1. How can you make the program run more slowly? What did you change to do this?

   Increase any wait time OR add a wait block anywhere (1 mark)

2. In the main programme the outer loop (repeat 4) draws four rectangles at right angles to each other. Change this to draw three rectangles evenly spaced. *HINT 360 divided by 3 = 120 degrees.* What did you change?

   In the main programme, change repeat 4 to repeat 3 AND change turn right 90 to turn right 120 (1 mark)

3. In the main programme, the inner nested loop (repeat 3) draws 3 squares at the end of each rectangle. Change this to draw five squares evenly spaced. *HINT 360 divided by 5 = 72 degrees.* What did you change?

   In the main programme, change repeat 3 to repeat 5 AND change turn right 120 to turn right 72 (1 mark)

4. What would you change to make the program draw smaller rectangles without changing the pattern? What did you change?

   In the rectangle procedure, change both move steps to smaller numbers or just one (1 mark)

5. What would you add to make the pattern multicoloured? *HINT Pen commands.* What did you change/add?

   Either add a change colour by pen block somewhere inside a loop or inside a shape procedure loop or build new code with the same block inside a separate loop. You could also have used separate set pen colour blocks inside another loop with waits in between them. (1 mark for any method that works)

PROGRAMMING MODULES THAT USE VARIABLES (ALL TYPES)

> **Overview**
> Pupils explore how variables can be used in different ways before adding variables to previous projects.

To do before the session

1. Look at the grid below and decide which **optional** and **SEN** activities you are going to include and exclude.
2. Print pupil worksheets for each activity chosen and staple into a booklet, one for each pupil.
3. Print marksheets for activities chosen to be placed where pupils can access them.
4. Download the code needed and place in a templates folder on your school network or add to a Scratch Studio or link on your learning platform.
5. Download the slides that go with the concept introduction.
6. Study the notes that go with the slides.
7. Examine the teacher help notes that are provided alongside every activity.

To do at the start of the session

If you have not introduced **variables** with this class before, do this first using the resources on page 23 as a whole class activity.

To do after the concept has been introduced

Each activity has whole class notes to help you explain what is needed if it is the first time pupils have carried out this type of activity. There are also core instructions underneath in case you are sticking to the core activities only.

It can also be helpful to show pupils how to create a variable if they haven't already done so and give them 20 mins to experiment with creating and using a variable without any directed theme. However useful this time is, don't be tempted to believe that pupils have good understanding even if they can use variables in simple ways. They will need careful code comprehension to broaden their understanding.

Variables

Make a variable

See card at end of module for reminder

How this module fits into a programming progression

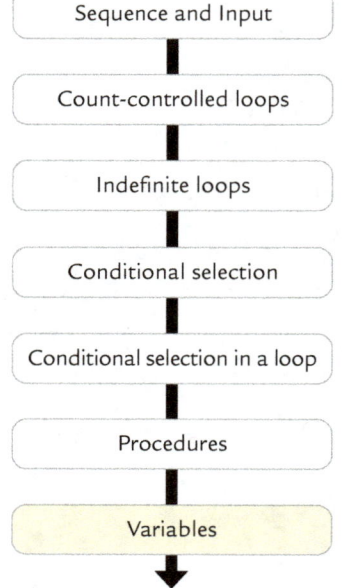

Sequence and Input

Count-controlled loops

Indefinite loops

Conditional selection

Conditional selection in a loop

Procedures

Variables

> **Vocabulary**
> variable, assign, set, value, name

Resource Name	Core Optional SEN	Teacher	Pupil Grouping	How Assessed	SCRATCH ACCESS
CONCEPT Variables	CORE	Leads Session	Solo whole class activity	Formative	NO
PARSONS	OPTIONAL SEN OPTIONAL ALL	Support Poor Readers	Solo or Paired (Teacher choice)	Pupil Marked Marksheet Provided	YES Parsons Variable fun
PREDICT	OPTIONAL ALL (predict or parsons not both)	Support Poor Readers	Paired	Pupil Marked Marksheet Provided	NO
INVESTIGATE	OPTIONAL ALL (predict or parsons not both)	Support Poor Readers	Paired	Pupil Marked Marksheet Provided	YES Variable fun
CHANGE	CORE	Support Poor Readers	Paired	Pupil Marked Marksheet Provided	YES Variable fun
CREATE	CORE	Assesses Pupil Work and Checks Pupil Self-Assessment	Solo	Pupil Assessed & Teacher Assessed	YES Variable fun
FLOW ASSESSMENT LOGICAL ASSESSMENT	OPTIONAL ALL	Assesses Logical Understanding	Solo or Paired (Teacher Choice)	Pupil Marked Marksheet Provided	NO

Core activities general instructions

1. Group pupils in roughly same ability pairs. For **investigate** and **change** worksheets pupils will work in pairs, for **create** they will work separately.

2. Give out the pupil booklets and explain that pupils need to follow the instructions on the sheets to explore how **variables** work.

3. Explain that each pupil will record separately whilst working alongside their partner and keeping to the same pace as their partner.

4. Demonstrate where they can find the template code and explain that pupils will share one device for investigate and change.

5. Explain that during each question only one person should touch the shared device and they should swap who that person is when there is a new questions.

6. Encourage them to discuss their answers with their partner. If they disagree with their partner they can record a different answer in their own booklet.

7. Show pupils where it says they should mark their work on the sheet and where the answer sheets are in the classroom.

8. Remind pupils to return marksheets after marking, because there are not enough for every pair to have their own.

Key Programming Knowledge

Variables are used to store information to be referred to and changed in a computer programme or algorithm

Variables

- Have a name and a value
- read the name but act on the value
- Values can be changed during the algorithm or programme
- When writing the value of a variable we call it assigning

Variable Naming

- Always name a variable after the data that it stores or the task that it does
- Avoid naming variables with spaces – teamScore (camelCase) or user_name (underscore)
- Avoid using the same name as a procedure

Resources

Variable fun https://scratch.mit.edu/projects/583590770/
Parsons Variable fun https://scratch.mit.edu/projects/644630478/

	On the sheet, if it says no Scratch, they must work only on the sheet.
	If it says Scratch with a green tick, they can use one device between the pair.
	If it says work with a partner, they must work at the same speed as their partner.
	If it says work on their own, they must do this using a separate device each working alone.

There is a flow of control sheet for teachers to use with pupils at the end of the module to help discuss flow problems

Scottish Curriculum for Excellence Technologies

I understand the instructions of a visual programming language and can predict the outcome of a program written using the language. TCH 1-14a

I can explain core programming language concepts in appropriate technical language. TCH 2-14a

I can demonstrate a range of basic problem solving skills by building simple programs to carry out a given task, using an appropriate language. TCH 1-15a

I can create, develop and evaluate computing solutions in response to a design challenge. TCH 2-15a

English Computing National Curriculum Programs of Study

Pupils should be taught to:

- **design, write and debug programs that accomplish specific goals,** including controlling or simulating physical systems; solve problems by decomposing them into smaller parts.

- **use sequence, selection and repetition in programs;** work with **variables and various forms of input and output.**

- **use logical reasoning to explain how some simple algorithms work and to detect and correct errors in algorithms and programs.**

Welsh National Curriculum Relevant Strands

Progression Step 3.

- I can use conditional statements to add control and decision-making to algorithms.
- I can explain and debug algorithms.

VARIABLE FUN
PARSONS

Work with a partner

Start Scratch and Load
PARSONS VARIABLE FUN

Use the algorithms below to help you connect the Scratch blocks in the correct places in PARSONS VARIABLE FUN

Start when sprite clicked	Start when sprite clicked
Assign 0 to num1	Set rotation left and right
Assign 0 to num2	Point –90 (left)
Assign 0 to total	Assign 0 to count
Ask user to type in first number	Say counting to 10
Assign answer to num1	Loop 10 times
Ask user to type in second number	Add 1 to count variable
Assign answer to num2	Say count variable
Add num1 and num2 and assign to total	
Say num1 + num2 = total	

Adding   Counting

Now mark your work using the parsons marksheet

photocopiable page

SUPPORTING PARSONS

Whole class advice

Load Parsons variables fun code and then use the algorithm on this page to build the code. When you have completed it, run the code and check your answer with the Parsons marking sheet.

Understanding programming

You can find out more about Parsons problems in the teacher book.

Individual advice adding

Assign is the same as set in Scratch.

Individual advice counting

Point out that the code inside a loop is indented in the planning algorithm.

Notes on the activity

This allow pupils to build the code first before investigating, modifying and creating code of their own. The algorithm is written in language similar but also different to the code. This helps pupils by enabling them to see an example of planning which will help them when they come to plan their own project. On its own, it is not enough deep thinking about the code to enable agency, but as a starter or SEN activity it is useful to see how code can be built.

Send advice

Parsons problems can be made less complex by connecting more blocks in the example Scratch code and saving that version as a new template.

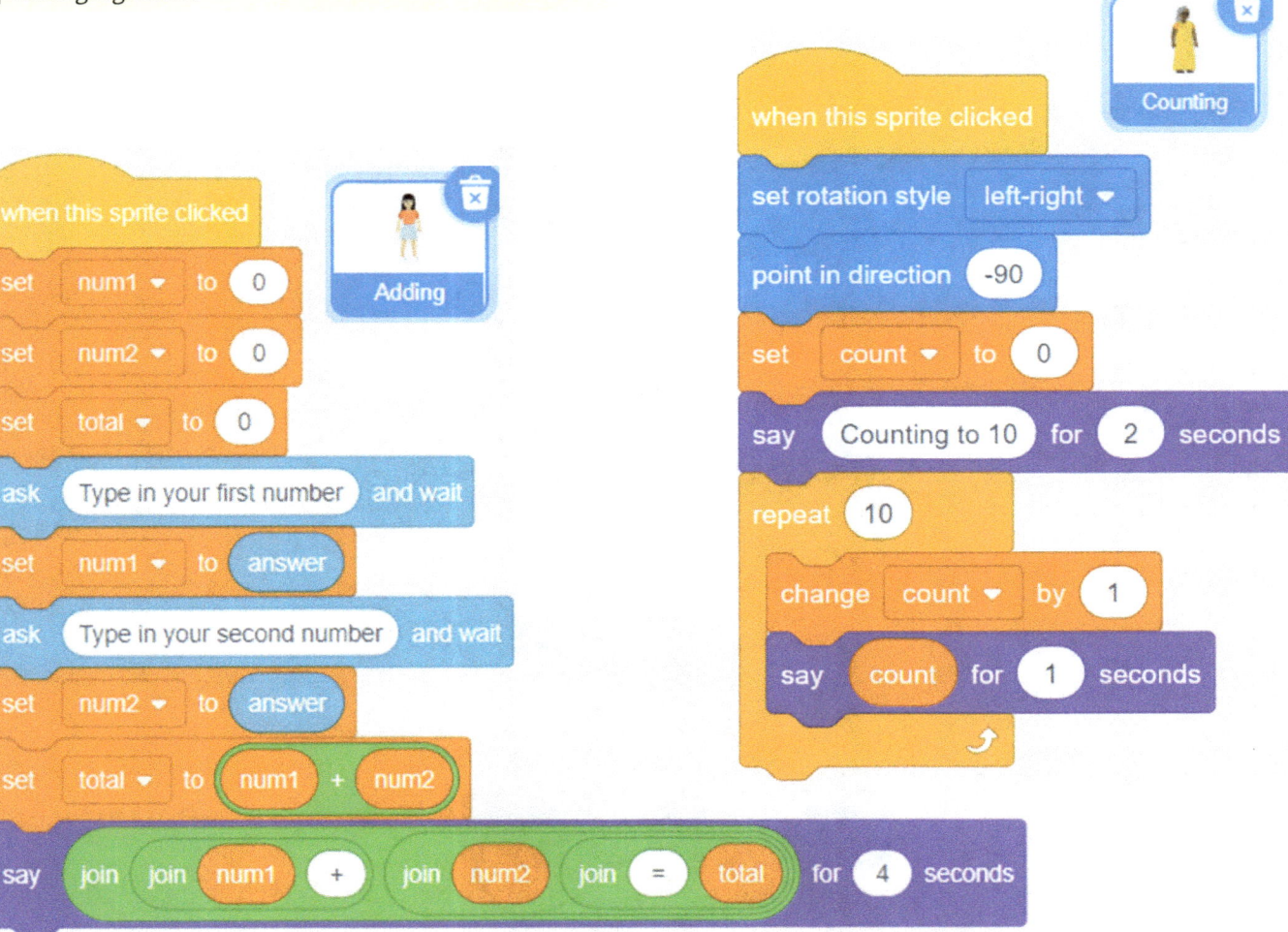

VARIABLE FUN

Work with a partner

PREDICT

Read the code carefully with your partner.
Write down what you think the programme is for.

Initialisation
Sets all the variables back to 0 getting rid of any values assigned when the program was last used

```
when this sprite clicked
set num1 to 0
set num2 to 0
set total to 0
```

Collects two numbers from the users and assigns them to two variables

```
ask Type in your first number and wait
set num1 to answer
ask Type in your second number and wait
set num2 to answer
```

Adds values of num1 to num2 and stores this in total

```
set total to (num1 + num2)
```

Shows the user all the variable values

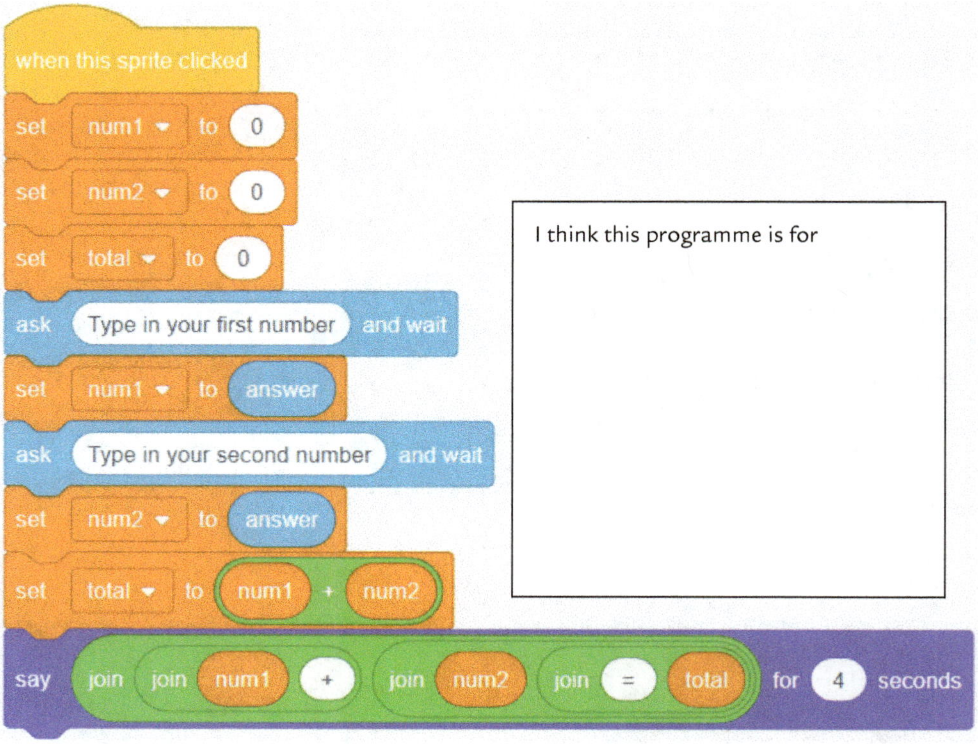

```
say (join (join num1 (join + (join num2 (join = total)))) for 4 seconds
```

I think this programme is for

Initialisation
Sets the variable back to 0 getting rid of any values assigned when the program was last used

```
when this sprite clicked
set rotation style left-right
point in direction -90
set count to 0
```

Add one to the count variable every time it is run in the loop and then tell the user what the value of count is on the screen

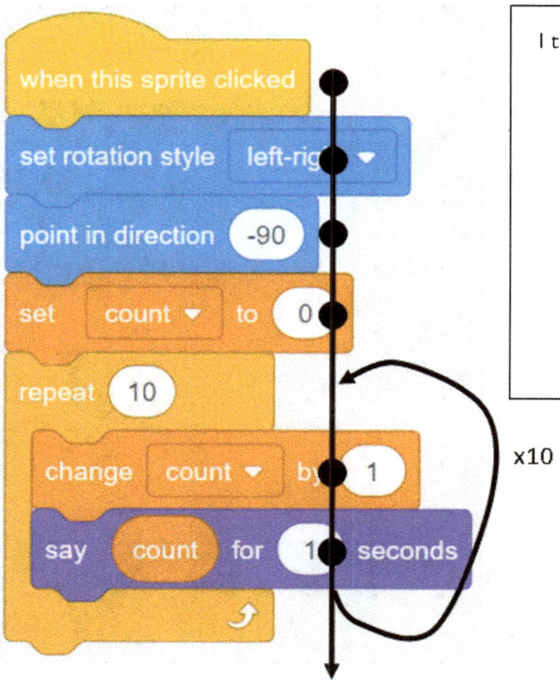

```
repeat 10
  change count by 1
  say count for 1 seconds
```

x10

I think this programme is for

HINT Go through the loop and change the count variable value as you do

Now mark your work using the predict marksheet

photocopiable page

SUPPORTING PREDICT

I think this programme is for

Any answer that indicates that this programme adds two numbers together (1 mark)

Send advice
Simplifying the language can help. The simplifications below are not the best computer science language but can act as a stepping stone for some pupils.

Initialisation Sets all the variables back to 0 getting rid of any values assigned when the program was last used

Rubs out all the numbers stored in these variables and replaces them with 0.

Collects two numbers from the users and assigns them to two variables

Collects a number from the user and puts it inside num1 variable.

Collects a number from the user and puts it inside num2 variable.

Adds values of num1 to num2 and stores this in total

Adds what is inside of num1 to num2 and puts this in total variable.

Shows the user all the variable values

Shows everyone the sum including what is inside the variables.

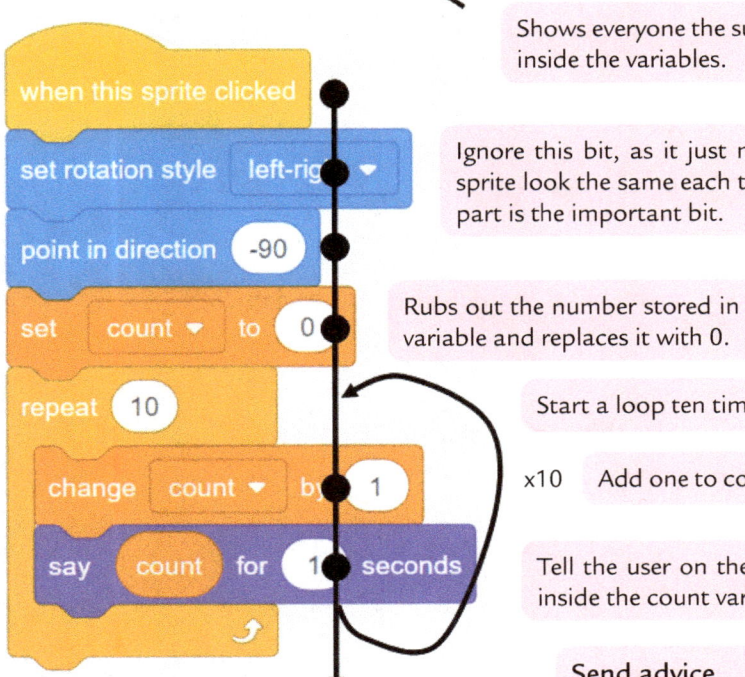

Initialisation Sets the variable back to 0 getting rid of any values assigned when the program was last used

Ignore this bit, as it just makes the sprite look the same each time. Next part is the important bit.

Rubs out the number stored in count variable and replaces it with 0.

Add one to the count variable every time it is run in the loop and then tell the user what the value of count is on the screen

Start a loop ten times.

x10   Add one to count variable.

Tell the user on the screen what is inside the count variable.

I think this programme is for

Any answer that mentions counting (1 mark)
Any answer that mentions counting to 10 (2 marks)

HINT Go through the loop and change the count variable value as you do

Send advice
Do this on a whiteboard as you go through this and go through the loop 3 times.

VARIABLE FUN
INVESTIGATE

Work with a partner

Work with a partner. Open Scratch and load Variable Fun

Run the program as many times as you want. Work with a partner to answer these questions.
Look inside the placeholder sprite

1. Which two lines of code collect the user's name and assign it to the variable **user_name**?
    A
    B

2. How many times is the (user_name) variable block used in the program?

Look inside accumulator sprite

3. If you get the answer correct what happens to the score?

4. If you get the answer wrong what happens to the score?

Look inside adding sprite

5. Name all three variables
    A   B   C

6. Which line of code adds num1 to num2?

Look inside counting

7. What line of code says what is inside the count variable?

8. Which block initialises the count variable?
    HINT Sets it back to what it was at the start

Now mark your work using the investigate marksheet

photocopiable page

SUPPORT INVESTIGATE

Send advice
Support pairs of pupils who are poor readers by reading questions, reading code samples and covering up questions until they get to them.

Whole class advice
Work in pairs, one device between the pair. Take it in turns every question to swap who runs code. You must work at the same pace as your partner and not move on to the next question until you have both written your answer down. If you disagree, write a different answer. You must mark your work before moving on to the next section.

Look inside the placeholder sprite
1. Which two lines of code collect the user's name and assign it to the variable **user_name**?

    A Ask what is your name and wait (1 mark)

    B Set user_name to answer (1 mark)

2. How many times is the **user_name** variable block used in the program?

    4 (1 mark)

Look inside accumulator sprite
3. If you get the answer correct what happens to the score?

    Add 1 (1 mark)

4. If you get the answer wrong what happens to the score?

    Minus 1 (1 mark)

Look inside adding sprite
5. Name all three variables

    A num1 (1mark)   B num2 (1 mark)

    C total (1 mark)

6. Which line of code adds num1 to num2?

    Set total to num1 + num2 (1 mark) the line below only tells you the answer

Look inside counting
7. What line of code says what is inside the count variable?

    Say count for 1 second (1 mark)

8. Which block initialises the count variable?

    HINT Sets it back to what it was at the start

    Set count to 0 (1 mark)

Notes on the activity
Investigating the code encourages pupils to think deeply about how it works. Check that every pupil is filling in and marking the questions individually but at the pace of the slowest in the pair. Sometimes a pair decides not to mark to speed up their efforts. Marking gives valuable information, so I recommend sending them back to mark their work. A class instruction to come and talk to you if they have over half of the questions wrong or they do not understand the answer after they have marked it helps to check progress is being made correctly. There is real value in collecting these scores to build up a summative picture of pupil progress.

Individual advice all
There is a sheet to print at the end of the chapter that has the flow of control for all the code examples which might help if pupils get stuck on any question.

Individual advice Q1
Ask how you would know their name. You would ask for it and then you would store their answer in your memory.

Individual advice Q2
Setting the variable assigns value. The variable is only used when we read the name but act on the value using this block.

Individual advice Q3
Which block of code checks to see if the answer is correct? Answer = 24. It reads if the answer is same as 24. What happens to the score after this?

Individual advice Q4
Which block of code checks to see if the answer is **not** correct? NOT Answer = 24. It reads if the answer is NOT same as 24. What happens to the score after this?

Individual advice Q6
Some pupils mistake adding the numbers with reading the answer out.

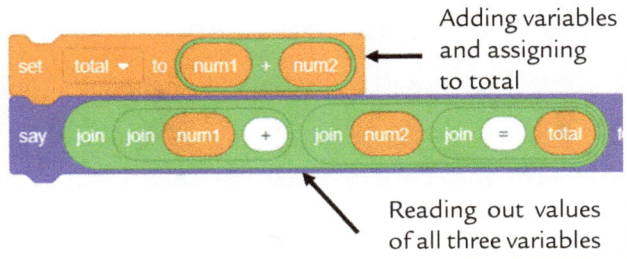

Adding variables and assigning to total

Reading out values of all three variables

VARIABLE FUN
CHANGE

Work with a partner

Work with a partner. Open Scratch and load
Variable Fun

Make changes to the code to answer these questions
Make changes to accumulator

1. Change the code to give 5 points for every correct answer.
   What did you change?

2. Change the code to start with 10 points
   What did you change?

Make changes to Adding

3. Change the code to multiply both numbers
   Circle the block you changed it to?

Make changes to Counting. *HINT Duplicate code and then change*

4. Change the code to count slower
   What did you change?

5. Change the code to count in 2s.
   What did you change?

6. Change the code to count in halves. *HINT decimal halves*
   What did you change?

7. Change the code to count backwards from 10.
   What things did you change?

Now mark your work using the change marksheet

photocopiable page

SUPPORTING CHANGE

Whole class advice

Work in pairs, one device between the pair. Take it in turns every question to swap who runs code. You must work at the same pace as your partner and not move on to the next question until you have both written your answer down. If you disagree, write a different answer. You must mark your work before moving on to the next section.

Notes on the activity

Changing or modifying code is a core part of this module, so I suggest you do not leave it out. It is an important step towards creation of their own code, as parts they have modified they will feel more ownership of. Recording marks will help with assessment.

Send advice

Support pairs of pupils who are poor readers by reading questions, reading code samples and covering up questions until they get to them.

Make changes to the code to answer these questions

Make changes to Accumulator

1. Change the code to give 5 points for every correct answer.

   What did you change? Change score by 1 to change score by 5 (1 mark)

2. Change the code to start with 10 points.

   What did you change? Change set score to 0 to set score to 10 (1 mark)

Make changes to Adding

3. Change the code to multiply both numbers.

   What did you change it to?

   (1 mark)

Make changes to Counting *HINT Duplicate and then change*

4. Change the code to count slower.

   What did you change? Change say count for 1 second to a higher seconds number (1 mark)

   Or add a wait block into the loop (1 mark)

5. Change the code to count in 2s.

   What did you change? Change-count-by-1 to change-count-by-2

6. Change the code to count in halves. *HINT decimal halves*

   What did you change? Change-count by 1 to change count by 0.5 (1 mark)

7. Change the code to count backwards from 10.

   What things did you change? Change set count to 0 to set count to 10 and change-count-by 1 to change-count-by –1 (2 marks)

Individual advice Q1

Ask what blocks do they think change the score variable?

Individual advice Q2

Encourage pupils to run the code two or three times. What makes the score go back to 0 every time the code restarts?

Individual advice Q3

Pupils can think that the last line actually carries out the maths rather than just saying what is assigned to the variables. If they do believe this ask them what the line above does? You can always ask them to remove the penultimate line and see what the code does without it.

Individual advice Q4

Mention that slower is a time word. Are there any time words in the code?

Individual advice Q5

Ask what makes it count in 1s? You can always use the flow of control sheets to help pupils think through what is happening in each script.

Individual advice Q6

You may need to remind pupils that 0.5 is a decimal half.

Individual advice Q7

Ask pupils to decompose the problem into Starting from 10 and counting backwards.

Individual advice all

There is a sheet to print at the end of the chapter that has the flow of control for all the code examples which might help if pupils get stuck on any question.

VARIABLE FUN
CREATE

Work on
your own

Work within variable fun to complete Tasks 1, 2 and 3

Task 1

Add a new maths question to the bottom of the **Placeholder** maths quiz and personalise it using the user_ name variable

Task 2

Add a new maths quiz question to the bottom of the **Accumulator** maths quiz and increase the score if the user is correct

Task 3

Work within **Adding** to make the program add three numbers together

Now work outside variable fun to complete Task 4 OR 5

Task 4

Find any previous program created in the past and add variables to make it work better

Task 5

Build your own program that uses variables

Teacher and Pupil Assessment

Circle one column on each row to show what you think you have achieved

	Not used a variable in my program	copied a variables idea exactly	Adapted a variable idea	Used variables in a way not shown in the example program
Variables	0 marks	1 mark	2 marks	3 marks
			Not used previous programming concepts for real purpose	Used previous programming concepts for real purpose
Used previous programming concept such as loops or conditions correctly			0 marks	1 mark

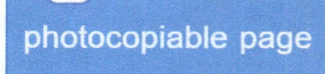
photocopiable page

SUPPORTING CREATE

Task 1

An answer that simply copies the code and adapts the question and answer (1 mark only)

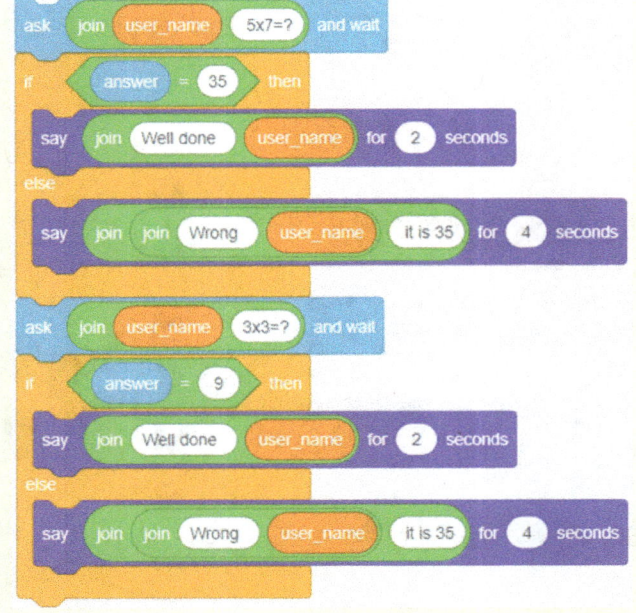

Work within variable fun to complete Tasks 1, 2 and 3

Task 1

Add a new maths question to the bottom of the **Placeholder** maths quiz and personalise it using the user_name variable

Task 2

Add a new maths quiz question to the bottom of the **Accumulator** maths quiz and increase the score if the user is correct

Task 3

Work within **Adding** to make the program add three numbers together

Now work outside variable fun to complete Task 4 OR 5

Task 3

You would also need to change how the answer is reported in the say blocks

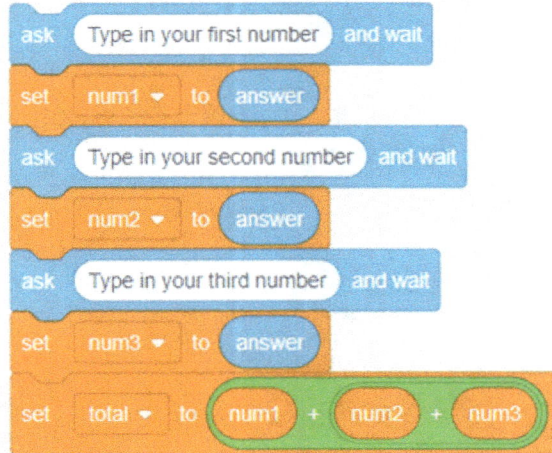

Notes on the activity

The make part of a project is really important and teachers should always make sure that pupils have time to make their own project, even if that means reducing the time spent on other stages for pupils who work slowly. It helps if pupils work on their own for this while supporting their partner.

Whole class advice

Work on your own, one device each. You can discuss the work with your former partner but you are responsible for creating your own projects. Save your work regularly. Read the instructions carefully. Assess your own work by circling where you think you are in the assessment grid at the bottom of the page.

Task 1

An answer that adapts the question (2 marks)

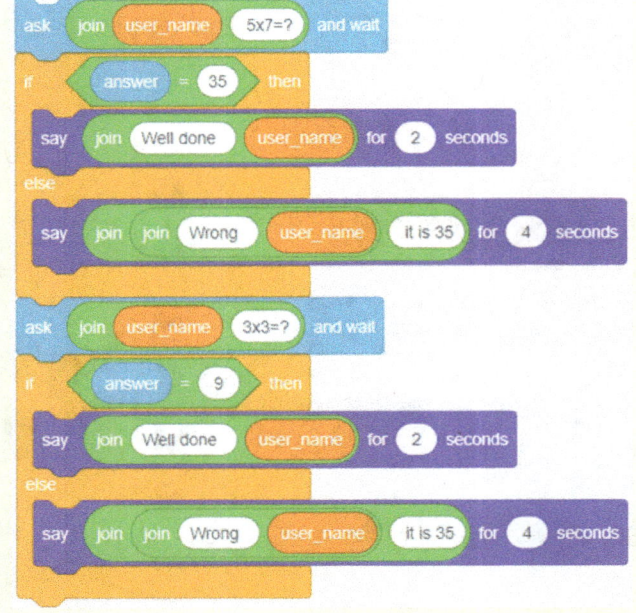

Task 2

New question example

Task 2

New question example 2

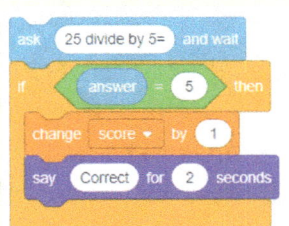

VARIABLE FUN
FLOW ASSESSMENT

Read the code carefully and follow the order the code is run with your finger.

Doug said the code took a different red dashed line path – – – – – – – in both scripts

Doug was wrong! Tick the red dashed pathway that it is **impossible** for the code to follow

HINT It is impossible for any number to be both 24 and NOT 24

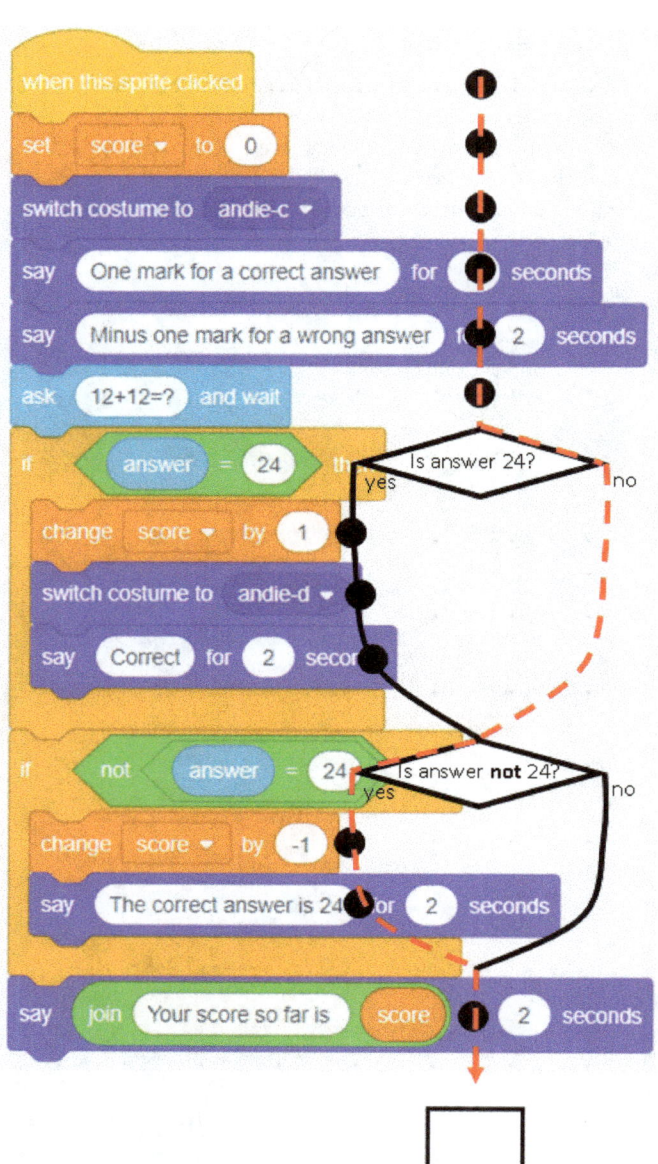
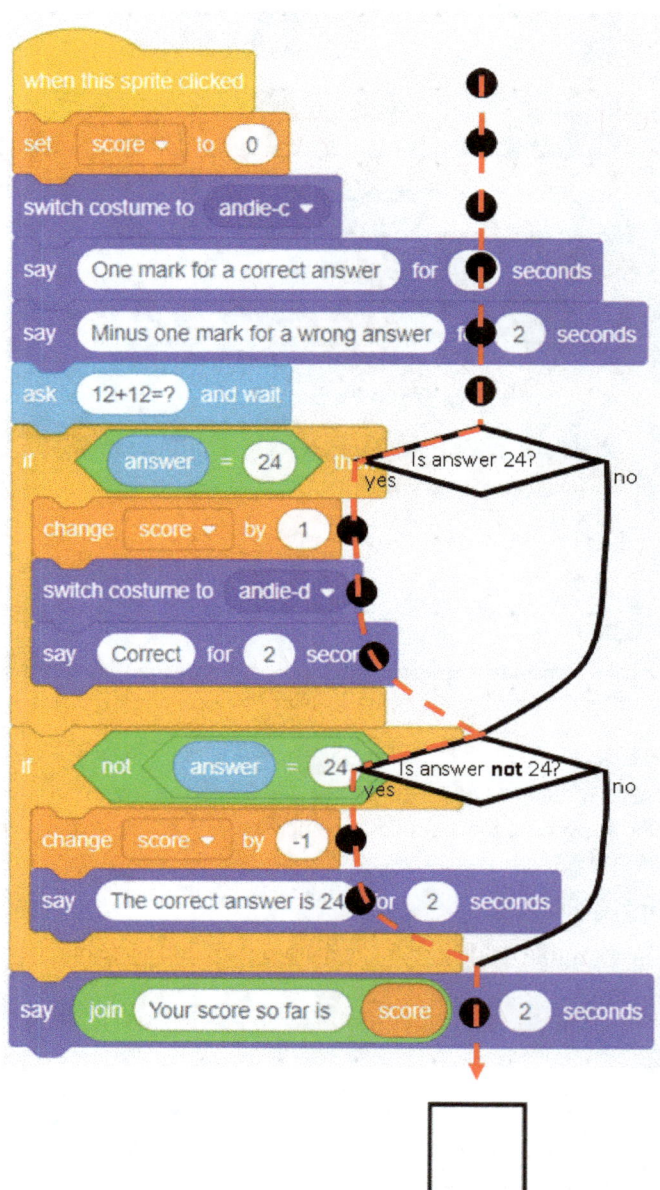

SUPPORTING FLOW ASSESSMENT 1

Whole class instructions

Look at this code carefully. Trace the flow of the code making sure that when you get to one of the diamonds you ask the question and then go down one of the two pathways.

Now look at the two dashed paths which are different on both code examples.

One of the dashed paths is impossible to go down. Which one is it?

FLOW

Read the code carefully with your partner and follow the order the code is run with your finger.

Doug said the code took a different red dashed line path ▬ ▬ ▬ ▬ ▬ ▬ in both scripts

Doug was wrong! Tick the red dashed pathway that it is impossible for the code to follow

HINT *It is impossible for any number to be both 24 and NOT 24*

Notes on the activity

This assessment checks pupils' understanding of conditional selection, which they learnt about in Year 5 and their logical understanding of what can and can't happen.

Send advice

Some pupils will really benefit from going through this in a group with you.

The simplifications below are not the best computing science language but can help some SEN pupils.

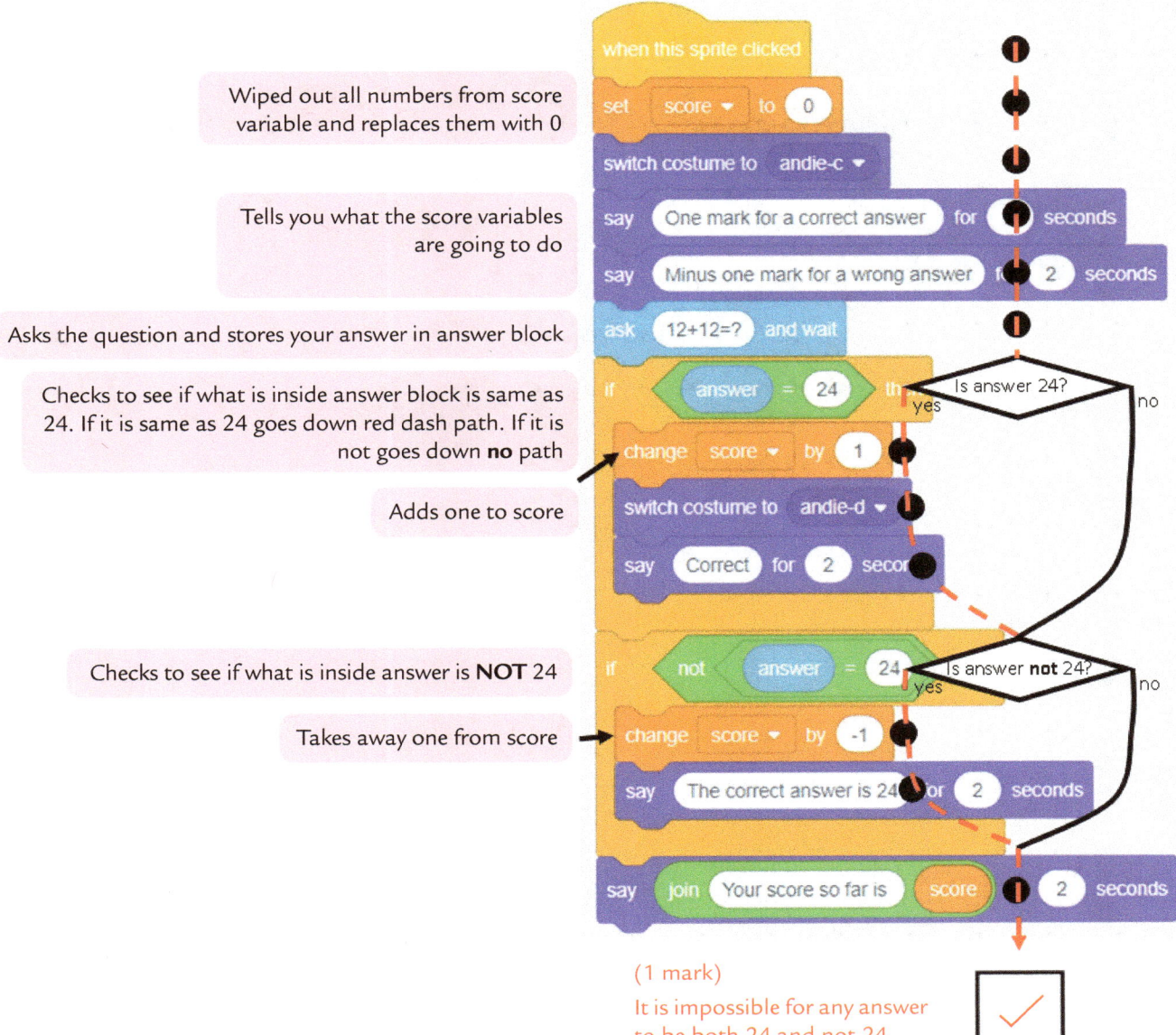

Wiped out all numbers from score variable and replaces them with 0

Tells you what the score variables are going to do

Asks the question and stores your answer in answer block

Checks to see if what is inside answer block is same as 24. If it is same as 24 goes down red dash path. If it is not goes down **no** path

Adds one to score

Checks to see if what is inside answer is **NOT** 24

Takes away one from score

(1 mark)

It is impossible for any answer to be both 24 and not 24

VARIABLE FUN
LOGICAL ASSESSMENT

Read the code carefully

Three outcome have been created

Tick the outcome that is impossible (it will never happen)

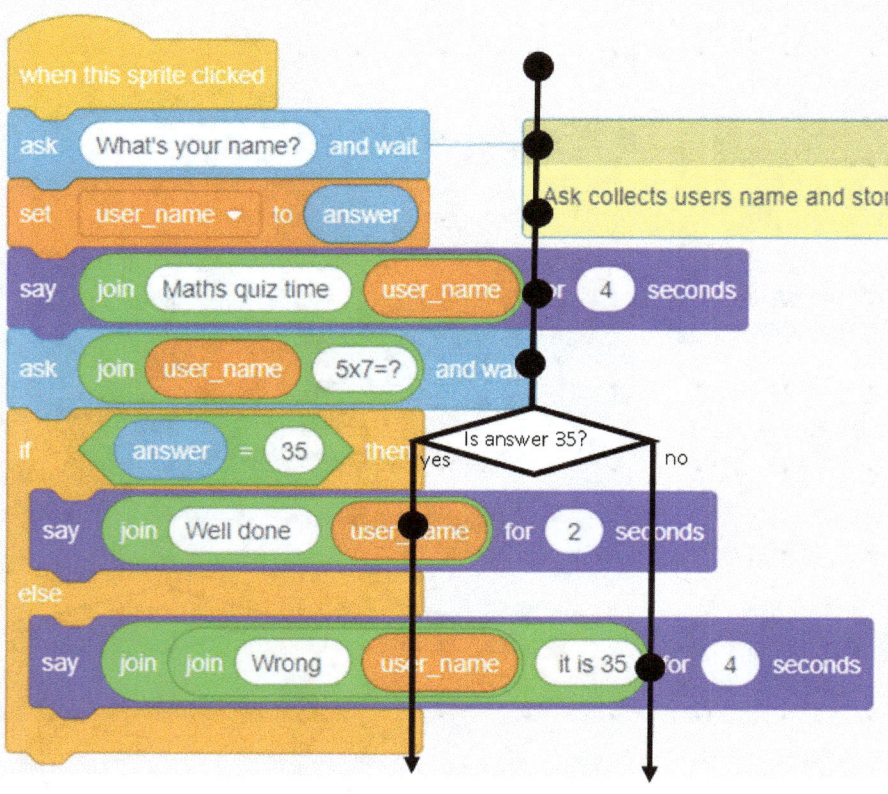

Now mark your work using the logical assessment marksheet

Outcome 1

Start program

             Type in name

Maths quiz time **Lizzy**

Lizzy 5x7=?

             Type in answer

Well done **Lizzy**

Outcome 2

Start program

             Type in name

Maths quiz time **Aki**

Aki 5x7=?

             Type in answer

Wrong **Aki** it is 35

Outcome 3

Start program

             Type in name

Maths quiz time **Mike**

Darla 5x7=?

             Type in answer

Well done **Don**

photocopiable page

SUPPORTING LOGICAL ASSESSMENT

Notes on the activity
This optional activity helps to assess pupils' understanding of conditions and variables.

Whole class advice
Make sure you work with your partner on this sheet. Read the outcomes together. Which outcome is impossible?

Send advice
Ask where in the code can someone type in their name? Answer blocks 2

Ask where is users name is in the program? Answer assigned to user_name orange variable blocks

Say if the user typed in Bob what would it say on line 5? Answer Bob 5x7=?

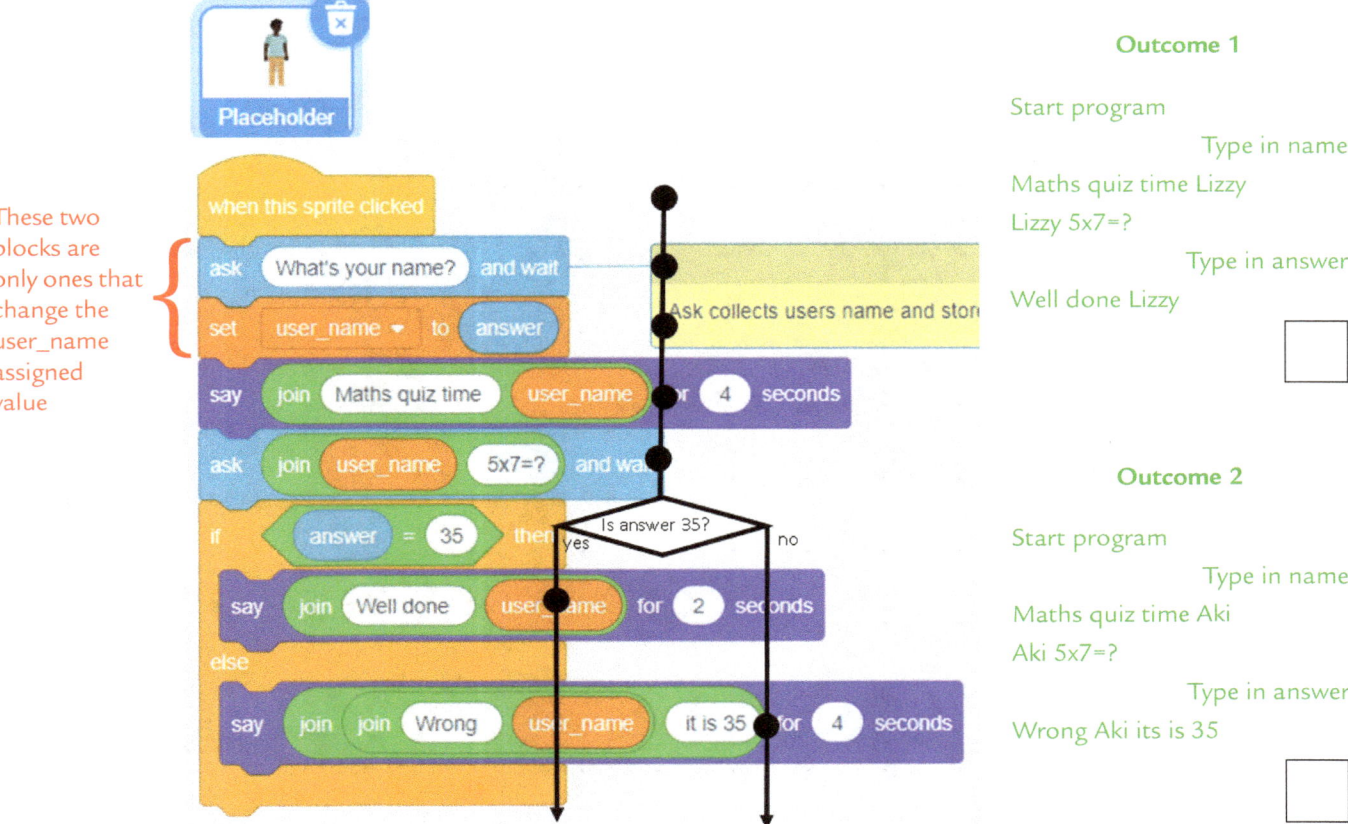

These two blocks are only ones that change the user_name assigned value

Outcome 1

Start program

Type in name

Maths quiz time Lizzy

Lizzy 5x7=?

Type in answer

Well done Lizzy

Outcome 2

Start program

Type in name

Maths quiz time Aki

Aki 5x7=?

Type in answer

Wrong Aki its is 35

Outcome 3

Start program

Type in name

Maths quiz time **Mike**

Darla 5x7=?

Type in answer

Well done **Don**

Individal advice question
Sometimes just rephrasing the question helps.

Point towards the three outcomes and explain that in this code one is impossible. Which one is it?

Individal advice question
HINT Look at the names in each outcome.

(1 mark)

It is impossible for the user_name variable to change name without programming opportunities to do so.

PARSONS MARKSHEET

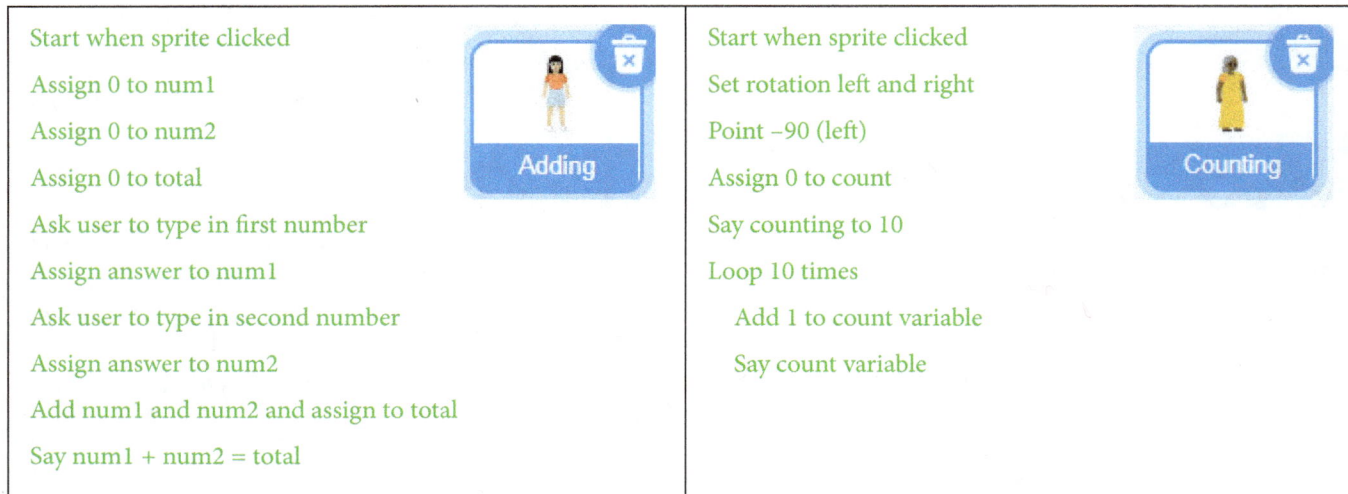

Start when sprite clicked	Start when sprite clicked
Assign 0 to num1	Set rotation left and right
Assign 0 to num2	Point –90 (left)
Assign 0 to total	Assign 0 to count
Ask user to type in first number	Say counting to 10
Assign answer to num1	Loop 10 times
Ask user to type in second number	Add 1 to count variable
Assign answer to num2	Say count variable
Add num1 and num2 and assign to total	
Say num1 + num2 = total	

```
when this sprite clicked
set rotation style [left-right ▼]
point in direction (-90)
set [count ▼] to (0)
say (Counting to 10) for (2) seconds
repeat (10)
    change [count ▼] by (1)
    say (count) for (1) seconds
```

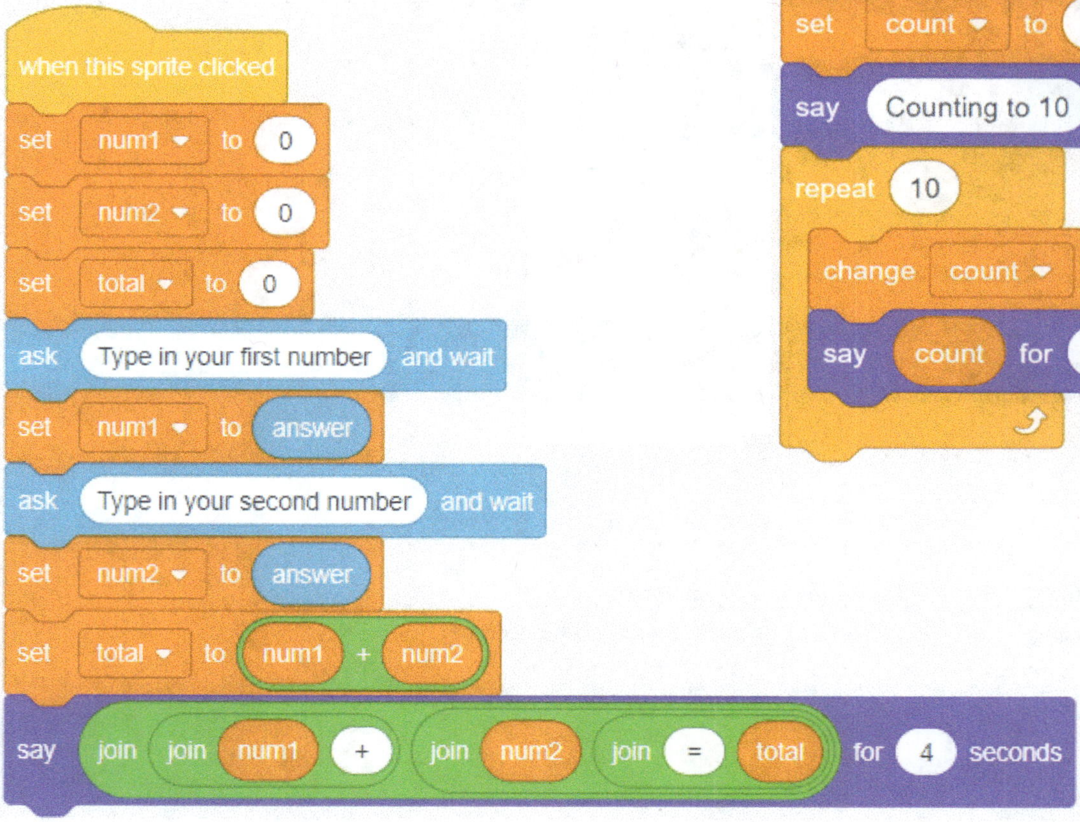

```
when this sprite clicked
set [num1 ▼] to (0)
set [num2 ▼] to (0)
set [total ▼] to (0)
ask (Type in your first number) and wait
set [num1 ▼] to (answer)
ask (Type in your second number) and wait
set [num2 ▼] to (answer)
set [total ▼] to (num1 + num2)
say (join (join (num1) (+) (join (num2) (join (=) (total)))) for (4) seconds
```

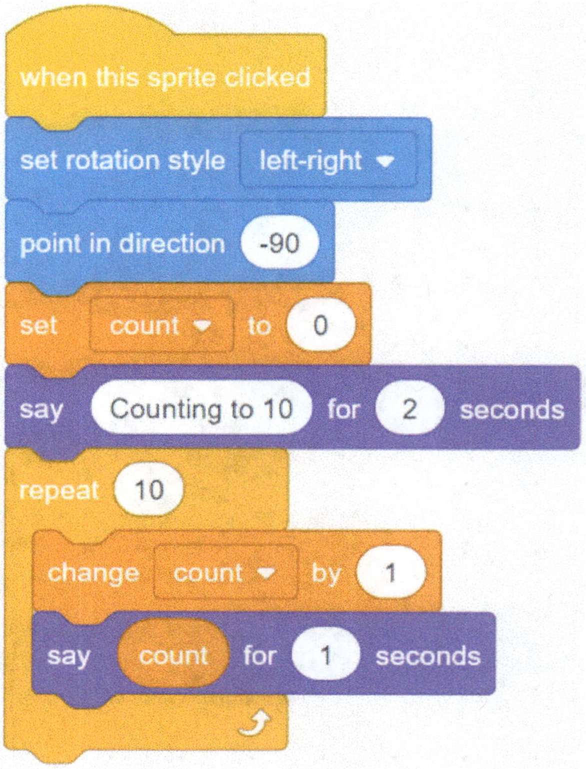

photocopiable page

PREDICT MARKSHEET

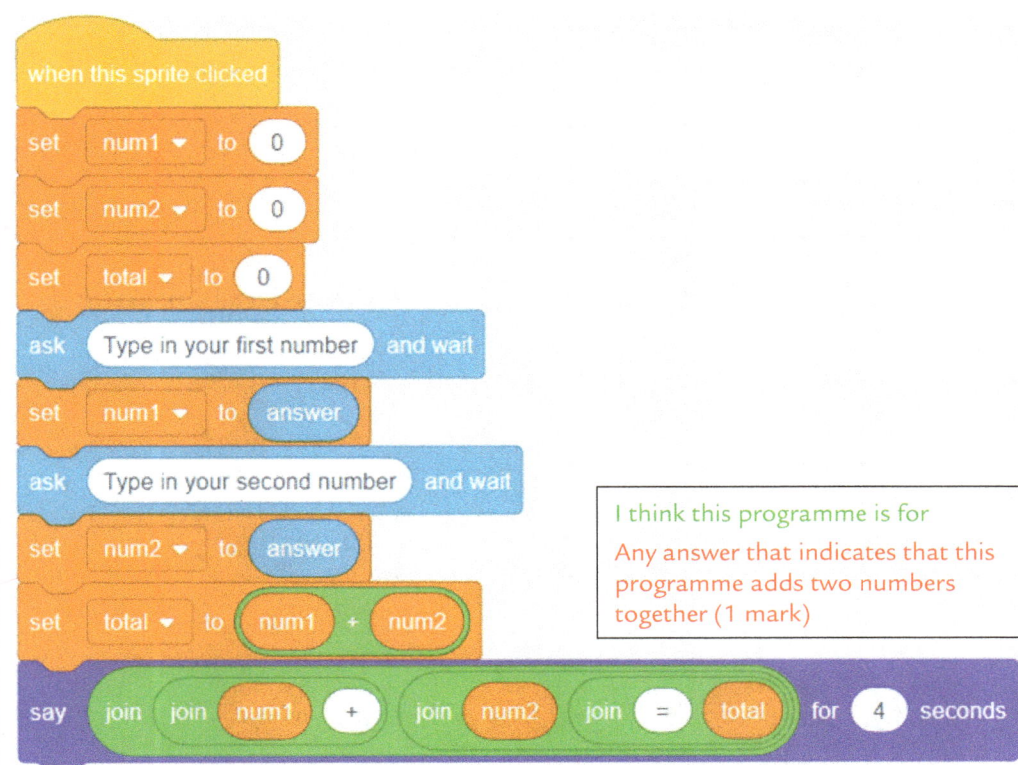

Initialisation
Sets all the variables back to 0 getting rid of any values assigned when the program was last used

Collects two numbers from the users and assigns them to two variables

Adds values of num1 to num2 and stores this in total

Shows the user all the variable values

I think this programme is for

Any answer that indicates that this programme adds two numbers together (1 mark)

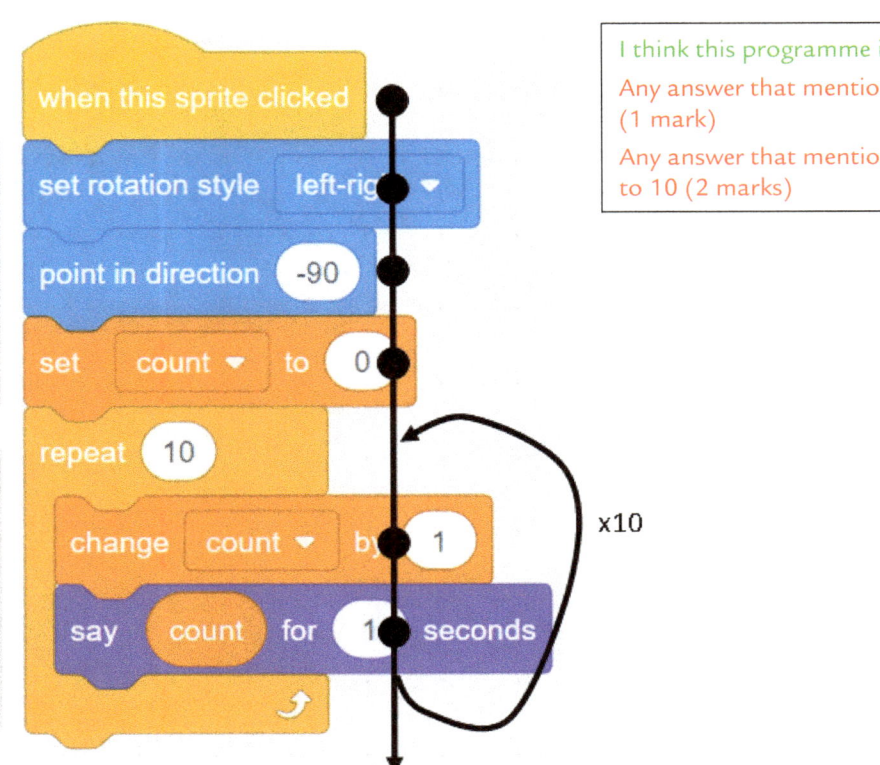

Initialisation
Sets the variable back to 0 getting rid of any values assigned when the program was last used

Add one to the count variable every time it is run in the loop and then tell the user what the value of count is on the screen

I think this programme is for

Any answer that mentions counting (1 mark)

Any answer that mentions counting to 10 (2 marks)

HINT Go through the loop and change the count variable value as you do

photocopiable page

INVESTIGATE MARKSHEET

Look inside the Placeholder sprite

1. Which two lines of code collect the users name and assign it to the variable **user_name**?

   A   Ask what is your name and wait (1 mark)

   B   Set user_name to answer (1 mark)

2. How many times is the **user_name** variable block used in the program?

   4 (1 mark)

Look inside Accumulator sprite

3. If you get the answer correct what happens to the score?

   Add 1 (1 mark)

4. If you get the answer wrong what happens to the score?

   Minus 1 (1 mark)

Look inside Adding sprite

5. Name all three variables

   A   num1 (1mark)   B   num2 (1 mark)   C   total (1 mark)

6. Which line of code adds num1 to num2?

   Set total to num1 + num2 (1 mark) the line below only tells you the answer

Look inside Counting

7. What line of code says what is inside the count variable?

   Say count for 1 second (1 mark)

8. Which block initializes the count variable?

   HINT Sets it back to what it was at the start

   Set count to 0 (1 mark)

photocopiable page

CHANGE MARKSHEET

Make changes to the code to answer these questions
Make changes to Accumulator

1. Change the code to give 5 points for every correct answer.
    What did you change? Change score by 1 to change score by 5 (1 mark)

2. Change the code to start with 10 points
    What did you change? Change set score to 0 to set score to 10 (1 mark)
    Make changes to Adding

3. Change the code to multiply both numbers
    What did you change it to? (1 mark)
    Make changes to Counting. *HINT Duplicate and then change*

4. Change the code to count slower
    What did you change? Change say count for 1 second to a higher seconds number (1 mark)
    Or add a wait block into the loop (1 mark)

5. Change the code to count in 2s.
    What did you change? Change change-count-by-1 to change-count-by-2

6. Change the code to count in halves. *HINT decimal halves*
    What did you change? Change change-count by 1 to change count by 0.5 (1 mark)

7. Change the code to count backwards from 10.
    What things did you change? Change set count to 0 to set count to 10 and change change-count-by 1 to change-count-by −1 (2 marks)

FLOW ASSESSMENT MARKSHEET

Read the code carefully with your partner and follow the order the code is run with your finger

The code took the dashed line path **– – – – – –**

Tick the pathway that is impossible for the code to follow

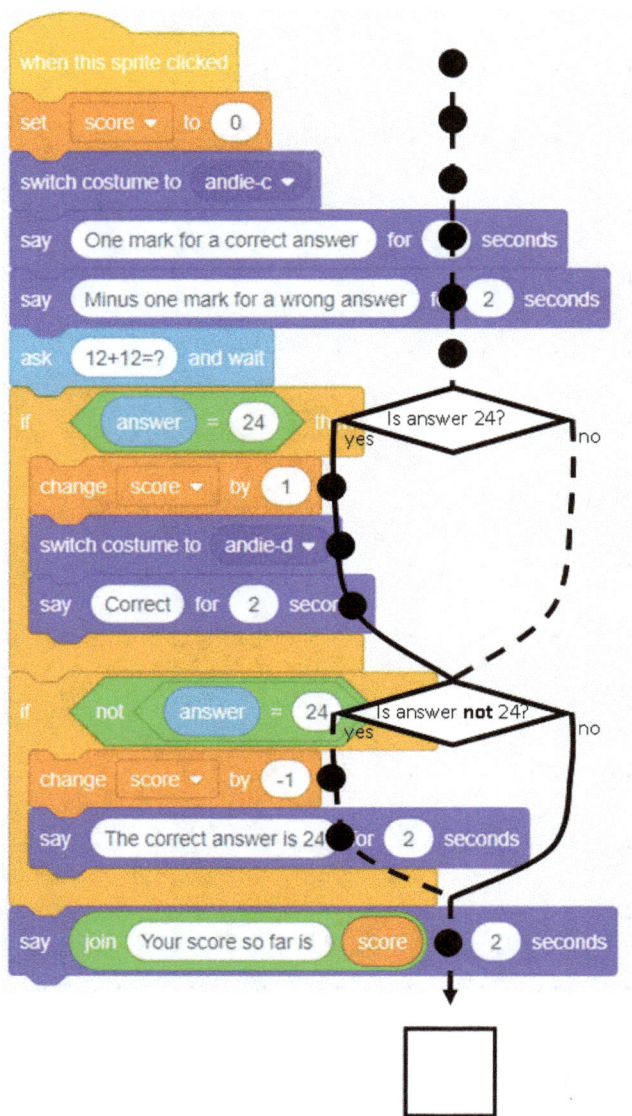

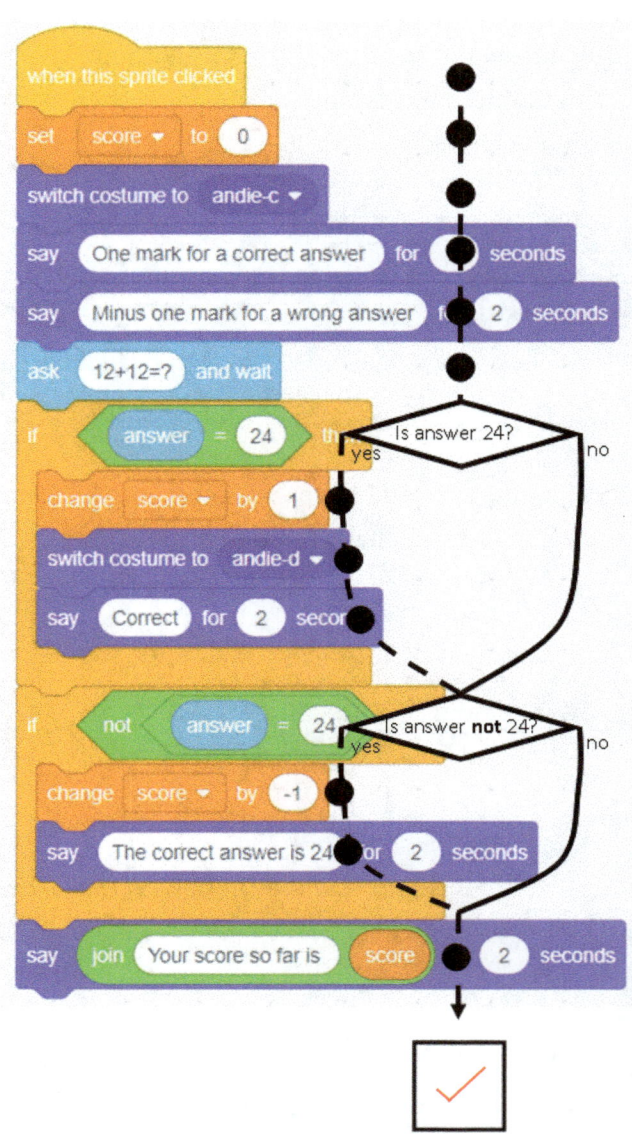

(1 mark)

It is impossible for any answer to be both 24 and not 24

VARIABLE FUN
LOGICAL ASSESSMENT MARKSHEET

Read the code carefully with your partner
Three outcomes have been created
Tick the one that is **impossible**

Placeholder

when this sprite clicked

These two blocks are only ones that change the user_name assigned value

ask **What's your name?** and wait

set **user_name** to **answer**

Ask collects users name and store

say join **Maths quiz time** **user_name** for 4 seconds

ask join **user_name** **5x7=?** and wait

if **answer** = **35** then

say join **Well done** **user_name** for 2 seconds

else

say join join **Wrong** **user_name** **it is 35** for 4 seconds

Is answer 35?   yes   no

Outcome 1

Start program

Type in name

Maths quiz time Lizzy

Lizzy 5x7=?

Type in answer

Well done Lizzy

Outcome 2

Start program

Type in name

Maths quiz time Aki

Aki 5x7=?

Type in answer

Wrong Aki its is 35

Outcome 3

Start program

Type in name

Maths quiz time **Mike**

Darla 5x7=?

Type in answer

Well done **Don**

(1 mark)
It is impossible for the user_name variable
to change name without programming
opportunities to do so.

VARIABLE FUN
FLOW OF CONTROL

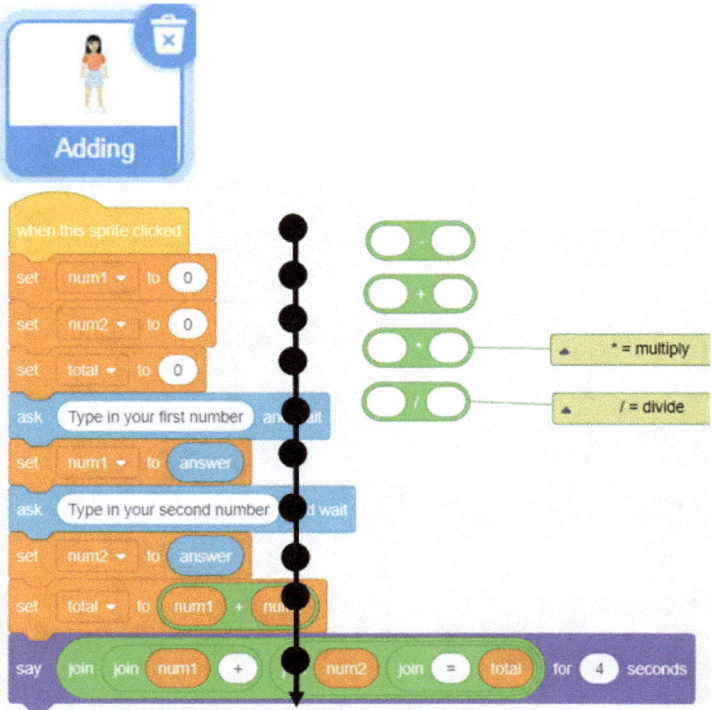

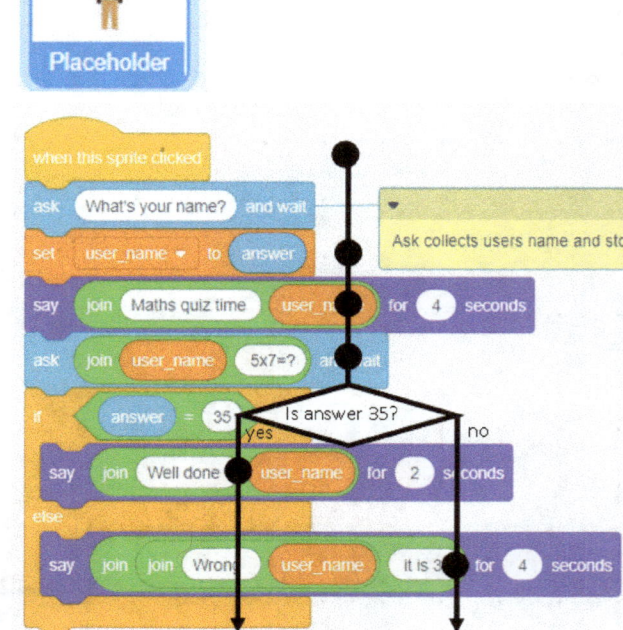

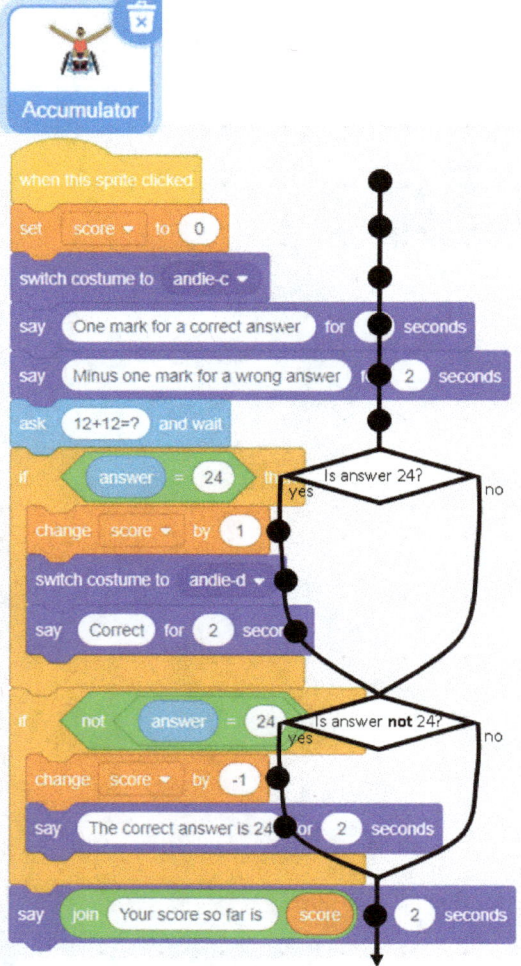

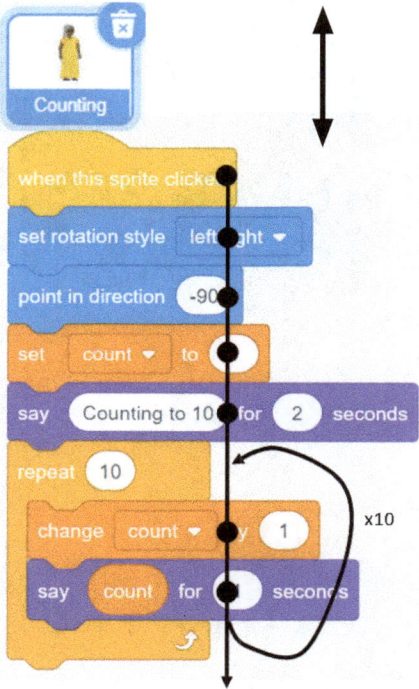

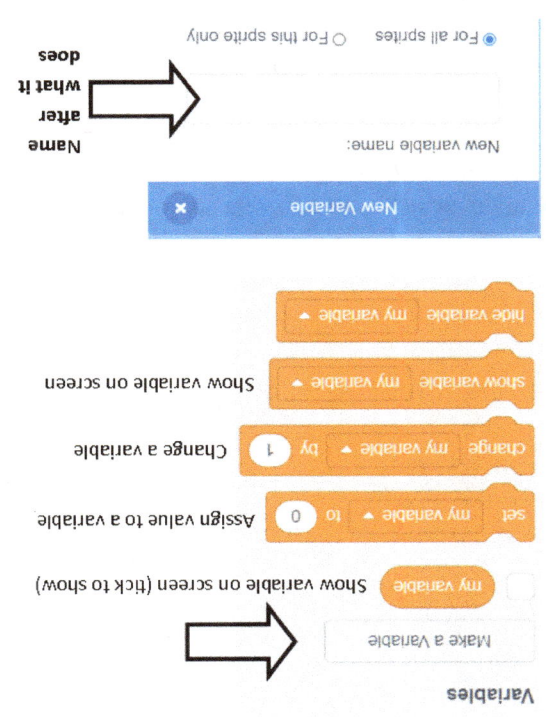

Name
after
what it
does

New variable name:

● For all sprites   ○ For this sprite only

New Variable

hide variable my variable ▾

Show variable on screen   show variable my variable ▾

Change a variable   change my variable ▾ by 1

Assign value to a variable   set my variable ▾ to 0

Show variable on screen (tick to show)   my variable

Make a Variable

Variables

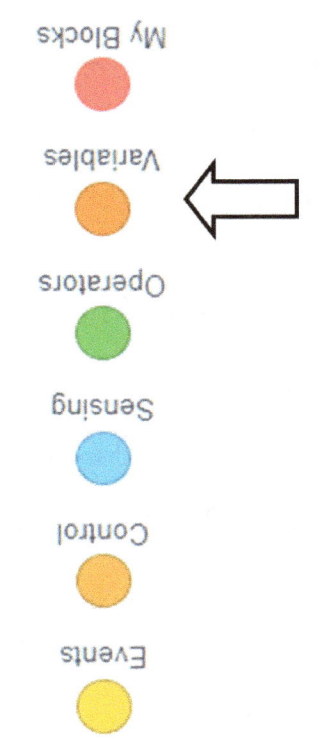

My Blocks

Variables

Operators

Sensing

Control

Events

Create Variables Back

Create Variable

Overview

Pupils learn about changing variables. They then examine a programme that counts in different ways by changing a variable within a loop and adds numbers input by the user.

This uses pupils' Year 5 knowledge about conditions as well as variables, which make it a great additional variable project.

To do before the session

1. Look at the grid below and decide which optional and SEN activities you are going to include and exclude.
2. Print pupil worksheets for each activity chosen and staple into a booklet, one for each pupil.
3. Print marksheets for activities chosen to be placed where pupils can access them.
4. Download the code needed and place in a templates folder on your school network or add to a Scratch Studio or link on your learning platform.
5. Download the slides that go with the concept introduction.
6. Study the notes that go with the slides.
7. Examine the teacher help notes that are provided alongside every activity.

To do at the start of the session

If you have not introduced **variables** with this class before, do this first as a whole class activity. If you used placeholder variables prior to this activity this resource build on that understanding rather than replacing it.

To do after the concept has been introduced

Each activity has whole class notes to help you explain what is needed if it is the first time pupils have carried out this type of activity. There are also core instructions underneath in case you are sticking to the core activities only.

How this module fits into a programming progression

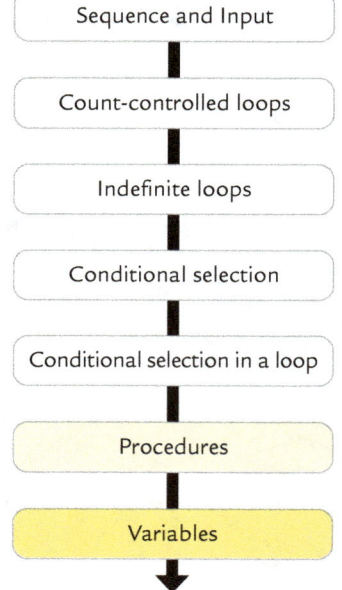

Sequence and Input

Count-controlled loops

Indefinite loops

Conditional selection

Conditional selection in a loop

Procedures

Variables

Vocabulary

Variable, assign, change variable, add to variable, subtract from variable, condition, conditional selection, condition-starts-action.

Resource Name	Core Optional SEN	Teacher	Pupil Grouping	How Assessed	SCRATCH ACCESS
CONCEPT Variables	CORE	Leads Session	Solo Whole Class Activity	Formative	NO
PARSONS	OPTIONAL SEN OPTIONAL ALL	Support Poor Readers	Solo or Paired (Teacher choice)	Pupil Marked Marksheet Provided	YES Parsons Ada Lovelace
PREDICT	OPTIONAL ALL	Support Poor Readers	Paired	Pupil Marked Marksheet Provided	NO
INVESTIGATE	CORE	Support Poor Readers	Paired	Pupil Marked Marksheet Provided	YES Ada Lovelace
FLOW	OPTIONAL ALL OPTIONAL ABLE	Leads Session with Whole Class or Works with Poor Readers	Paired	Pupil Marked Marksheet Provided	NO
CHANGE	CORE	Support Poor Readers	Paired	Pupil Marked Marksheet Provided	YES Ada Lovelace
CREATE	CORE	Assesses Pupil Work and Checks Pupil Self-Assessment	Solo	Pupil Assessed & Teacher Assessed	YES Ada Lovelace

Core activities general instructions

1. Group pupils in roughly same ability pairs. For **investigate** and **change** worksheets pupils will work in pairs, for **create** they will work separately.

2. Give out the pupil booklets and explain that pupils need to follow the instructions on the sheets to explore how **variables** work.

3. Explain that each pupil will record separately whilst working alongside their partner and keeping to the same pace as their partner.

4. Demonstrate where they can find the template code and explain that pupils will share one device for investigate and change.

5. Explain that during each question only one person should touch the shared device and they should swap who that person is when there is a new questions.

6. Encourage them to discuss their answers with their partner. If they disagree with their partner, they can record a different answer in their own booklet.

7. Show pupils where it says they should mark their work on the sheet and where the answer sheets are in the classroom.

8. Remind pupils to return marksheets after marking, because there are not enough for every pair to have their own.

Key Programming Knowledge
Variables are used to store information to be referred to and changed in a computer programme or algorithm

Variables
Have a name and a value
read the name but act on the value

Values can be changed during the algorithm or programme
When writing the value of a variable we call it assigning

Variable Naming
Always name a variable after the data that it stores or the task that it does
Avoid naming variables with spaces – teamScore (camelCase) user_name (underscore)
Avoid using the same name as a procedure

Resources

Ada Lovelace & the difference engine   https://scratch.mit.edu/projects/521923255/
Parsons Ada Lovelace & the Difference Engine   https://scratch.mit.edu/projects/612225397/
Sub Goal Labelled Ada Lovelace & the difference engine (useful for SEN)
https://scratch.mit.edu/projects/664087395/editor

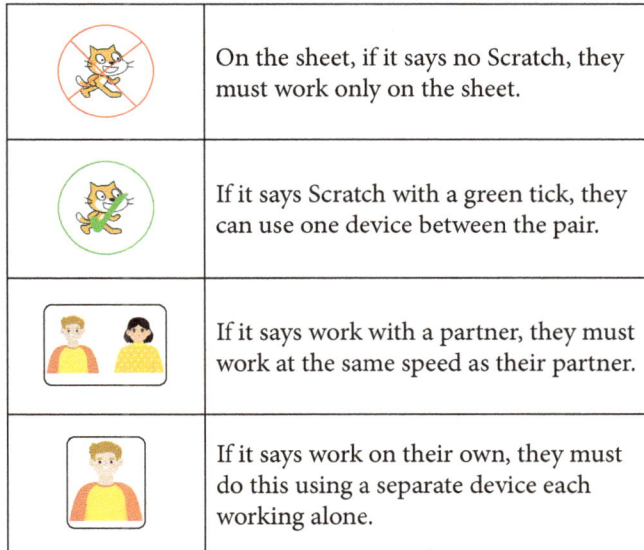

	On the sheet, if it says no Scratch, they must work only on the sheet.
	If it says Scratch with a green tick, they can use one device between the pair.
	If it says work with a partner, they must work at the same speed as their partner.
	If it says work on their own, they must do this using a separate device each working alone.

English Computing National Curriculum Programs of Study

Pupils should be taught to:

- **design, write and debug programs that accomplish specific goals,** including controlling or simulating physical systems; solve problems by decomposing them into smaller parts.

- **use sequence, selection and** repetition **in programs**; work **with variables and various forms of input and output**.

- **use logical reasoning to explain how some simple algorithms work and to detect and correct errors in algorithms and programs.**

Scottish Curriculum for Excellence Technologies

I understand the instructions of a visual programming language and can predict the outcome of a program written using the language. TCH 1-14a

I can explain core programming language concepts in appropriate technical language TCH 2-14a

I can demonstrate a range of basic problem solving skills by building simple programs to carry out a given task, using an appropriate language. TCH 1-15a

I can create, develop and evaluate computing solutions in response to a design challenge. TCH 2-15a

Welsh National Curriculum Relevant Strands

Progression Step 3.

- I can use conditional statements to add control and decision-making to algorithms.

- I can explain and debug algorithms.

ADA LOVELACE
PARSONS

Work with a partner

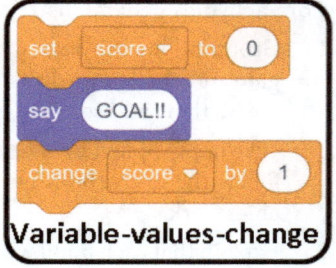

Variable-values-change

Start Scratch and load
Parsons Ada Lovelace and the
difference engine

Algorithm in blue means the code in the program is already built

Algorithm in orange means the code in the program needs assembling

Start with an A key

Loop always

    Assign 0 to count variable

    Assign 0 to num1 variable

    Assign 0 to num2 variable

    Assign 0 to total variable

    Ask press 1 = count, 2 = count back, 3 = 2x table, 4 = add 2 numbers

    If answer is = 1

Remember
Indents mean

It is affected by a
condition or inside
a loop.

        Say counting to 10

        Assign 0 to count variable

        Do 10 time

            Add 1 to count variable

            Say count variable

    If answer is = 2

        Say counting back

        Assign 11 to count variable

        Do 10 time

            subtract 1 from count variable

            Say count variable

    If answer is = 3

        Say counting in 2 times table

        Assign 1 to count variable

        Assign 2 to total variable

        Do 12 times

            Say count x 2 = total

            Add 1 to count variable

            Add 2 to total variable

    If answer is = 4

Now mark your work using the Parsons marksheet

photocopiable page

PARSONS TEACHERS NOTES

Notes on the activity

Parsons problems were originally designed for university students to make sense of text-based programming by ordering chunks of code rather than writing all the code out. It was designed as a scaffold to reduce the time spent in the minute detail of code and concentrate on the logical order needed to solve a problem.

This example makes pupils think about how an algorithm can be written differently than the code, as it uses similar language to the code but not always the same. An algorithm is designed for another human to understand and can be created with a wide variety of language, commands and symbols. A machine can only follow the precise code language that the blocks are written in.

If pupils still need time to develop their code-connecting skills, it can be a good activity to start with. It is popular with pupils as it is hands-on activity. If this is the case, you might ask pupils to complete this in pairs, but with both having a device to do this individually.

Alternatively, it could be an option you only give to pupils who have struggled in other modules to help them familiarize themselves with the code first before moving on to investigating and modifying code.

Whole class advice

Remember an algorithm plan does not have to be written in code, so the algorithm will not be the same as the code in every line.

Individual advice

Do not forget to look for coding concepts? Are there any loops or conditions? You can tell these from the indents. There are both in this Parsons problem.

Algorithm in blue means the code in the program is already built

Algorithm in orange means the code in the program needs assembling

Start with an A key
Loop always
    Assign 0 to count variable
    Assign 0 to num1 variable
    Assign 0 to num2 variable
    Assign 0 to total variable
    Ask press 1 = count, 2 = count back, 3 = 2x table, 4 = add 2 numbers
    If answer is = 1
        Say counting to 10
        Assign 0 to count variable
        Do 10 time
            Add 1 to count variable
            Say count variable
    If answer is = 2
        Say counting back
        Assign 11 to count variable
        Do 10 time
            subtract 1 from count variable
            Say count variable
    If answer is = 3
        Say counting in 2 times table
        Assign 1 to count variable
        Assign 2 to total variable
        Do 12 times
            Say count x 2 = total
            Add 1 to count variable
            Add 2 to total variable
    If answer is same as 4

Individual advice

Don't forget to run your code to check that it works before moving on.

Send advice

Use something to block out all of the algorithm but the section pupils are working on. There are brackets to suggest a division opposite.

This makes it easier to concentrate on the immediate task rather than be overwhelmed by all of the algorithm.

If supporting pupils one to one you could also get them to work with just three bits of code, one of which must be the code they need.

You could also part-build some of the code so there are even fewer sections.

Understanding programming

The downside of Parsons problems is that if they are the only activity that pupils use in coding they can encourage pupils to believe that there is only one right way to program.

NOTE
The correct code is on the Parsons answer sheet.

ADA LOVELACE
PREDICT

Work with a partner

Match the program letter to a description of what you think
the code does below.

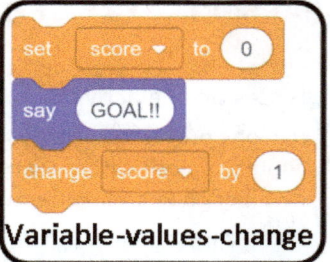

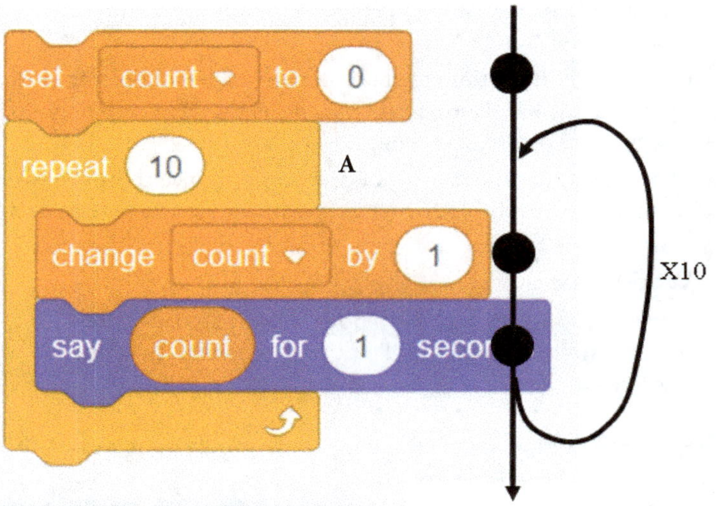

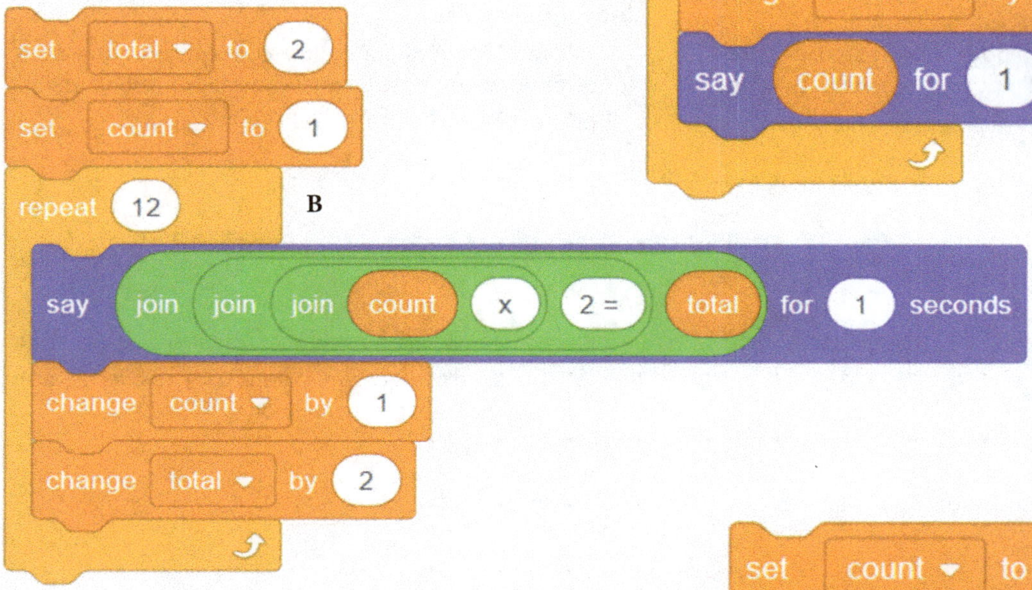

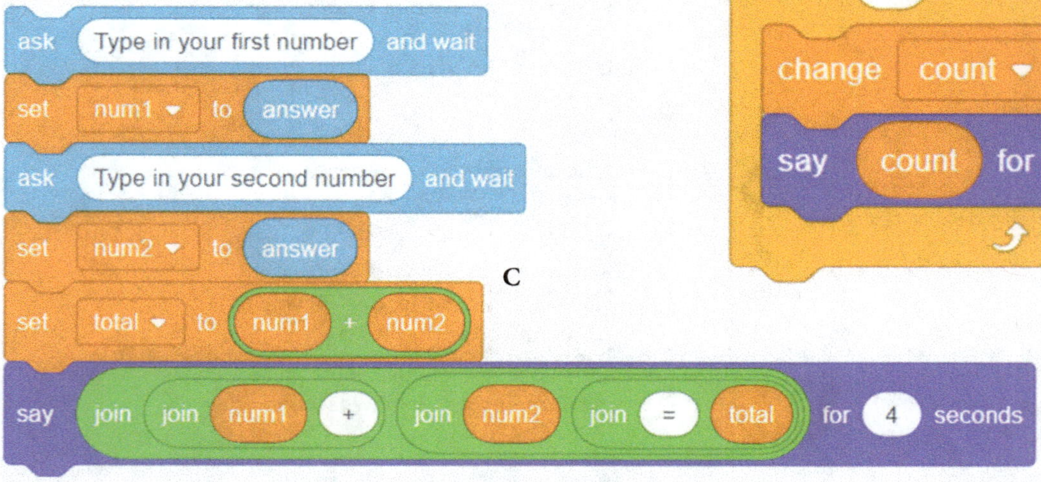

Variable-values-change

A
```
set count to 0
repeat 10
    change count by 1
    say count for 1 seconds
```
X10

B
```
set total to 2
set count to 1
repeat 12
    say join join join count x 2 = total for 1 seconds
    change count by 1
    change total by 2
```

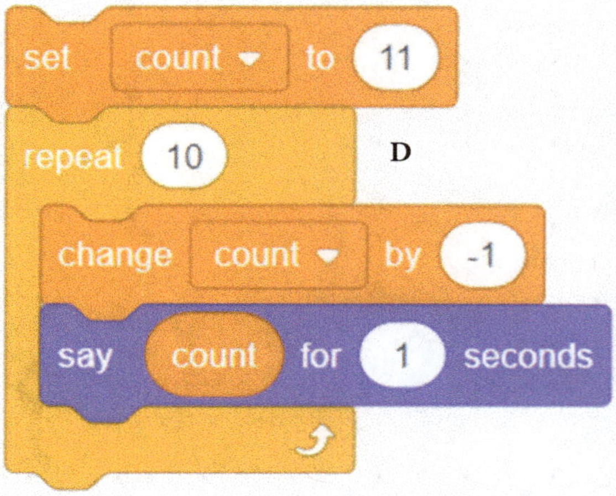

C
```
ask Type in your first number and wait
set num1 to answer
ask Type in your second number and wait
set num2 to answer
set total to num1 + num2
say join join num1 + join num2 join = total for 4 seconds
```

D
```
set count to 11
repeat 10
    change count by -1
    say count for 1 seconds
```

Count backwards	Count forwards	Say the two times tables	Add two numbers together
A, B, C or D	A, B, C or D	A, B, C or D	A, B, C or D

PREDICT TEACHER HELP NOTES

Whole class advice

Examine each section of code. I recommend that you start with A. What is happening to the count variable as it goes through the count-controlled loop? Use the flow of control diagram next to A to mime going round a loop and changing the variable.

Send advice

Cover up all the code apart from A at the top and the choices at the bottom. Read through the four choices. Write down what the variable will be when the program starts next to A. Now go through the count-controlled loop changing the variable as you go. Do the same for B and D. Examine C last.

Match the program letter to a description of what you think the code does below.

Individual advice B

Draw the flow of control first like the one drawn in A. Now write down what the variables will be when the program starts next to B. Go through the count-controlled loop changing the variables as you go. Changing a variable by one adding one and changing by two adding two will change count and score differently.

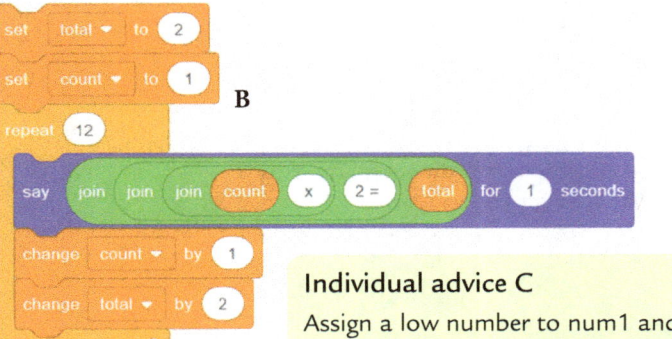

Notes on the activity

Prediction helps pupils to think about the bigger purpose of the code before they run the code and experience what it actually does. It is carried out away from a digital devices.

In this case, we are only looking at a subsection of the code rather than the framework that delivers it.

Individual advice A

Write down what the variable will be when the program starts next to A. Now go through the count-controlled loop changing the variable as you go.

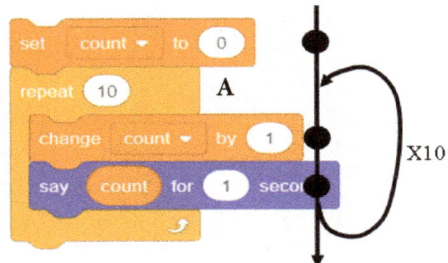

Individual advice D

Draw the flow of control first like the one drawn in A. Now write down what the variable will be when the program starts next to D. Go through the count-controlled loop changing the variable as you go. Do not forget to take away one rather than add one as you did in A!

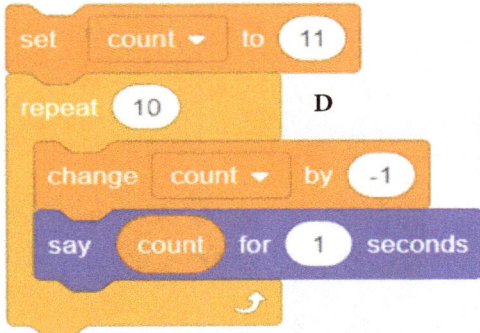

Individual advice C

Assign a low number to num1 and write it down next to C e.g. num1 = 8. Now assign a low number to num2 and write it down e.g. num2 = 4.

What does the fifth line do to num1 and num2?

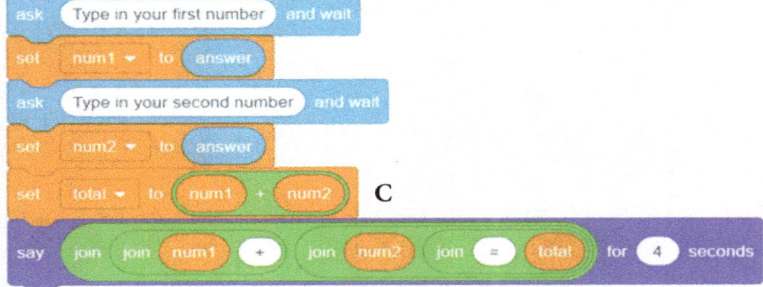

Remember

Variables have a name and a value

Setting a variable removes all previous values and replaces them with the new value

Changing a variable adapts the current value of the variable. Change by 1 would add 1. Change by 2 would add 2

Count backwards	Count forwards	Say the two times tables	Add two numbers together
A, B, C or D	A, B, C or D	A, B, C or D	A, B, C or D
(1 mark)	(1 mark)	(1 mark)	(1 mark)

ADA LOVELACE
INVESTIGATE CODE

Work with a partner

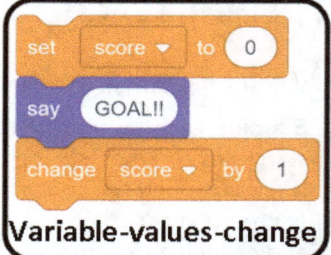

Variable-values-change

Start Scratch and load
Ada Lovelace

INVESTIGATE

(Run the programs lots of times but don't change the code)

Run the code inside sprite **Difference A OR Difference B** and answer these questions.

1. How many conditions are there?
    HINT all start with **if**

2. Name all four variables

    A   B   C   D

Find the code section that starts **Counting to 10**

3. Which code block assigns 0 to the count variable?

4. Which code block adds one to the count variable?

5. Which code block reports the value of count in a speech bubble for 1 second?

6. Complete this adapted flow of control on top of this *changed* code block from the program. Next to the dots write in the value of the count variable. Some have been done for you.

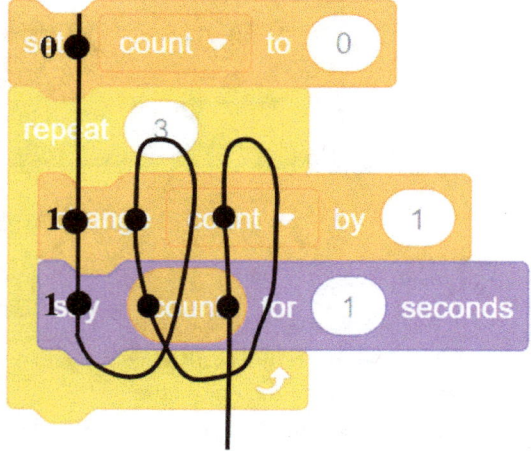

Find the code section that starts **Type in your first number**

7. Which code block adds num1 to num2?

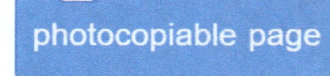

photocopiable page

Now mark your investigate answers using the marksheet provided

ADA LOVELACE
INVESTIGATE CODE TEACHER NOTES

INVESTIGATE

(Run the programs lots of times but don't change the code)

Run the code inside sprite **Difference A OR Difference B** and answer these questions.

1. How many conditions are there?
   HINT all start with **if**

   Q1 Is a revision question from Y5

   5 (1 mark)

2. Name all four variables

   Individual advice Q2

   Variables can be found on the screen as well as in the code.

   A count   B num1   C num2   D total

   (1 mark) if all four are named in any order

   Find the code section that starts **Counting to 10**

3. Which code block assigns 0 to the count variable?

   Set count to 0 (1 mark)

   Individual advice Q4

   If change has no number in front of it then it will add.

4. Which code block adds one to the count variable?

   Change count by 1 (1 mark)

5. Which code block reports the value of count in a speech bubble for 1 second?

   Say count for 1 seconds (1 mark)

6. Complete this adapted flow of control on top of this *changed* code block from the program. Next to the dots write in the value of the count variable. Some have been done for you.

   se**0** count ▼ to 0
   repeat 3
   1 **an**2 **c**3**t** ▼ by 1
   1**s** 2 **u**3 **r** 1 seconds

   (1 mark) if all numbers are the same

   Find the code section that starts **Type in your first number**

7. Which code block adds num1 to num2?

   Set total to num1 + num2 (1 mark)

Notes on the activity

Investigating code is a core activity in this modules, so I do not recommend that you skip this activity. If some pairs of pupils are taking much longer than their peers you can always cross out the last two questions. Sometimes one pupil in a pair decides to work faster than their partner; check that this is not happening and that every pupil is filling in and marking the questions individually but at the pace of the slowest in the pair. Sometimes a pair decides not to mark to speed up their efforts. Marking gives valuable information, so I recommend sending them back to mark their work if this is the case. A class instruction to come and talk to you if they have over half of the questions wrong or they do not understand the answer after they have marked it helps to check progress is being made correctly. There is real value in collecting these scores to build up a summative picture of pupil progress.

Individual advice Q5

HINT Speech bubble.

Whole class advice

Most of the questions will be about variables. Either set or change a variable or where the orange variable is referenced or used in the code shown as ovals with the variable name inside. It can be useful to show pupils briefly what variable look like in code if you have not already done so.

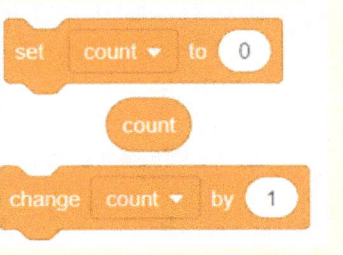

Individual advice Q6

This method of showing the loops in a count-controlled loop allows us to mark every individual instance of an action. It can be used instead of the normal method.

Individual advice Q7

HINT + add.

Individual advice all

There is a full flow of control sheet that you can use with pupils who struggle to understand how the loops and conditions work in the code on the last page of this module.

Now mark your investigate answers using the marksheet provided

ADA LOVELACE

Flow of Control

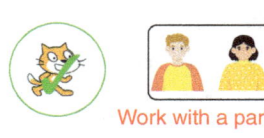

Work with a partner

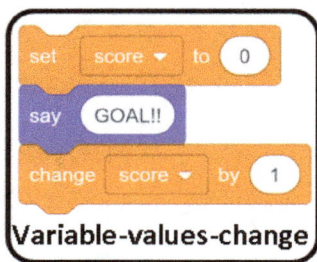

set score to 0
say GOAL!!
change score by 1
Variable-values-change

Work with your partner to explore the flow of control diagram. Start at the top and take it in turns to explain every **dot, condition** or **loop**. Now fill in the table below.

This table shows the value of the count variable in the repeat loop when used in say.

Initial value 0

repeat	1	2	3	4	5	6	7	8	9	10
count	1	2	3	4	5	6	7	8	9	10

Fill in the table below to show the value of the count variable in the repeat loop when used in say.

Initial value ☐ ***(HINT set count)***

repeat	1	2	3	4	5	6	7	8	9	10
count										

when a key pressed
forever
set count to 0
set num1 to 0
set num2 to 0
set total to 0
ask 1=count to 10, 2=count backwards, 3=2 x tabl
if answer = 1
Is answer 1?
yes
no
say Counting to 10 for 2 seconds
set count to 0
X10
repeat 10
change count by 1
say count for 1 seconds
if answer = 2
Is answer 2?
yes
no
say Counting backwards for 2 seconds
set count to 11
X10
repeat 10
change count by -1
say count for 1 seconds
if answer = 3
Is answer 3?
yes

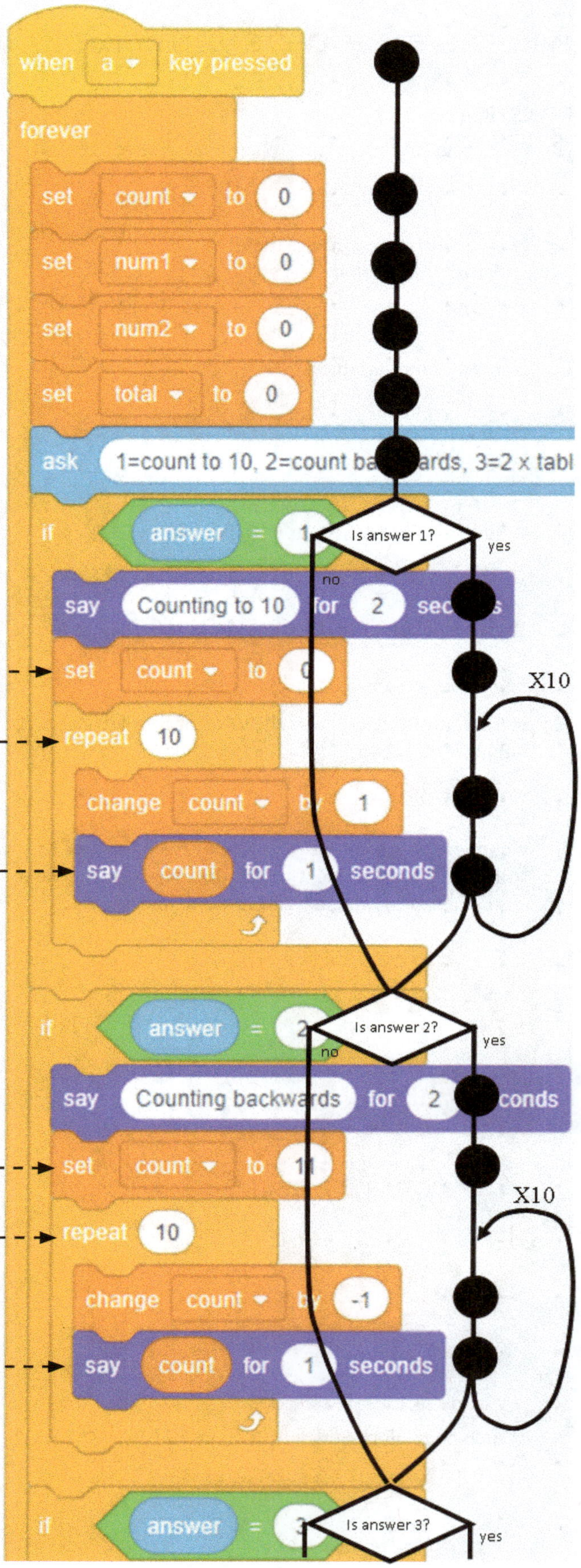

Now mark your work using the flow of control marksheet

photocopiable page

ADA LOVELACE
FLOW OF CONTROL TEACHER NOTES

Whole class advice

Explain that filling in the table is not as important as explaining the flow of control with your partner step by step. Say that you will be walking around and listening to them explain what is happening in the programme.

Work with your partner to explore the flow of control diagram. Start at the top and take it in turns to explain every **dot, condition** or **loop**. Now fill in the tables below.

This table shows the value of the count variable in the repeat loop when used in say.

Initial value 0

repeat	1	2	3	4	5	6	7	8	9	10
count	1	2	3	4	5	6	7	8	9	10

Fill in the table below to show the value of the count variable in the repeat loop when used in say.

Initial value 11 *(HINT set count)*

repeat	1	2	3	4	5	6	7	8	9	10
count	10	9	8	7	6	5	4	3	2	1

(1 mark) for initial value 11

(1 mark) for count numbers correctly descending

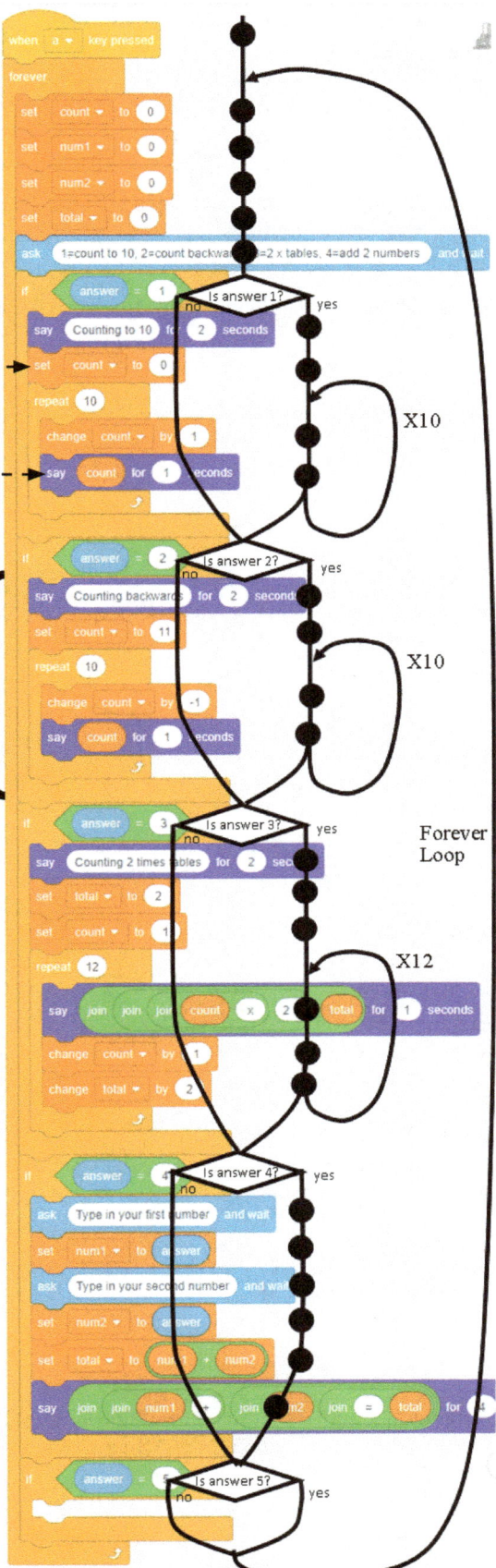

Individual advice

Have a really good look at the worked example above that counts to 10. That will help you fill in the table.

You can also run the programme option 2 to see what it does to help you.

Send advice

Some pupils will really benefit from you explaining the top part with them first.

Get a whiteboard and write down the four variables names.
When you get to set **count** to 0 write 0 next to **count**
When you get to set **num1** to 0 write 0 next to **num1**
When you get to set **num2** to 0 write 0 next to **num2**
When you get to set **total** to 0 write 0 next to **total**
Then ask shall we press 1 2 3 or 4?
Press 1
Ask is the answer 1?
Yes it is, so let us go down this path
Say counting to 10
set **count** to 0 write 0 next to count *(we don't really need to do this as the variable was initialised earlier as 0, but it helps to see it here. Now point out that this is the initial value in the top table)*

Explain that change **count** adds one and change count value on whiteboard to 1

Now say and look at whiteboard and point to value as you say one.

Now go round the loop for the second time.

Increase count to 2 on whiteboard and say 2. Continue for 10 repeats and then go through all the no paths

Then leave them to go through option 2

Individual advice all

There is a full flow of control sheet that you can use with pupils who struggle to understand how the loops and conditions work in the code on the last page of this module.

ADA LOVELACE
CHANGE CODE

Work with a partner

Run the code inside sprite Difference A OR Difference B ,or for an easier option use Change sprite and answer these questions.

1. Change **count to 10** so that it counts slower. What did you change?

2. Change **count to 10** so that it counts from 1 to 20. What two things did you need to change?

    A

    B

3. Change **count to 10** so that it counts in halves. What did you need to change? *HINT Half as a decimal fraction is 0.5* (If it adds an extra 0 to right it is still correct and it might be a bug in Scratch)

4. Change **count backwards** so that it counts from 30 to 0. What two things did you need to change?

    A

    B

5. Change **2xtable** so that it counts from 1 x 2 = 2 up to 30 x 2 = 60
    What thing did you need to change?

6. Change 2xtable so that it counts the seven times table.
    What four things do you need to change?

    A

    B

    C

    D

7. Change **add numbers** so that it multiplies num1 by num2. What did you change?
    *HINT Operators * is multiply. HINT You will need to change a block*

Now mark your work using the change code marksheet

photocopiable page

ADA LOVELACE
CHANGE CODE TEACHER NOTES

Whole class advice

Test your solution before moving on to the next question. Test it all the way through rather than just the start. It is easy to miss a part of a question through not testing fully.

Notes on the activity

Changing or modifying the code is a core part of this module, so I suggest you do not leave it out. It is an important step towards creation of their own code. Recording their marks can help with formative and summative assessment.

Send advice

Pupils can work on the code parts they need removed from the main program in the **change** sprite. Clicking on the code sections will run them. This will reduce cognitive load.

Change Code in Difference A OR Difference B

(Make small changes or small additions to the code)

1. Change **count to 10** so that it counts slower. What did you change?

   Either increase say seconds to more than 2 OR add a wait block into the loop (1 mark)

   Individual advice Q1

   HINT Are there any time words in this section of code?

2. Change **count to 10** so that it counts from 1 to 20. What two things did you need to change?

   A   Say counting to 20 instead of 10 (1 mark)

   B   Change repeat 10 to repeat 20 (1 mark)

   Individual advice Q2

   HINT What makes it count 10 times?

3. Change **count to 10** so that it counts in halves. What did you need to change? *HINT Half as a decimal fraction is 0.5 or 0.50 (If it adds an extra 0 to right it still correct and it might be a bug in Scratch)*

   Change count by 1 to count by 0.5 OR .5 (1 mark)

   Individual advice Q3

   HINT 0.5, 1, 1.5, 2. 2.5, etc.

4. Change **count backwards** so that it counts from 30 to 0. What two things did you need to change?

   A   Change set count to 11 to 31 (1 mark)

   B   Change repeat 10 to repeat 31 (1mark)

   Individual advice Q4

   HINT What makes it start counting at 10? Have you tested it all the way through from 30 up to 0?

5. Change **2xtable** so that it counts from $1 \times 2 = 2$ up to $30 \times 2 = 60$
   What did you need to change?

   Change repeat from 12 to 30 (1 mark)

   Individual advice Q5

   HINT What makes it count 12 times?

6. Change **2xtable** so that it counts the seven times table.
   What four things do you need to change?

   A   Change say counting from 2 to 7 times table (1 mark)

   B   Change set total from 2 to 7 (1 mark)

   C   Change say count × 2 = total to say count × 7 = total (1 mark)

   D   Change change total by 2 to change total by 7 (1 mark)

   Individual advice Q6

   Testing is key in this question, as there are so many things to change and you can easily miss some.

7. Change **add numbers** so that it multiplies num1 by num2. What did you change? *HINT Operators * is multiply. HINT You will need to change a block.*

   A   Change set total to num1 * num2 replacing green + block (1 mark)

   B   Change say num1 + num1 = total to num1 × num2 = total (1 mark)

   Individual advice Q7

   HINT You will need a new block, a multiplication block.

   Send advice

   Cover up sheet with a page and only reveal top question you are working on.

Now mark your work using the change code marksheet

ADA LOVELACE
CREATE

Work on
your own

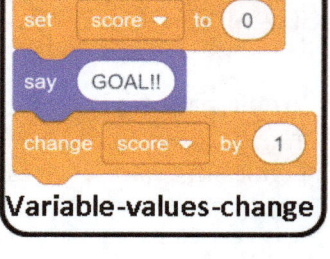

Variable-values-change

FIRST CREATIONS (Do either Option 1 or Option 2)

1. Create new code to say the 5x tables and add it into the menu as option 5.

2. Create your own mathematical procedure and add it into the menu as option 5.
    Ideas for maths procedures
    -   *Subtract a number from another number*
    -   *Divide a number by another number*
    -   *Find perimeter of square by inputting distance of one side*

LONGER PROJECTS (Do either Option 3 or Option 4)

3. Create a class countdown timer from 30 to 0.
    Prepare three different effects to show when the timer counts within
    30–20 seconds
    20–10 seconds
    10–0 seconds
    Additionally provide teacher controls so that the length of the timer can be changed.

4. Design and create your own project that uses variables to do mathematical operations.

Planning Space

	Not used **a variable that changes** through the program	Copied a **variable** that changes idea	Adapted a variable that changes idea	Used variables in a way not shown in the example program
Variable-values-change	0 marks	1 mark	2 marks	3 marks
			Not used previous programming concepts for real purpose	Used previous programming concepts for real purpose
Used previous programming concept such as loops or conditions correctly			0 marks	1 mark
			No theme in planning or code	Has a theme in planning or code
Has a project theme in longer projects			0 marks	1 mark

photocopiable page

ADA LOVELACE
CREATE TEACHER NOTES

FIRST CREATIONS

1. Create new code to say the 5x tables and add it into the menu as option 5.

2. Create your own mathematical procedure and add it into the menu as option 5.

   Ideas for maths procedures

   - *Subtract a number from another number*
   - *Divide a number by another number*
   - *Find perimeter of square by inputting distance of one side*

LONGER PROJECTS

3. Create a class countdown timer from 30 to 0.

   Prepare three different effects to show when the timer counts within

   30–20 seconds

   20–10 seconds

   10–0 seconds

   Additionally provide teacher controls so that the length of the timer can be changed.

4. Design and create your own project that uses variables to do mathematical operations.

   > Planning Space

Whole class advice

Work on your own, one device each. You can discuss the work with your former partner but you are responsible for creating your own projects. Save your work regularly. Read the instructions carefully. Assess your own work by circling where you think you are in the assessment grid at the bottom of the page.

Notes on the activity

The make part of a project is really important and teachers should always make sure that pupils have time to make their own project, even if that means reducing the time spent on other stages for pupils who work slowly. It helps if pupils work on their own for this while supporting their partner.

Individual advice first creation 1 & 2

These projects are easy to adapt existing code to make, which makes them easier to complete first. If pupils are stuck, suggest adapting existing code.

Individual advice 3

Count backwards is a shorter countdown timer. This will help pupils to have a good initial starting point that thy can adapt.

Individual advice 4

Add numbers uses mathematical operations. This will help pupils to have a good initial starting point that thy can adapt.

Assessment

Do a preliminary assessment halfway through their creation time, as this will give them time to improve their projects. You can also ask them to self-assess their creations first.

	Not used **a variable that changes** through the program	Copied a **variable** that changes idea	Adapted a variable that changes idea	Used variables in a way not shown in the example program
Variable-values-change	0 marks	1 mark	2 marks	3 marks
			Not used previous programming concepts for real purpose	Used previous programming concepts for real purpose
Used previous programming concept such as loops or conditions correctly			0 marks	1 mark
			No theme in planning or code	Has a theme in planning or code
Has a clear countdown timer in the longer project			0 marks	1 mark

ADA LOVELACE
PARSONS ANSWERS

Algorithm in blue means the code in the program is already built

Algorithm in orange means the code in the program needs assembling

Start with an A key

Loop always

    Assign 0 to count variable

    Assign 0 to num1 variable

    Assign 0 to num2 variable

    Assign 0 to total variable

    Ask press 1 = count, 2 = count back, 3 = 2x table, 4 = add 2 numbers

    If answer is same as 1

        Say counting to 10

        Assign 0 to count variable

        Do 10 time

            Add 1 to count variable

            Say value of count variable

    If answer is same as 2

        Say counting back

        Assign 11 to count variable

        Do 10 time

            subtract 1 from count variable

            Say value of count variable

    If answer is same as 3

        Say counting in 2 times table

        Assign 2 to total variable

        Assign 1 to count variable

        Do 12 times

            Say count x 2 = total

            Add 1 to count variable

            Add 2 to total variable

    If answer is same as 4

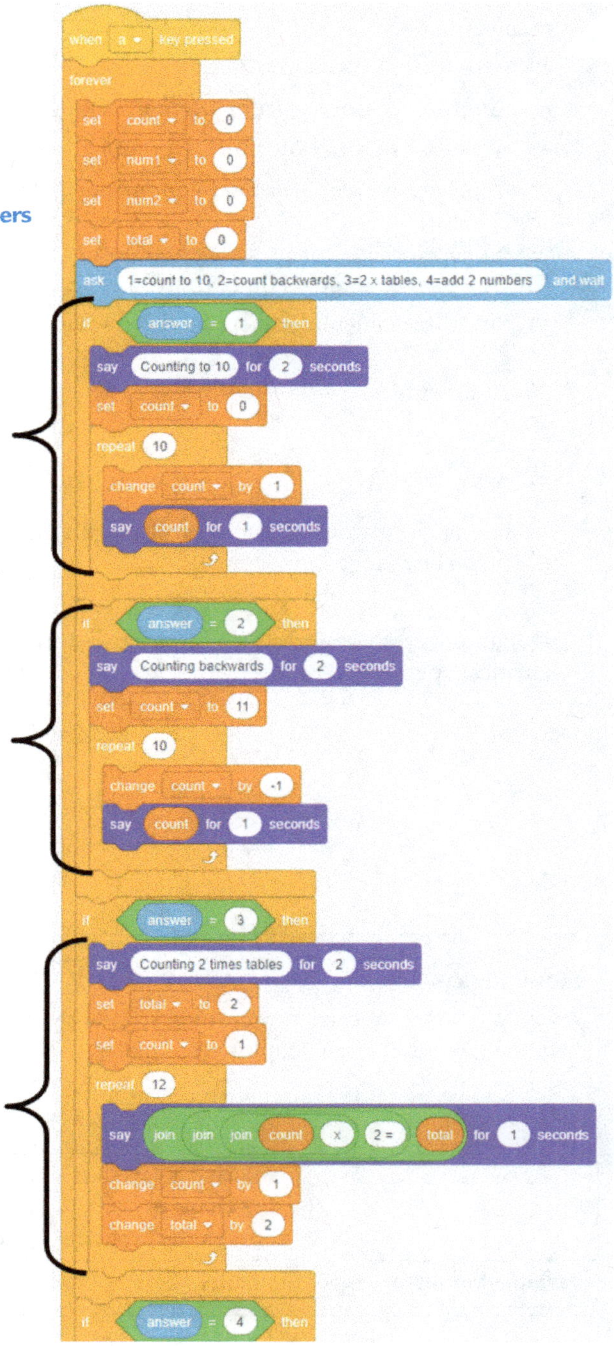

photocopiable page

ADA LOVELACE
PREDICT ANSWERS

Match the program letter to a description of what you think
the code does below.

Count backwards	Count forwards	Say the two times tables	Add two numbers together
A, B, C or (D)	(A), B, C or D	A, (B), C or D	A, B, (C) or D

(1 mark)   (1 mark)   (1 mark)   (1 mark)

ADA LOVELACE
INVESTIGATE CODE MARKSHEET

INVESTIGATE

(Run the programs lots of times but don't change the code)

Run the code inside sprite **Difference A OR Difference B** and answer these questions.

1. How many conditions are there?
    *HINT all start with **if***

    5 (1 mark)

2. Name all four variables

    A   count   B   num1   C   num2   D   total

    (1 mark) if all four are named in any order

    Find the code section that starts **Counting to 10**

3. Which code block assigns 0 to the count variable?

    Set count to 0 (1 mark)

4. Which code block adds one to the count variable?

    Change count by 1 (1 mark)

5. Which code block reports the value of count in a speech bubble for 1 second?

    Say count for 1 seconds (1 mark)

6. Complete this adapted flow of control on top of this *changed* code block from the program. Next to the dots write in the value of the count variable. Some have been done for you.

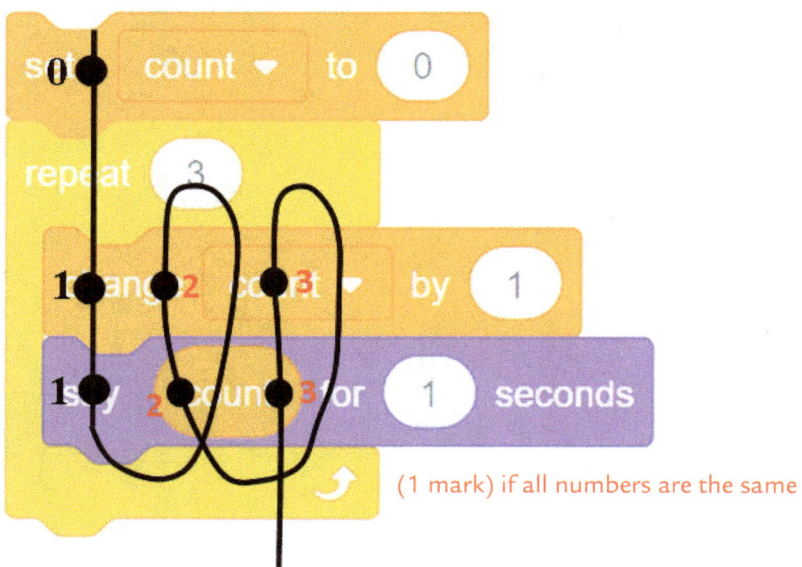

    (1 mark) if all numbers are the same

    Find the code section that starts **Type in your first number**

7. Which code block adds num1 to num2

    Set total to num1 + num2 (1 mark)

ADA LOVELACE
FLOW OF CONTROL MARKSHEET

Fill in the table below to show the value of the count
variable in the repeat loop when used in say.

Initial value [11] *(HINT set count)*

repeat	1	2	3	4	5	6	7	8	9	10
count	10	9	8	7	6	5	4	3	2	1

(1 mark) for initial value 11

(1 mark) for count numbers correctly descending

ADA LOVELACE
CHANGE CODE MARKSHEET

Change Code in Difference A OR Difference B
(Make small changes or small additions to the code)

1. Change **count to 10** so that it counts slower.
    What did you change?

    Either increase say seconds to more than 2 OR add a wait block into the loop (1 mark)

2. Change **count to 10** so that it counts from 1 to 20.
    What two things did you need to change?
    A   Say counting to 20 instead of 10 (1 mark)
    B   Change repeat 10 to repeat 20 (1 mark)

3. Change **count to 10** so that it counts in halves
    What did you need to change? *HINT Half as a decimal fraction is 0.5 or 0.50 (If it adds an extra 0 to right it still correct and it might be a bug in Scratch)*
    Change count by 1 to count by 0.5 OR .5 (1 mark)

4. Change **count backwards** so that it counts from 30 to 0.
    What two things did you need to change?
    A   Change set count to 11 to 31 (1 mark)
    B   Change repeat 10 to repeat 31 (1 mark)

5. Change **2xtable** so that it counts from $1 \times 2 = 2$ up to $30 \times 2 = 60$.
    What did you need to change?
    Change repeat from 12 to 30 (1 mark)

6. Change **2xtable** so that it counts the seven times table.
    What four things do you need to change?
    A   Change say counting from 2 to 7 times table (1 mark)
    B   Change set total from 2 to 7 (1 mark)
    C   Change say count $\times$ 2 = total to say count $\times$ 7 = total (1 mark)
    D   Change change total by 2 to change total by 7 (1 mark)

7. Change **add numbers** so that it multiplies num1 by num2.
    What did you change?
    *HINT Operators * is multiply*
    A   Change set total to num1 * num2 replacing green + block (1 mark)
    B   Change say num1 + num1 = total to num1 $\times$ num2 = total (1 mark)

photocopiable page

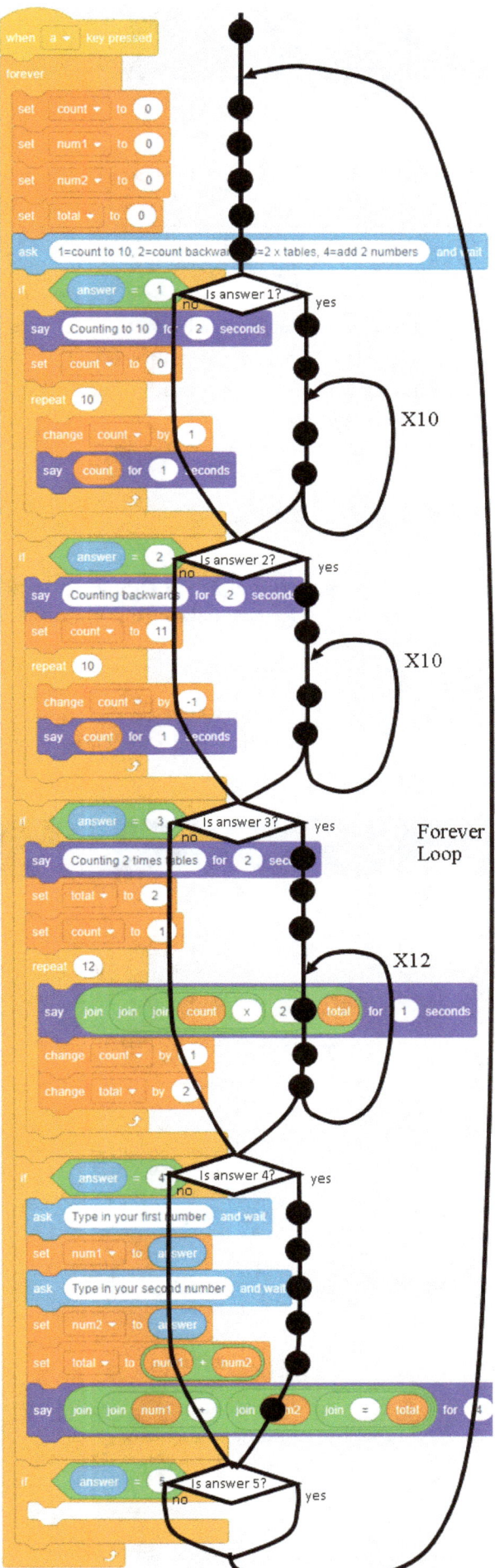

photocopiable page

> **Overview**
>
> Pupils learn about variables before examining three programs that use variables to predict a match between two teams. This uses pupils' Year 5 knowledge about conditions as well as variables, which make it a great additional variable project.

To do before the session

1. Look at the grid below and decide which optional and SEN activities you are going to include and exclude.
2. Print pupil worksheets for each activity chosen and staple into a booklet, one for each pupil.
3. Print marksheets for activities chosen to be placed where pupils can access them.
4. Download the code needed and place in a templates folder on your school network or add to a Scratch Studio or link on your learning platform.
5. Download the slides that go with the concept introduction.
6. Study the notes that go with the slides.
7. Examine the teacher help notes that are provided alongside every activity.

To do at the start of the session

If you have not introduced variables with this class before, do this first as a whole class activity. If you used placeholder variables prior to this activity, this resource build on that understanding rather than replacing it.

To do after the concept has been introduced

Each activity has whole class notes to help you explain what is needed if it is the first time pupils have carried out this type of activity. There are also core instructions underneath in case you are sticking to the core activities only.

How this module fits into a programming progression

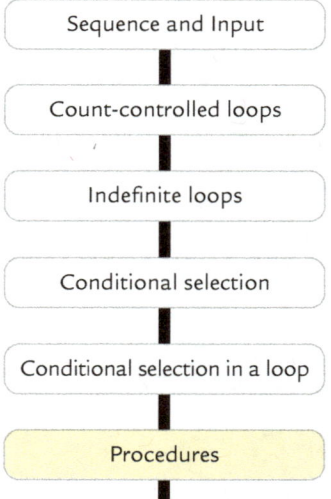

Sequence and Input

Count-controlled loops

Indefinite loops

Conditional selection

Conditional selection in a loop

Procedures

Variables

Vocabulary

Variable, assign, change variable, add to variable, subtract from variable, condition, conditional selection, condition-starts-action.

I recommend you do one of these

Resource Name	Core Optional SEN	Teacher	Pupil Grouping	How Assessed	SCRATCH ACCESS
CONCEPT variables	CORE	Leads Session	Solo Whole Class Activity	Formative	NO
PARSONS	OPTIONAL SEN OPTIONAL ALL	Support Poor Readers	Solo or Paired (Teacher choice)	Pupil Marked Marksheet Provided	YES Parsons Predict the score
PREDICT	OPTIONAL ALL	Support Poor Readers	Paired	Pupil Marked Marksheet Provided	NO
FLOW	OPTIONAL ALL	Leads session with whole class or works with poor readers	Paired	Pupil Marked Marksheet Provided	NO
INVESTIGATE	CORE	Support Poor Readers	Paired	Pupil Marked Marksheet Provided	YES Predict the score
CHANGE	CORE	Support Poor Readers	Paired	Pupil Marked Marksheet Provided	YES Predict the score
CREATE	CORE	Assesses Pupil Work and Checks Pupil Self-assessment	Solo	Pupil Assessed & Teacher Assessed	YES Predict the score
PARTS OF CODE ASSESSMENT	OPTIONAL	Support Poor Readers	Solo	Pupil Marked Marksheet Provided	No

Core activities general instructions

1. Group pupils in roughly same ability pairs. For **investigate** and **change** worksheets pupils will work in pairs, for **create** they will work separately.

2. Give out the pupil booklets and explain that pupils need to follow the instructions on the sheets to explore how **variables** work.

3. Explain that each pupil will record separately whilst working alongside their partner and keeping to the same pace as their partner.

4. Demonstrate where they can find the template code and explain that pupils will share one device for investigate and change.

5. Explain that during each question only one person should touch the shared device and they should swap who that person is when there is a new questions.

6. Encourage them to discuss their answers with their partner. If they disagree with their partner, they can record a different answer in their own booklet.

7. Show pupils where it says they should mark their work on the sheet and where the answer sheets are in the classroom.

8. Remind pupils to return marksheets after marking, because there are not enough for every pair to have their own.

Key Programming Knowledge
Variables are used to store information to be referred to and changed in a computer programme or algorithm

Variables
Have a name and a value
read the name but act on the value
Values can be changed during the algorithm or programme
When writing the value of a variable we call it assigning
Variable Naming
Always name a variable after the data that it stores or the task that it does
Avoid naming variables with spaces teamScore (camelCase) user_name (underscore)
Avoid using the same name as a procedure

Resources

Predict the score https://scratch.mit.edu/projects/609399844/
Parsons Predict the Score https://scratch.mit.edu/projects/611557610/

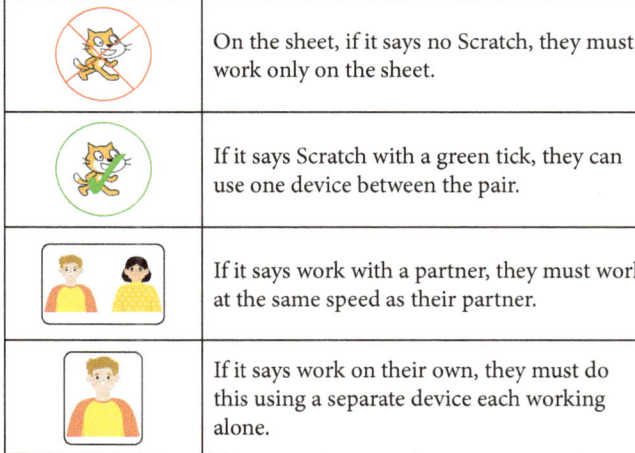

	On the sheet, if it says no Scratch, they must work only on the sheet.
	If it says Scratch with a green tick, they can use one device between the pair.
	If it says work with a partner, they must work at the same speed as their partner.
	If it says work on their own, they must do this using a separate device each working alone.

English Computing National Curriculum Programs of Study

Pupils should be taught to:

- **design, write and debug programs that accomplish specific goals**, including controlling or simulating physical systems; solve problems by decomposing them into smaller parts.

- **use sequence, selection and** repetition **in programs;** work **with variables and various forms of input and output**.

- **use logical reasoning to explain how some simple algorithms work and to detect and correct errors in algorithms and programs**

Scottish Curriculum for Excellence Technologies

I understand the instructions of a visual programming language and can predict the outcome of a program written using the language. TCH 1-14a

I can explain core programming language concepts in appropriate technical language. TCH 2-14a

I can demonstrate a range of basic problem solving skills by building simple programs to carry out a given task, using an appropriate language. TCH 1-15a

I can create, develop and evaluate computing solutions in response to a design challenge. TCH 2-15a

Welsh National Curriculum Relevant Strands

Progression Step 3.

- I can use conditional statements to add control and decision-making to algorithms.

- I can explain and debug algorithms.

PREDICT THE SCORE PARSONS

Work with a partner

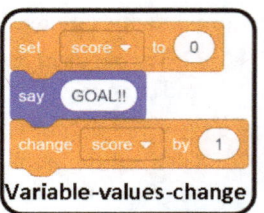

Variable-values-change

Start Scratch and load
Parsons Predict the score

Use the algorithm below to help you connect the Scratch blocks in the correct places in First Attempt

Start the program with a green flag

Assign 0 to Manchester City variable
Assign 0 to Man U variable

Referee Costume
Say Man U v Man C
Say 100% works

Do 10 times
      Assign 1 or 2 to attack variable randomly
      If attack variable = 1
            Add 1 to Man U variable score
            Say Man U score
      If attack variable = 2
            Add 1 to Man U variable score
            Say Man C score
      Pause

Run the code and check your answer using the PARSONS ANSWERS sheet

photocopiable page

PARSONS TEACHER NOTES

Whole class advice

Remember an algorithm plan does not have to be written in code, so the algorithm will not be the same as the code in every line.

Send advice

Use something to block out all of the algorithm but the line pupils are working on, thus revealing one line of the algorithm at a time.

This makes it easier to concentrate on the immediate task rather than be overwhelmed by all of the algorithm.

If supporting pupils one to one you could also get them to work with just three bits of code, one of which must be the code they need.

You could also part-build some of the code so there are even fewer sections.

Individual advice

The first word in every line is often the most important and will often give you a good clue as to which block you need.

Don't forget to run your code to check that it works before moving on.

Whole class advice

Load Parsons Predict the Score code and then use the algorithm on this page to build the code. When you have completed it, run the code and check your answer with the marking sheet.

Use the algorithm below to help you connect the Scratch blocks in the correct places in First Attempt

Start the program with a green flag

Assign 0 to Manchester City variable
Assign 0 to Man U variable

Referee Costume
Say Man U v Man C
Say 100% works

Do 10 times
       Assign 1 or 2 to attack variable randomly
       If attack variable = 1
              Add 1 to Man U variable score
              Say Man U score
       If attack variable = 2
              Add 1 to Man U variable score
              Say Man C score
       Pause

Notes on the activity

Parsons problems were originally designed for university students to make sense of text-based programming by ordering chunks of code rather than writing all the code out. It was designed as a scaffold to reduce the time spent in the minute detail of code and concentrate on the logical order needed to solve a problem.

This example makes pupils think about how an algorithm can be written differently than the code, as it uses similar language to the code but not always the same. An algorithm is designed for another human to understand and can be created with a wide variety of language, commands and symbols. A machine can only follow the precise code language that the blocks are written in.

If pupils still need time to develop their code-connecting skills it can be a good activity to start with. It is popular with pupils, as it is a hands-on activity. If this is the case ,you might ask pupils to complete this in pairs, but with both having a device to do this individually.

Alternatively, it could be an option you only give to pupils who have struggled in other modules to help them familiarise themselves with the code first, before moving on to investigating and modifying code.

Understanding programming

The downside of Parsons problems is that if they are the only activity that pupils use in coding they can encourage pupils to believe that there is only one right way to program.

Predict the Score
PREDICT

Work with a partner

Variable-values-change

Read the labelled code carefully. Write below what you think the program does,

Flow of control

```
when [flag] clicked
```

Initialise the variables
```
set Manchester City ▾ to 0
set Man U ▾ to 0
```

Introduce the programme
```
switch costume to Referee ▾
say Man U vs Manchester City for 2 seconds
say 100% Accurate always! for 2 seconds
```

Loop 10 times
```
repeat 10
```
Repeat 10 times

Randomly assign 1 or 2 to attack variable
```
set attack ▾ to pick random 1 2
```

If 1 is assigned to attack variable Man U scores a goal
```
if attack = 1 then
```
Is 1 assigned to attack variable? Yes No
```
change Man U ▾ by 1
say Manchester United has scored for 2 seconds
```

If 2 is assigned to attack variable Manchester City scores a goal
```
if attack = 2 then
```
Is 2 assigned to attack variable? Yes No
```
change Manchester City ▾ by 1
say Manchester City has scored for 2 seconds
```

```
wait 1 seconds
```
Leave the loop after 10 goes

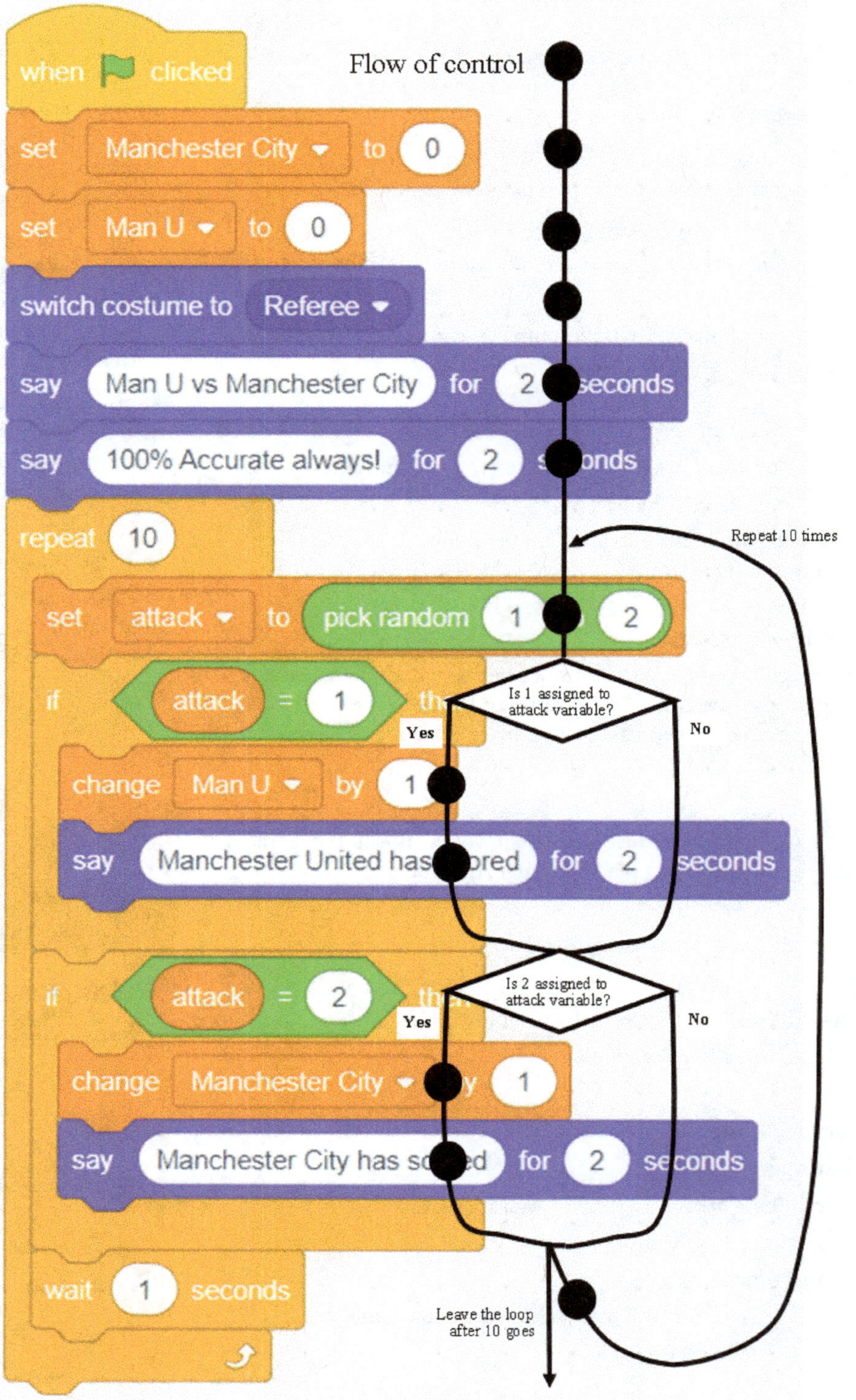

This programme

Randomly choose 1 or 2 is like throwing a coin that can either be heads or tails. We don't know which one will turn up.

HINT Go through the loop a few times to help you understand what is happening

photocopiable page

SUPPORTING PREDICT

Read the labelled code carefully. Write below what you think it is for.

Send advice
Alternative narrative below. This does not use the best computing science language but can help.

Whole class advice
Make sure you work with your partner on this sheet.

Notes on the activity
Prediction helps pupils to think about the bigger purpose of the code before they run the code and experience what it actually does. It is carried out away from a digital devices.

This rubs out any numbers in the variables from the last time the program was run.

This is like flipping a coin to see if 1 or 2 will turn up. (Flip a coin to show).

If 1 turns up on our random choice earlier Man U will score a goal.

The goal is stored in the Man U variable.

If 2 turns up on our random choice earlier Manchester City will score a goal.

The goal is stored in the Manchester City variable.

Initialise the variables

Introduce the programme

Loop 10 times

Randomly assign 1 or 2 to attack variable

If 1 is assigned to attack variable Man U scores a goal

If 2 is assigned to attack variable Manchester City scores a goal

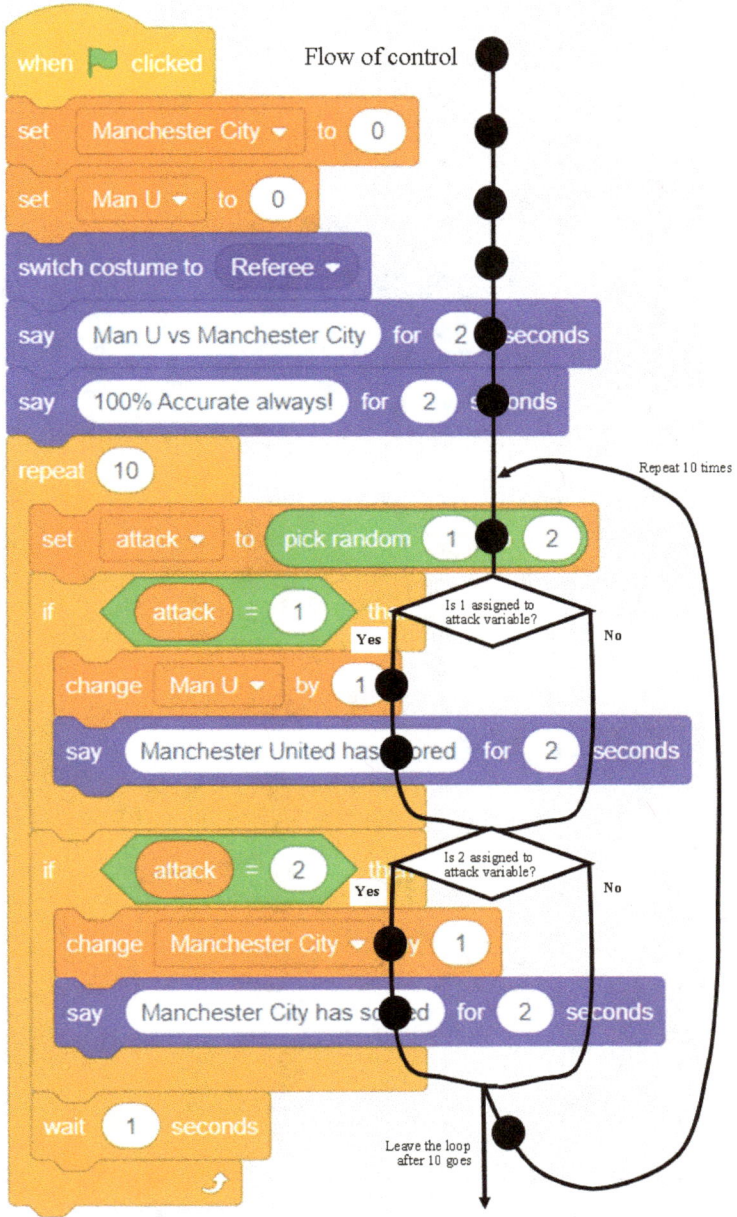

This programme

Randomly choose 1 or 2 is like throwing a coin that can either be heads or tails. We don't know which one will turn up

HINT Go through the loop a few times to help you understand what is happening

Individual advice
Have pupils read these helps?

FLOW

Work with a partner

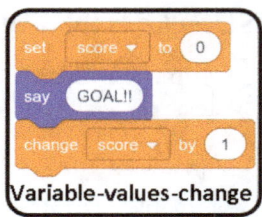

Variable-values-change

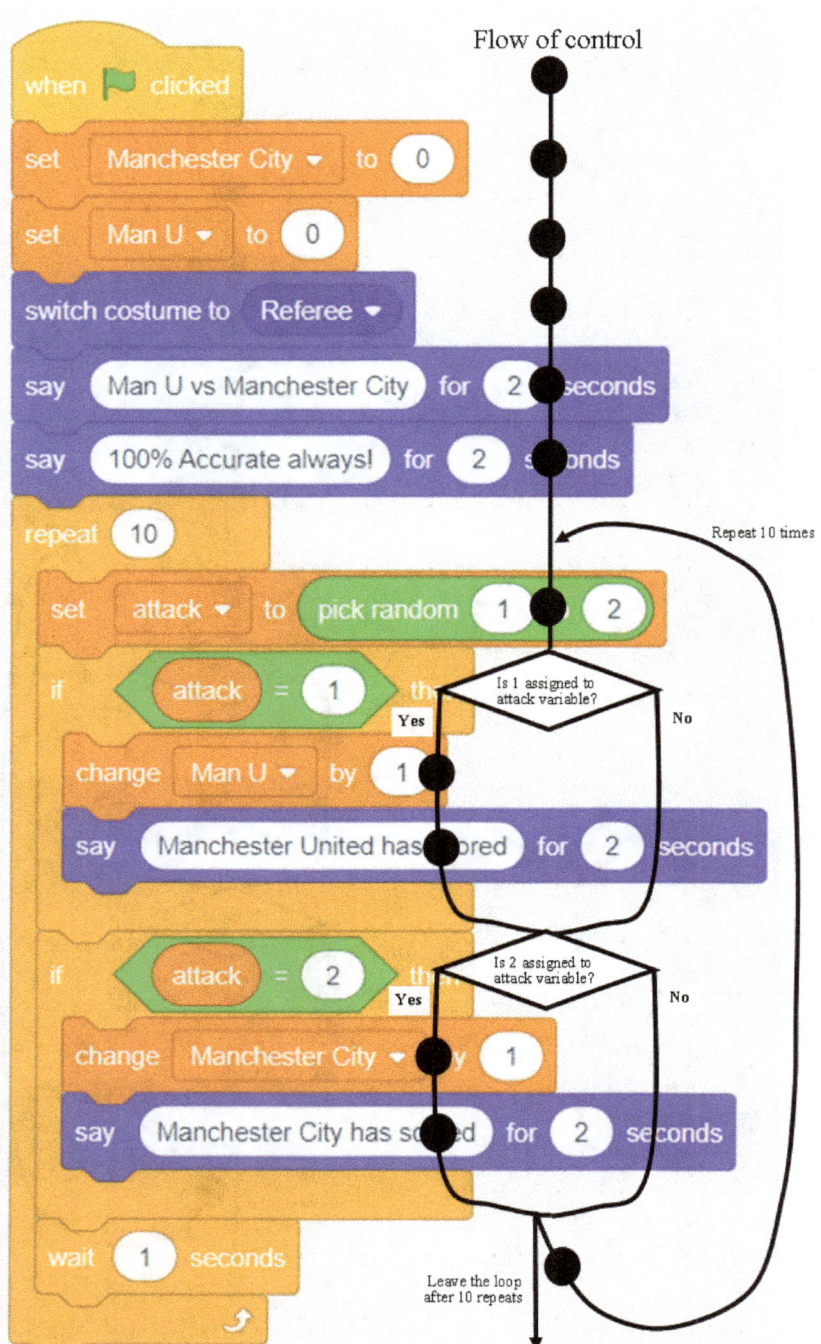

Flow of control

Do First

Use the space below to write in the values of the variables

Manchester City _____

Man U _____

Attack _____

Go through the flow of control and change the variable values (above) as they need to be changed. Make sure you go through all 10 loops.

Do Second

1. How many actions (dots) are there before the first ◇ condition?

2. How many actions (dots) are started by conditions ◇?

3. If 1 is randomly chosen and assigned to the attack variable, what will happen to the Man U score variable?

4. If 2 is randomly chosen and assigned to the attack variable, what will happen to the Manchester City score variable?

5. How many times will the attack variable be assigned a random number? *HINT Loop*

photocopiable page

SUPPORTING FLOW

Send advice

Work with your SEND pupils to go through Do First together.

Whole class instructions

Work together to do first make sure you record the value of all three variables as you go.

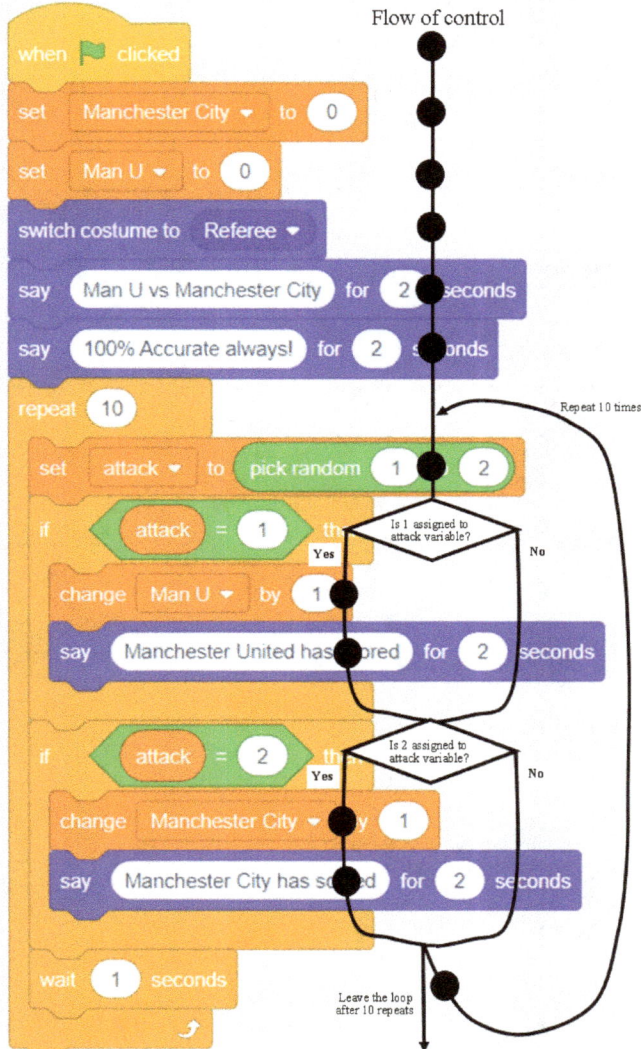

Notes on the activity

Do First can be done with the whole class instead of in pairs. Talk it through with the whole class following the flow of control.

When you get to set **Manchester City to 0** get class to write in 0 next to its name. When you get to set **Man U to 0** get class to write in 0 next to its name.

When you get to set attack, flip a coin to simulate random heads = 1 tails = 2

Get the class to assign the number chosen by the coin.

Check the condition and go down the correct pathway.

Add one to variable if needed. Go through the loop one more time and encourage the class to continue for 10 repetitions.

Do First

Use the space below to write in the values of the variables

Manchester City _____

Man U _____

Attack _____

Go through the flow of control and change the variable values (above) as they need to be changed. Make sure you go through all 10 loops.

Do Second

1. How many actions (dots) are there before the first ◇ condition?

   7 (1 mark)

2. How many actions (dots) are started by conditions ◇?

   4 (1 mark)

3. If 1 is randomly chosen and assigned to the attack variable what will happen to the Man U score variable?

   Add 1 or increase by 1 (1 mark)

4. If 2 is randomly chosen and assigned to the attack variable what will happen to the Manchester City score variable?

   Add 1 or increase by 1 (1 mark)

5. How many times will the attack variable be assigned a random number? *HINT Loop*

   10 (1 mark)

PREDICT THE SCORE
INVESTIGATE

Start Scratch and load
Predict the Score

Work with a partner

INVESTIGATE (Run the programs lots of times but don't change the code)
Run the code inside sprite **First Attempt** and answer these questions.

First Attempt

1. Match the variable to the job that it does by drawing a line

Manchester City   assigned either 1 or 2 randomly

         Man U   keeps the Manchester City score

         attack   keeps the Man U score

2. Which code block adds 1 to the Man U score?

3. What number needs to be assigned to the attack variable so Manchester City can score?

4. Name both conditions
    HINT if

Run the code inside sprite **2nd Attempt** AND OR **3rd Attempt** and answer these questions.

5. Name the code which asks the user the name of the first team and then
    assign it to a variable called team1name. *HINT Two blocks*

6. What is the minimum and maximum number of goal attempts?

7. Name the code which decides how many goal attempts there will be.

8. What condition does NOT lead to a score? *Hint*

Circle the code that you found easiest to use   2nd attempt   3rd attempt

Now mark these questions using the INVESTIGATE ANSWER sheet

photocopiable page

INVESTIGATE TEACHER HELP NOTES

NOTES ON THE ACTIVITY

Investigating code is a core activity in this modules, so I do NOT recommend that you skip this activity. Questions and code in first attempt are less complex than second and third attempts. If some pairs of pupils are taking much longer than their peers you can always cross out the questions in the last section. Sometimes one pupil in a pair decides to work faster than their partner; check that this is not happening and that every pupil is filling in and marking the questions individually but at the pace of the slowest in the pair. Sometimes a pair decides not to mark to speed up their efforts. Marking gives valuable information, so I recommend sending them back to mark their work if this is the case. A class instruction to come and talk to you if they have over half of the questions wrong or they do not understand the answer after they have marked it helps to check progress is being made correctly. There is real value in collecting these scores to build up a summative picture of pupil progress.

Whole Class Advice

Work in pairs, one device between the pair. Take it in turns every question to swap who runs code. You must work at the same pace as your partner and not move on to the next question until you have both written your answer down. If you disagree, write a different answer. You must mark your work before moving on to the next section.

INVESTIGATE (Run the programs lots of times but don't change the code)

Run the code inside sprite **First Attempt** and answer these questions.

First Attempt

Individual Advice Q1

Point out where the variables are used in the code. Now point out where the values appear on the screen.

1. Match the variable to the job that it does by drawing a line

Manchester City — assigned either 1 or 2 randomly (1 mark)

Man U — keeps the Manchester City score (1 mark)

attack — keeps the Man U score (1 mark)

Individual Advice Q2

Point out that there is an invisible + sign in front of every change by variable block.

2. Which code block adds 1 to the Man U score?
   change Man U by 1 (1 mark)

3. What number needs to be assigned to the attack variable so Manchester City can score?
   2 (1 mark)

Individual Advice Q3

Change the wait block to 10 seconds so pupils can see the value that needs to be assigned to attack for Manchester City to score. Now can they find that in the code?

4. Name both conditions *HINT if*
   1f attack = 1 and if attack =2 (1 mark) or attack = 1 and attack = 2 (1 mark)

Individual Advice Q4

Draw the shape of the condition as a hint.

Run the code inside sprite **2nd Attempt** AND OR **3rd Attempt** and answer these questions.

2nd attempt   3rd attempt

5. Which code asks the user the name of the first team and then assign it to a variable called team1name. *HINT Two blocks*
   Ask Type the name of the first team and wait set team1name to answer (1 mark for both blocks)

Send Advice

You can remove questions 5-8 if pupils are falling behind and will not have enough time to modify and make.

6. What is the minimum and maximum number of goal attempts?
   Minimum 3, Maximum 10 or 3 to 10 (1 mark)

7. Name the code which decides how many goal attempts there will be.
   Set randomgoalattempts to pick random 3 to 10 (1 mark)

Individual Advice Q5

HINT Look for code that creates a pop-up box that the user can type into.

8. What condition does NOT lead to a score? *HINT*
   If attack =3 or attack = 3 (1 mark)

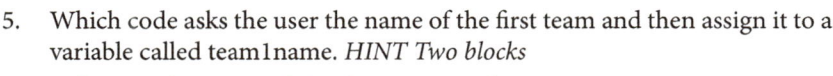

Circle the code that you found easiest to use 2nd attempt 3rd attempt
   No marks for this one just interested in your choice

Individual Advice Q8

What condition does not have a change teamscore by 1 block after it?

PREDICT THE SCORE
CHANGE

Work with a partner

Variable-values-change

First Attempt

Change Code in First Attempt (Make small changes or small additions to the code)

1. Change the code to make the wait between attacks longer. Describe what you changed.

2. Change the code so that Man U score two goals if they attack. I know that is impossible in a real match. Describe what you changed.

3. Change the code so that Manchester City have a goal subtracted if they attack. I know that is impossible in a real match. Describe what you changed. *HINT – (minus).*

4. Change the code so that Manchester City start the match with two goals. I know that is impossible in a real match. Describe what you changed. *HINT Initialisation code.*

5. Add code so that the crowd cheer when there is a goal.
   What did you add and where did you add it? *HINT Goal Cheer Sound.*

Change Code in 2nd attempt or 3rd attempt

(Make small changes or small additions to the code)

2nd attempt

3rd attempt

6. Modify the code so that a new attack option is created which leads to a penalty for one team. *HINT Things to think about.*
   Pick random
   If attack = 4
   Change score by
   Say penalty for…

Now mark the these questions using the CHANGE ANSWER sheet.

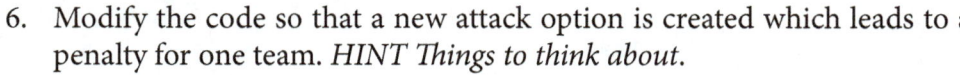

photocopiable page

CHANGE TEACHER HELP NOTES

Whole Class Advice

Work in pairs, one device between the pair. Take it in turns every question to swap who runs code. You must work at the same pace as your partner and not move on to the next question until you have both written your answer down. If you disagree, write a different answer. You must mark your work before moving on to the next section.

Change Code in First Attempt

(Make small changes or small additions to the code)

1. Change the code to make the wait between attacks longer. Describe what you changed

   Change wait 1 second to a higher number (1 mark)

2. Change the code so that Man U score two goals if they attack. I know that is impossible in a real match. Describe what you changed

   Change Man U by **2** (1 mark)

3. Change the code so that Manchester City have a goal subtracted if they attack. I know that is impossible in a real match. Describe what you changed. *HINT – (minus)*

   Change Manchester City by –1 (1 mark)

4. Change the code so that Manchester City start the match with two goals. I know that is impossible in a real match. Describe what you changed. *HINT Initialisation code*

   Set Manchester City to 2 (1 mark)

5. Add code so that the crowd cheer when there is a goal.

   What did you add and where did you add it? *HINT Goal Cheer Sound*

   Any code similar to this that has a sound block added which only plays when the condition is met (1 mark)

Change Code in 2nd attempt or 3rd attempt (with procedures)

(Make small changes or small additions to the code)

6. Modify the code so that a new attack option is created which leads to a penalty for one team. *HINT Things to think about.* Pick random 1 to…, If attack = 4, Change score by, Say penalty for…

Both options need this changed (1 mark)

2nd attempt needs code like this. To get the mark it must include attack = 4, mention a penalty and change score by 1 (1 mark)

Now mark the these questions using the CHANGE ANSWER sheet

Notes on the activity

Changing or modifying the code is a core part of this module, so I suggest you do not leave it out. It is an important step towards creation of their own code. Recording their marks can help with formative and summative assessment.

Send Advice

Programs like this can seem daunting because there is so much code. Only reveal one question at a time. Leave out question 6 if the pupil will not get time to create.

Individual Advice Q1

Key word is **wait**.

Individual Advice Q2

Point out the change Man U by one block and ask what part of the code increases the score by 1.

Individual Advice Q3

Point out that when we change a score by 1 there is an invisible + sign in front of the number. What might we need to do to subtract a number?

Individual Advice Q4

Say if only there was some code that set what the score was at the start of the program? I am sure that is called initialisation.

Individual Advice Q5

This is a revision question, so you may want to remind pupils of conditional selection projects they covered previously.

Individual Advice Q6

Point pupils to the HINTS as all the parts that need to be changed are there.

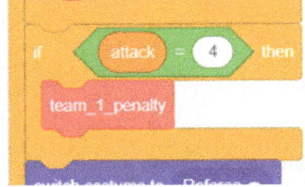

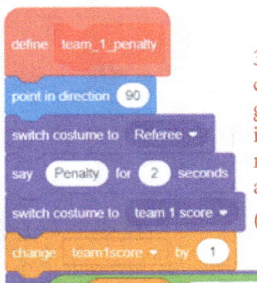

3rd attempt needs code like this. To get the mark it must include attack = 4, mention a penalty and change score by 1 (1 mark)

PREDICT THE SCORE
CREATE

Work on your own

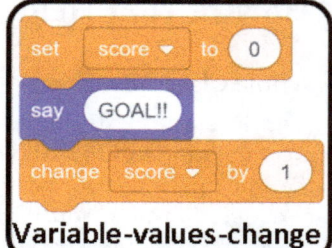

Variable-values-change

Create First (If you have worked with variables before you can leave this section out)

1. Create one variable and use it is a simple story. You must initialise the variable and change it at least twice. The values must all be numbers.

    Possible Program Ideas team score, shopping, racing, amount drunk.

    HINT To add or subtract values the variable must only be a number. No £ or L or KG. Avoid pence as 16.50 will be shortened to 16.5.

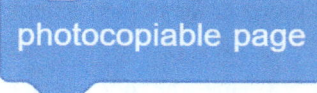

photocopiable page

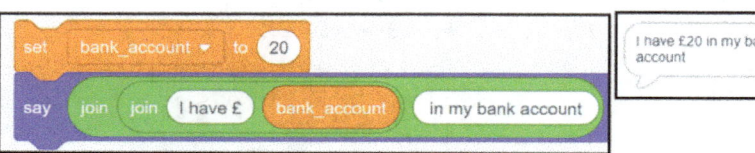

Create Second

2. Plan a program that checks the value of a randomly chosen variable value and uses **condition-starts-actions** (if else) blocks to trigger different responses.

Possible Program Ideas

A random sport pundit that tells you about a game through randomly chosen comments which include changes of score.

A random party commentator that tells you about a party through randomly chosen comments.

Set variable to pick random 1 to 4

If variable =1

> *Say cool party*

If variable =2

> *Someone spills their drink*

If variable =3 **etc**

Your own idea

Plan your program algorithms here

Teacher and Pupil Assessment

Circle one column on each row to show what you think you have achieved

	Not used **a variable that changes** through the program	Used score **variables** that change	Also used a variable to randomly choose an outcome	Used variables in a way not shown in the example program
Variable-values-change	0 marks	1 mark	2 marks	3 marks

		Not used previous programming concepts for real purpose	Used previous programming concepts for real purpose
Used previous programming concept such as loops or conditions correctly		0 marks	1 mark

		No theme in planning or code	Has a theme in planning or code
Has a project theme in create second		0 marks	1 mark

SUPPORTING CREATE

Sen Advice

Even if SEND pupils have worked with variables before, Create First is a simple way of initially engaging with some pupils who may struggle with jumping into a complex project.

Create First (If you have worked with variables before you can leave this section out)

1. Create one variable and use it in a simple story. You must initialise the variable and change it at least twice. The values must all be numbers.

   Possible Program Ideas team score, shopping, racing, amount drunk.

   HINT To add or subtract values the variable must only be a number. No £ or L or KG. Avoid pence, as 16.50 will be shortened to 16.5.

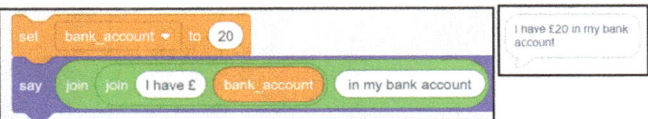

Create Second

2. Plan a program that checks the value of a randomly chosen variable value and uses **condition-starts-actions** (if else) blocks to trigger different responses.

Possible Program Ideas

A random sport pundit that tells you about a game through randomly chosen comments which include changes of score.

A random party commentator that tells you about a party through randomly chosen comments.

Set variable to pick random 1 to 4

If variable =1

   Say cool party

If variable =2

   Someone spills their drink

If variable =3 etc

Your own idea

NOTES ON THE ACTIVITY

The make part of a project is really important and teachers should always make sure that pupils have time to make their own project, even if that means reducing the time spent on other stages for pupils who work slowly. It helps if pupils work on their own for this whilst supporting their partners.

Whole Class Advice

Work on your own, one device each. You can discuss the work with your former partner but you are responsible for creating your own projects. Save your work regularly. Read the instructions carefully. Assess your own work by circling where you think you are in the assessment grid at the bottom of the page.

Individual Advice Create Second

Remind pupils that this is a similar way to the code being used in all the template code.

Plan your program algorithms here
Simple Plan
For example
Initialise variables
Explain what program does
Say how to use it
Set variable to pick random 1 to 4
If variable =1
Say cool party
If variable =2
Someone spills their drink
Have the variables been named after what they do?
Is there initialisation?
Are their score variables of some type?
Has a variable been used randomly to choose different options?
Is there a clear theme to the planning?

Teacher and Pupil Assessment

Circle one column on each row to show what you think you have achieved

	Not used a **variable that changes** through the program	Used score **variables** that change	Also used a variable to randomly choose an outcome	Used variables in a way not shown in the example program
Variable-values-change	0 marks	1 mark	2 marks	3 marks

		Not used previous programming concepts for real purpose	Used previous programming concepts for real purpose
Used previous programming concept such as loops or conditions correctly		0 marks	1 mark

		No theme in planning or code	Has a theme in planning or code
Has a project theme in create second		0 marks	1 mark

Predict the Score
PARTS OF CODE ASSESSMENT

Work with a partner

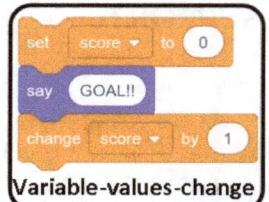

Variable-values-change

Match the code to the description of what it does. One example has been done for you.

A Check to see if attack variables value is 2. If it is a goal is added to the Manchester City variable

B Reset the team variables back to 0 at the start of the program (initialisation)

C Introduce the score prediction program

D Repeat 10 times so there are ten attack opportunities

E Randomly assign either 1 or two to the attack variable

F Check to see if attack variables value is 1. If it is a goal is added to the Man U variable

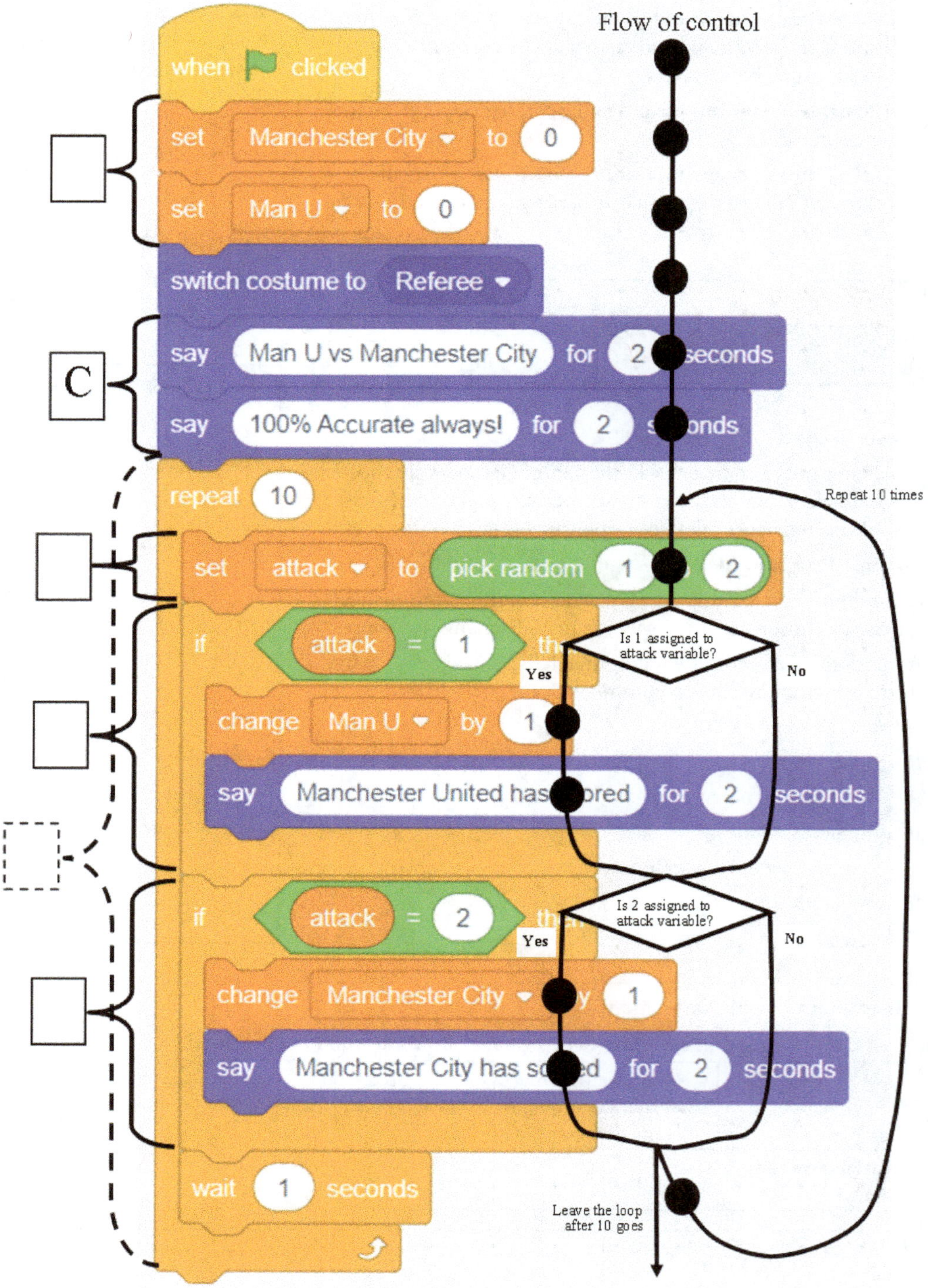

Flow of control

```
when ⚑ clicked
set Manchester City ▾ to 0
set Man U ▾ to 0
switch costume to Referee ▾
say Man U vs Manchester City for 2 seconds
say 100% Accurate always! for 2 seconds
repeat 10
  set attack ▾ to pick random 1 2
  if attack = 1 then
    change Man U ▾ by 1
    say Manchester United has scored for 2 seconds
  if attack = 2 then
    change Manchester City ▾ by 1
    say Manchester City has scored for 2 seconds
  wait 1 seconds
```

C

Repeat 10 times

Is 1 assigned to attack variable?   Yes   No

Is 2 assigned to attack variable?   Yes   No

Leave the loop after 10 goes

photocopiable page

SUPPORTING PARTS OF CODE ASSESSMENT

Whole Class Advice
Do individually without help.

Sen Advice
Cover up all the code apart from B at the top. Leave the choices down the side although you can exclude some to make it easier to choose. Then uncover C, E, etc.

Match the code to the description of what it does. One example has been done for you.

Individual Advice Whole
Use your whiteboard to jot down the names of all the variables and their assigned values.

Manchester City 0

Man U 0

Attack

Now go through the flow of control and change the variable values if they need to be changed. Go through the loop a couple of times changing variables where they need to be changed.

Individual Advice A
Remember = means the same as or assigned to.

A — Check to see if attack variables value is 2. If it is a goal is added to the Manchester City variable

B — Reset the team variables back to 0 at the start of the program (initialisation)

C — Introduce the score prediction program

D — Repeat 10 times so there are ten attack opportunities

E — Randomly assign either 1 or two to the attack variable

F — Check to see if attack variables value is 1. If it is a goal is added to the Man U variable

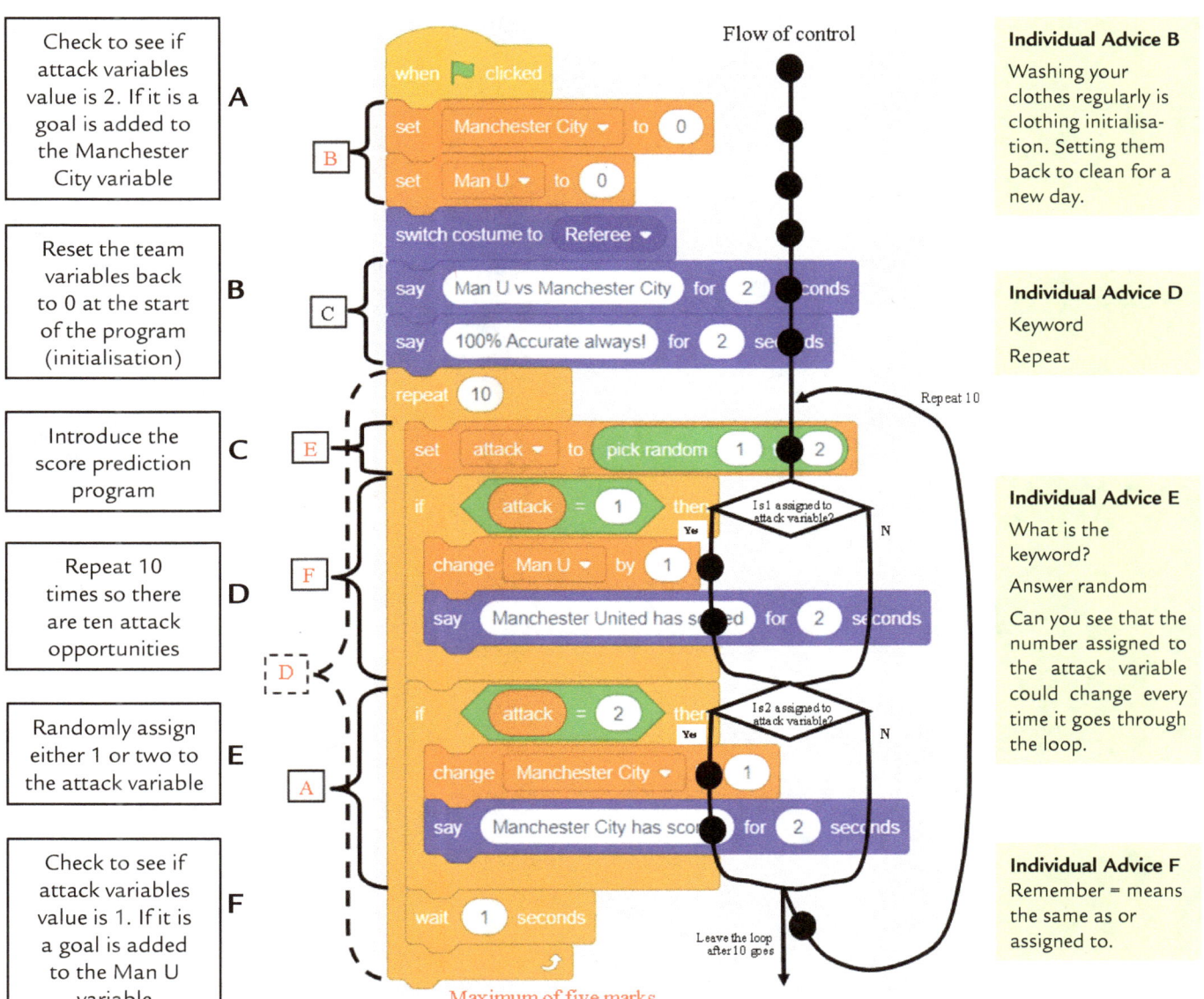

Maximum of five marks

Individual Advice B
Washing your clothes regularly is clothing initialisation. Setting them back to clean for a new day.

Individual Advice D
Keyword

Repeat

Individual Advice E
What is the keyword?

Answer random

Can you see that the number assigned to the attack variable could change every time it goes through the loop.

Individual Advice F
Remember = means the same as or assigned to.

129

PARSONS MARKSHEET

Start the program with a green flag

Assign 0 to Manchester City variable

Assign 0 to Man U variable

Referee Costume

Say Man U v Man C

Say 100% works

Do 10 times

    Assign 1 or 2 to attack variable randomly

    If attack variable = 1

        Add 1 to Man U variable score

        Say Man U score

    If attack variable = 2

        Add 1 to Man U variable score

        Say Man C score

    Pause

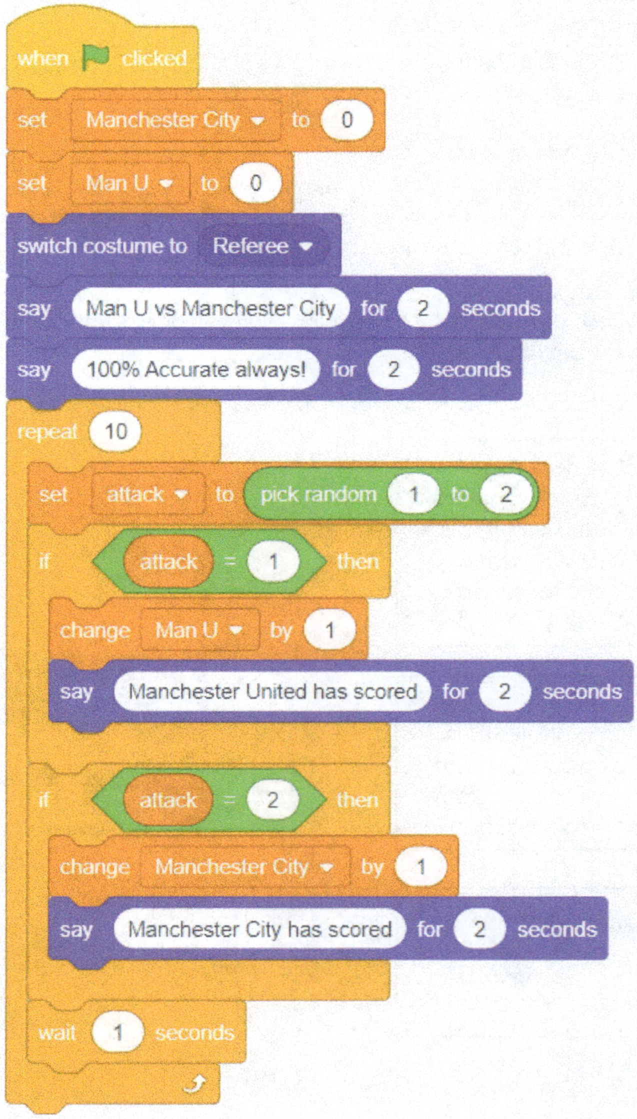

photocopiable page

PREDICT ANSWERSHEET

Any answer that says just predict the score (1 mark).

Any answer that explains that the predicted score will be chosen randomly (2 marks).

PREDICT MARKSHEET

Match the code to the description of what it does. One example has been done for you.

Check to see if attack variables value is 2. If it is a goal is added to the Manchester City variable	A
Reset the team variables back to 0 at the start of the program (initialisation)	B
Introduce the score prediction program	C
Repeat 10 times so there are ten attack opportunities	D
Randomly assign either 1 or two to the attack variable	E
Check to see if attack variables value is 1. If it is a goal is added to the Man U variable	F

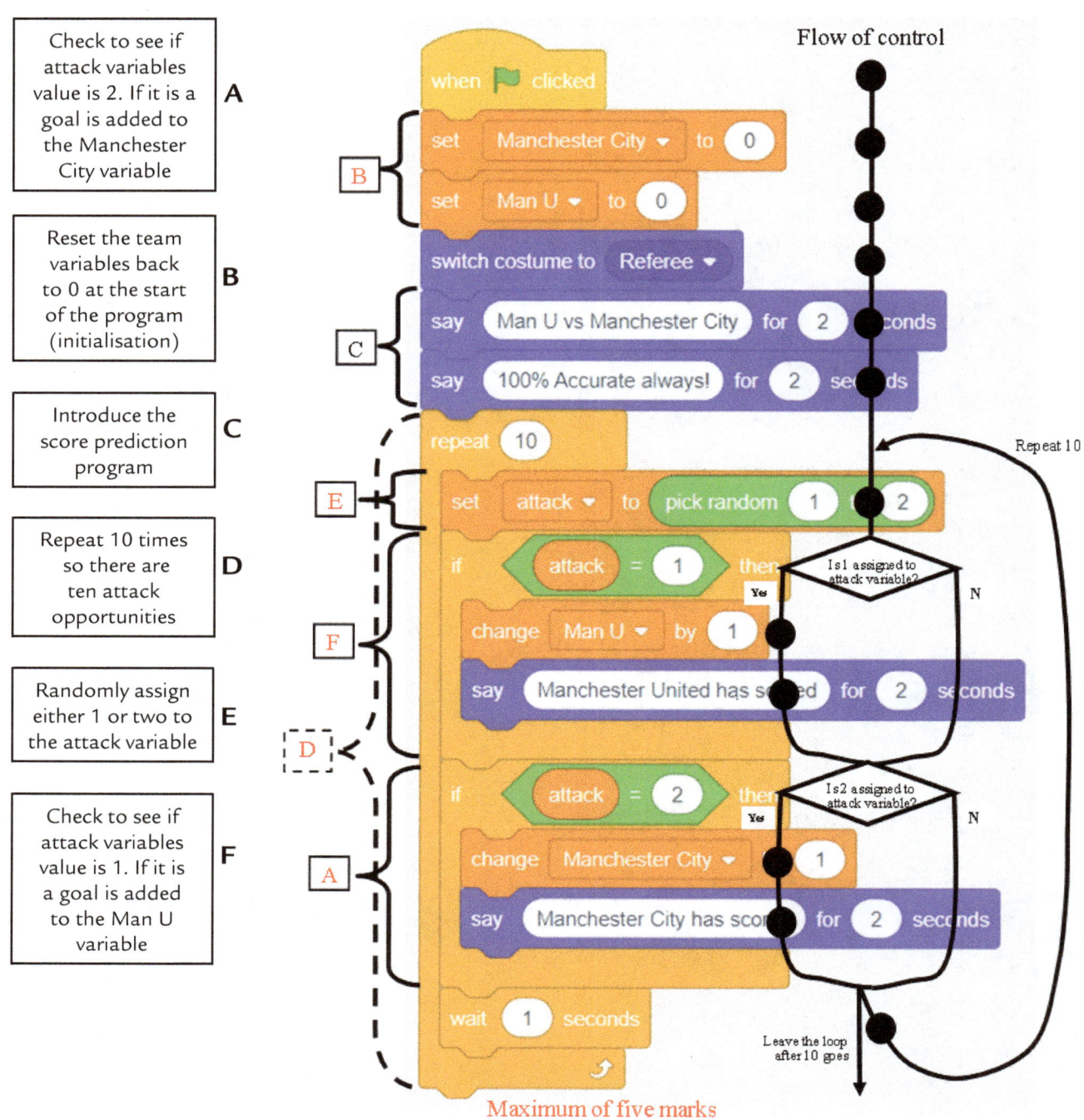

photocopiable page

FLOW MARKSHEET

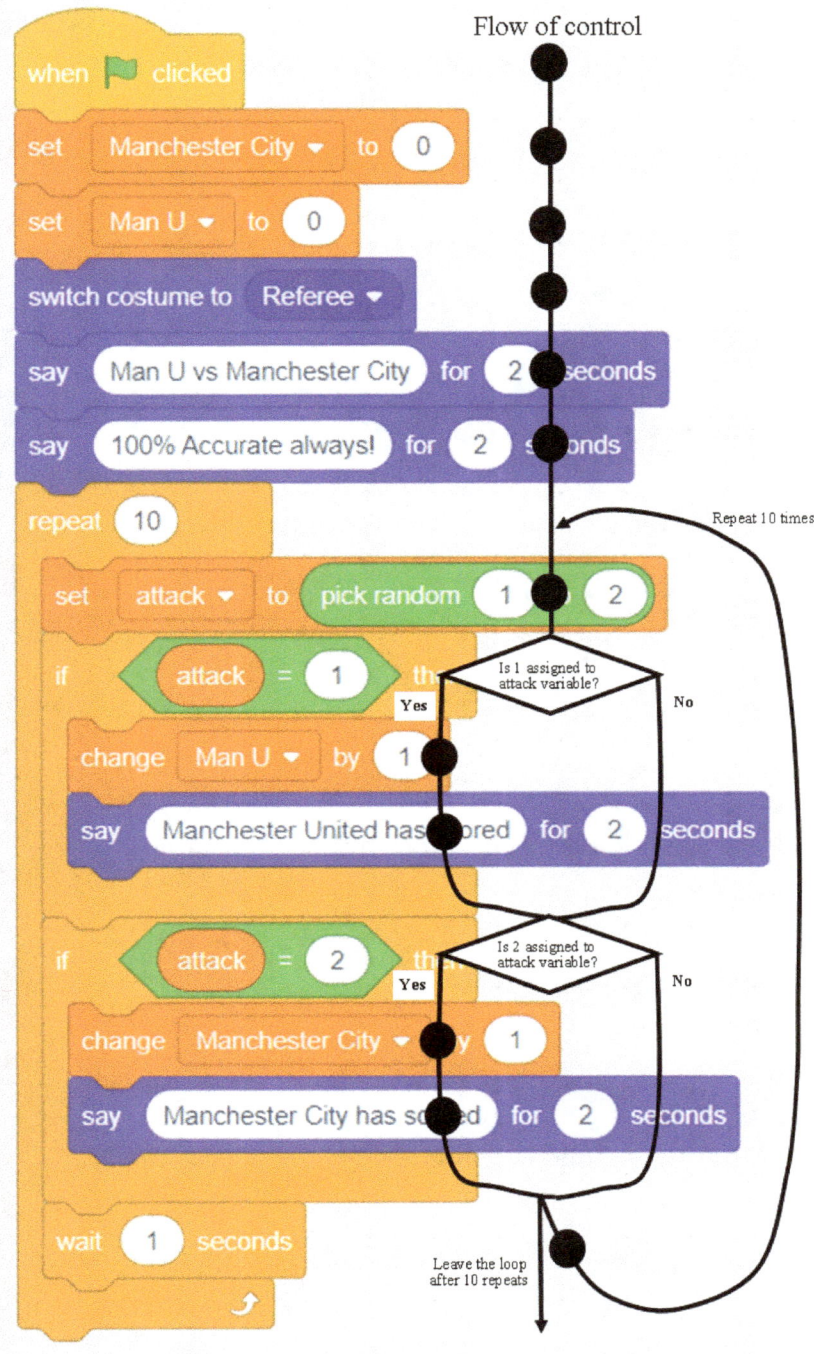

Do First

Use the space below to write in the values of the variables

Manchester City _____

Man U _____

Attack _____

Go through the flow of control and change the variable values (above) as they need to be changed. Make sure you go through all 10 loops.

Do Second

1. How many actions (dots) are there before the first ◇ condition?

    7 (1 mark)

2. How many actions (dots) are started by conditions ◇?

    4 (1 mark)

3. If 1 is randomly chosen and assigned to the attack variable, what will happen to the Man U score variable?

    Add 1 or increase by 1 (1 mark)

4. If 2 is randomly chosen and assigned to the attack variable, what will happen to the Manchester City score variable?

    Add 1 or increase by 1 (1 mark)

5. How many times will the attack variable be assigned a random number? *HINT Loop*

    10 (1 mark)

INVESTIGATE ANSWER SHEET

INVESTIGATE (Run the programs lots of times but don't change the code)
Run the code inside sprite **First Attempt** and answer these questions.

1. Match the variable to the job that it does by drawing a line

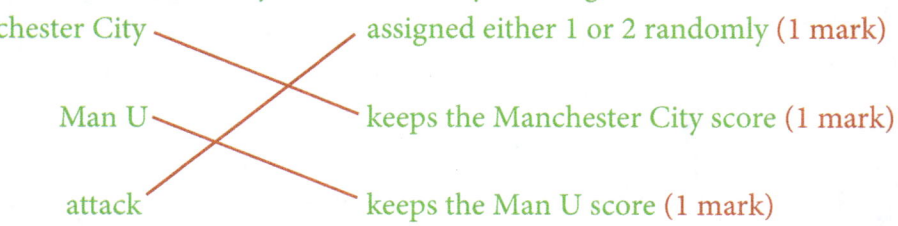

Manchester City — assigned either 1 or 2 randomly (1 mark)

Man U — keeps the Manchester City score (1 mark)

attack — keeps the Man U score (1 mark)

2. Which code block adds 1 to the Man U score?

    change Man U by 1 (1 mark)

3. What number needs to be assigned to the attack variable so Manchester City can score?

    2 (1 mark)

4. Name both conditions *HINT if*

    1f attack = 1 and if attack =2 (1 mark) or attack = 1 and attack = 2 (1 mark)

    Run the code inside sprite **2nd Attempt** AND OR **3rd Attempt** and answer these questions.

5. Which code asks the user the name of the first team and then assigns it to a variable called team1name? *HINT Two blocks*

    Ask Type the name of the first team and wait set team1name to answer (1 mark for both blocks)

6. What is the minimum and maximum number of goal attempts?

    Minimum 3, Maximum 10 or 3 to 10 (1 mark)

7. Name the code which decides how many goal attempts there will be.

    Set randomgoalattempts to pick random 3 to 10 (1 mark)

8. What condition does NOT lead to a score?

    If attack =3 or attack = 3 (1 mark)

    Circle the code that you found easiest to use 2nd attempt 3rd attempt

    No marks for this one, just interested in your choice

photocopiable page

CHANGE MARKSHEET

Change Code in First Attempt (Make small changes or small additions to the code)

1. Change the code to make the wait between attacks longer. Describe what you changed.

   Change wait 1 second to a higher number (1 mark)

2. Change the code so that Man U score two goals if they attack. I know that is impossible in a real match. Describe what you changed.

   Change Man U by **2** (1 mark)

3. Change the code so that Manchester City have a goal subtracted if they attack. I know that is impossible in a real match. Describe what you changed. *HINT – (minus)*

   Change Manchester City by –1 (1 mark)

4. Change the code so that Manchester City start the match with two goals. I know that is impossible in a real match. Describe what you changed. *HINT Initialisation code*

   Set Manchester City to 2 (1 mark)

5. Add code so that the crowd cheer when there is a goal.

   What did you add and where did you add it? *HINT Goal Cheer Sound*

   Any code similar to this that has a sound block added which only plays when the condition is met (1 mark)

Change Code in 2nd attempt or 3rd attempt (with procedures)

(Make small changes or small additions to the code)

6. Modify the code so that a new attack option is created which leads to a penalty for one team. *HINT Things to think about.* Pick random 1 to …, If attack = 4, Change score by, Say penalty for …

Both options need this changed (1 mark)

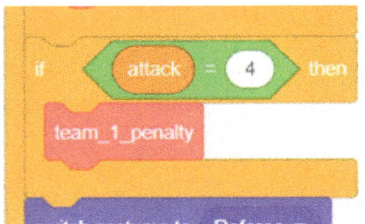

2nd attempt needs code like this. To get the mark it must include attack = 4, mention a penalty and change score by 1 (1 mark)

3rd attempt needs code like this. To get the mark it must include attack = 4, mention a penalty and change score by 1 (1 mark)

PROGRAMMING MODULE THAT USES PLACEHOLDER VARIABLES

Overview

Pupils explore how Scratch can use a variable as a placeholder in a karaoke, quiz and job prediction programme before pupils create their own programs that use a variable as a placeholder

To do before the session

1. Look at the grid below and decide which optional and SEN activities you are going to include and exclude.

2. Print pupil worksheets for each activity chosen and staple into a booklet, one for each pupil.

3. Print marksheets for activities chosen to be placed where pupils can access them.

4. Download the code needed and place in a templates folder on your school network or add to a Scratch Studio or link on your learning platform.

5. Download the slides that go with the concept introduction.

6. Study the notes that go with the slides.

7. Examine the teacher help notes that are provided alongside every activity.

To do at the start of the session

If you have not introduced **placeholder variables** with this class before, do this first as a whole class activity.

To do after the concept has been introduced

Each activity has whole class notes to help you explain what is needed if it is the first time pupils have carried out this type of activity. There are also core instructions underneath in case you are sticking to the core activities only.

How this module fits into a programming progression

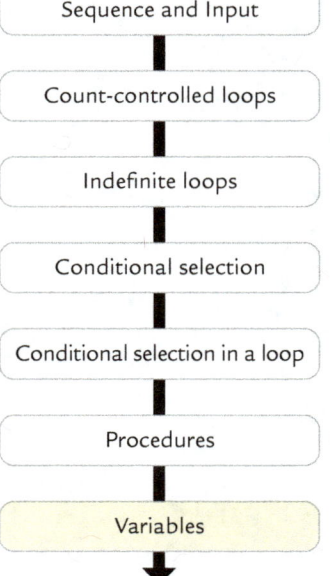

Sequence and Input

↓

Count-controlled loops

↓

Indefinite loops

↓

Conditional selection

↓

Conditional selection in a loop

↓

Procedures

↓

Variables

Vocabulary

variable, assign, set, value, name

Resource Name	Core Optional SEN	Teacher	Pupil Grouping	How Assessed	SCRATCH ACCESS
CONCEPT placeholder variables	CORE	Leads Session	Solo Whole Class Activity	Formative	NO
PARSONS	OPTIONAL SEN OPTIONAL ALL (predict or parsons not both)	Support Poor Readers	Solo or Paired (Teacher choice)	Pupil Marked Marksheet Provided	YES Placeholder Parsons
PREDICT	OPTIONAL ALL (predict or parsons not both)	Support Poor Readers	Paired	Pupil Marked Marksheet Provided	NO
INVESTIGATE	CORE	Support Poor Readers	Paired	Pupil Marked Marksheet Provided	YES Placeholder
CHANGE	CORE	Support Poor Readers	Paired	Pupil Marked Marksheet Provided	YES Placeholder
CREATE	CORE	Assesses Pupil Work and Checks Pupil Self-assessment	Solo	Pupil Assessed & Teacher Assessed	YES Placeholder

Core activities general instructions

1. Group pupils in roughly same ability pairs. For **investigate** and **change** worksheets, pupils will work in pairs, for **create** they will work separately.

2. Give out the pupil booklets and explain that pupils need to follow the instructions on the sheets to explore how **placeholder variables** work.

3. Explain that each pupil will record separately while working alongside their partner and keeping to the same pace as their partner.

4. Demonstrate where they can find the template code and explain that pupils will share one device for investigate and change.

5. Explain that during each question only one person should touch the shared device and they should swap who that person is when there is a new questions.

6. Encourage them to discuss their answers with their partner. If they disagree with their partner, they can record a different answer in their own booklet.

7. Show pupils where it says they should mark their work on the sheet and where the answer sheets are in the classroom.

8. Remind pupils to return marksheets after marking, because there are not enough for every pair to have their own.

Key programming knowledge

Variables are used to store information to be referred to and changed in a computer programme or algorithm

Variables

Have a name and a value

read the name but act on the value

Values can be changed during the algorithm or programme

When writing the value of a variable, we call it assigning

Variable Naming

Always name a variable after the data that it stores or the task that it does

Avoid naming variables with spaces – teamScore (camelCase) user_name (underscore)

Avoid using the same name as a procedure

Resources

Placeholder	https://scratch.mit.edu/projects/340972628/
Placeholder Parsons	https://scratch.mit.edu/projects/622844142/

	On the sheet, if it says no Scratch, they must work only on the sheet.
	If it says Scratch with a green tick, they can use one device between the pair.
	If it says work with a partner, they must work at the same speed as their partner.
	If it says work on their own, they must do this using a separate device each working alone.

English Computing National Curriculum Programs of Study

Pupils should be taught to:

- **design, write and debug programs that accomplish specific goals**, including controlling or simulating physical systems; solve problems by decomposing them into smaller parts.

- use **sequence, selection and** repetition **in programs**; work **with variables and various forms of input and output**.

- use **logical reasoning to explain how some simple algorithms work and to detect and correct errors in algorithms and programs.**

Scottish Curriculum for Excellence Technologies

I understand the instructions of a visual programming language and can predict the outcome of a program written using the language. TCH 1-14a

I can explain core programming language concepts in appropriate technical language TCH 2-14a

I can demonstrate a range of basic problem solving skills by building simple programs to carry out a given task, using an appropriate language. TCH 1-15a

I can create, develop and evaluate computing solutions in response to a design challenge. TCH 2-15a

Welsh National Curriculum Relevant Strands

Progression Step 3.

- I can use conditional statements to add control and decision-making to algorithms.

- I can explain and debug algorithms.

PLACEHOLDER
PARSONS

Work with a partner

set
variable
to
placeholder
Placeholder Variable
name
assigned value

Start Scratch and load placeholder Parsons

Use the algorithm below to help you connect the Scratch blocks in the correct places in the unfinished third quiz question (you might need to scroll down to find the code)

Say Third question user_name

Ask Double 13 is ? user_name and wait

if answer = 26 then

    Say That's right user_name

if answer = Twenty Six then

    Say That's right user_name

if answer is **NOT** answer = 26 **OR** answer = Twenty Six then

Say user_name the right answer is 26

(You will NOT need to type anything in anywhere)

SUPPORTING
PARSONS

Start Scratch and Load
Placeholder Parsons

Whole class advice

Load placeholder Parsons code and then use the algorithm on this page to build the code. When you have completed it, run the code and check your answer with the marking sheet.

Use the algorithm below to help you connect the Scratch blocks in the correct places in the unfinished third quiz question (you might need to scroll down to find the code).

Say Third question user_name

Ask Double 13 is ? user_name and wait

if answer = 26 then

    Say That's right user_name

if answer = Twenty Six then

    Say That's right user_name

if answer is **NOT** answer = 26 **OR** answer = Twenty Six then

Say user_name the right answer is 26

(You will NOT need to type anything in anywhere)

Notes on the activity

This allows pupils to build part of the code first before investigating, modifying and creating code of their own. The algorithm is written in language similar but also different to the code. This helps pupils by enabling them to see an example of planning which will help them when they come to plan their own project. On its own it is not enough deep thinking about the code to enable agency, but as a starter or SEN activity it is useful to see how code can be built.

Able advice

Parsons problems can be made more complex by separating more blocks in the example Scratch code and saving that version as a new template.

Send advice

Parsons problems can be made less complex by connecting more blocks in the example Scratch code and saving that version as a new template.

Understanding programming

You can find out more about Parsons problems in the teacher book, Chapter 19.

Individual advice

Pointing out that the code affected by the condition is indented once it is in the if block and it is indented in the planning algorithm can help some pupils.

Individual advice

Point out that the user_name code will need to embedded in other code blocks to be used. Then show pupils where that has been done in earlier questions.

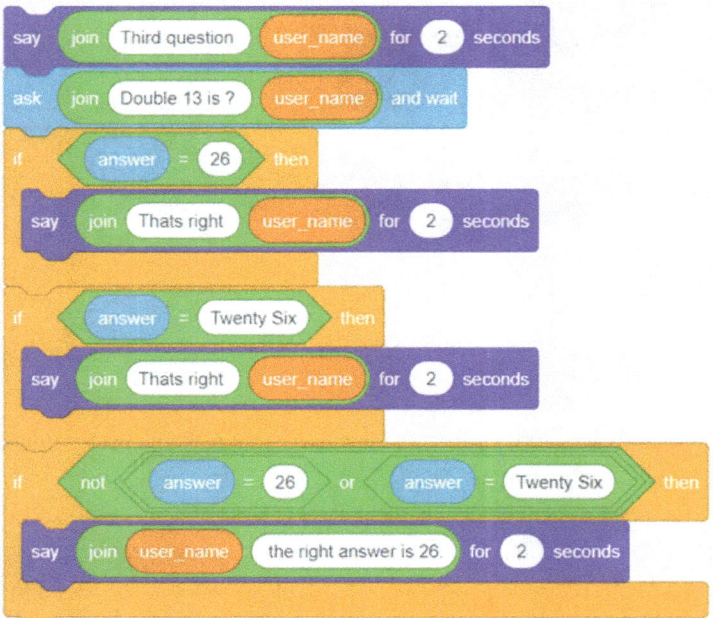

PLACEHOLDER
PREDICT

Read the code carefully with your partner

Work with a partner

set variable ▼ to placeholder
Placeholder Variable
name   assigned value

	when this sprite clicked
Initialisation	show variable user_name ▼
	switch backdrop to stage2 ▼
Collect the users name and assigns it to user_name variable	ask What's your name? and wait
	set user_name ▼ to answer
Introduce the quiz	say join join Try and answer the questions correctly user_name ( ) for
Quiz question 1	say join First question user_name for 2 seconds
	ask join user_name what is 12 x 2 = ? and wait
	if answer = 24 then
	say join That is a great answer user_name for 2 seconds
	else
	say join user_name you got this one incorrect! for 2 seconds
Quiz question 2	say join Second question user_name for 2 seconds
	ask join user_name what is 100 - 80 = ? and wait
	if answer = 20 then
	say join Correct user_name for 2 seconds
	else
	say join user_name the right answer is 20. for 2 seconds

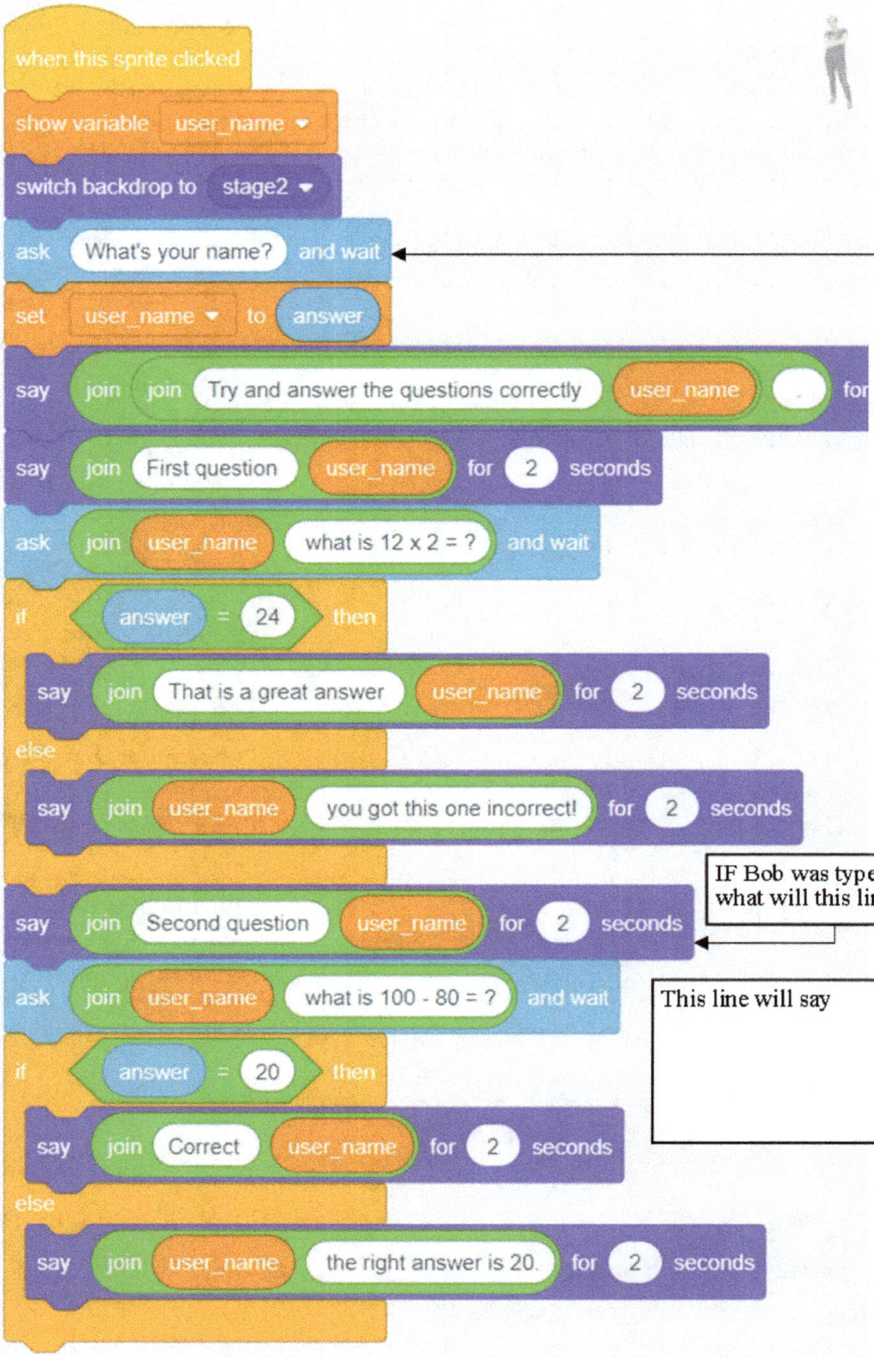

IF Bob was typed in here what will this line say?

This line will say

Personalised means addressed to you by using your name

Tick the most accurate prediction of what the code does

- Asks a two question quiz and gives answers if the quiz answers are correct or wrong.
- Asks a personalised two question quiz and gives personalised answers if the user's answers are the same as the programmer's correct answers.
- Asks a two question quiz and gives answers if the user's answers are the same as the programmer's correct answers.

Now mark your work using the predict marksheet

photocopiable page

SUPPORTING PREDICT

Read the code carefully with your partner

Notes on the activity

This optional activity helps pupils to think about the bigger purpose of the program before they start looking at parts of it in later sections.

This activity draws on pupils understanding of conditional selection that they learnt about in Year 5. It can be helpful for their teacher to find out what module of work they studied in Year 5 that covered this area of learning.

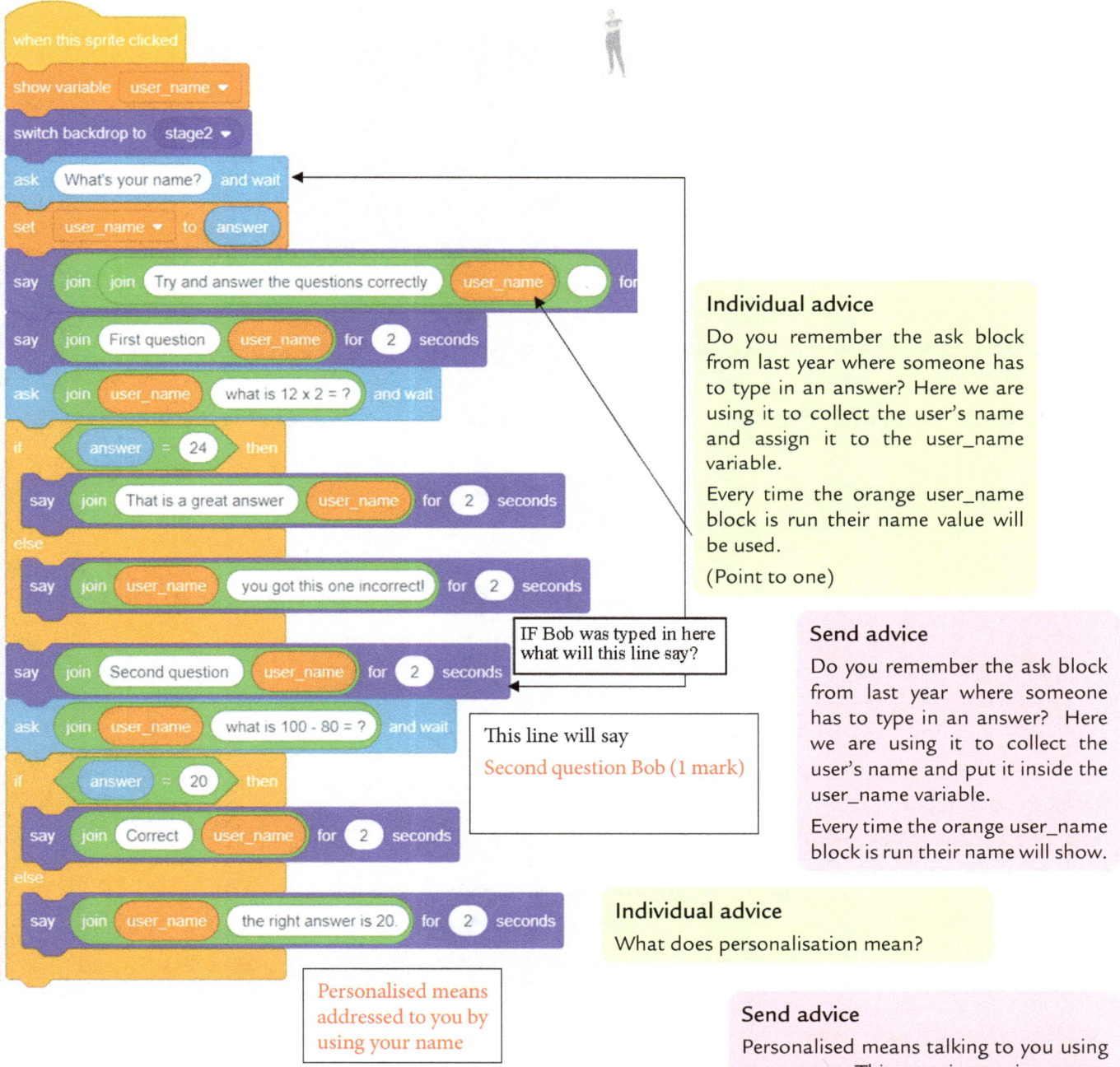

Individual advice

Do you remember the ask block from last year where someone has to type in an answer? Here we are using it to collect the user's name and assign it to the user_name variable.

Every time the orange user_name block is run their name value will be used.

(Point to one)

IF Bob was typed in here what will this line say?

This line will say
Second question Bob (1 mark)

Send advice

Do you remember the ask block from last year where someone has to type in an answer? Here we are using it to collect the user's name and put it inside the user_name variable.

Every time the orange user_name block is run their name will show.

Individual advice

What does personalisation mean?

Personalised means addressed to you by using your name

Send advice

Personalised means talking to you using your name. This part is very important for answering the bottom question.

Tick the most accurate prediction of what all the code does

- Asks a two question quiz and gives answers if the quiz answers are correct or wrong.
- Asks a personalised two question quiz and gives personalised answers if the user's answers are the same as the programmer's correct answers (1 mark).
- Asks a two question quiz and gives answers if the user's answers are the same as the programmer's correct answers.

INVESTIGATE

Start Scratch and load

Placeholder

Work with a partner

Placeholder Variable

name   assigned value

Look in karaoke

Run the code to answer the questions

1. What is the value of the **user_name** variable at the start of the program?

Karaoke

2. How many times is the user_name variable used in karaoke? Hint

3. Who **changes** the value of the user_name variable **half way** through the program?

Stop Karaoke running first using stop button ⬤

Look in quiz

Run the code to answer the questions

4. What value did you give to **user_name** in quiz when you first ran the program?

quiz

5. Does the value of **user_name** change after it has been assigned by the user in the beginning?

6. How many joins blocks are used inside the first say block?

7. List the four different ways the programmer use the user_name variable in the first quiz question? *HINT Add name to first question*

Add name   Add name

Add name   Add name

Stop quiz running first using stop button ⬤

Look in Which Job?

Run the code to answer the questions

Which Job?

8. Which block stops the variable **user_name** and value being shown on the screen?

9. Which blocks display the **user_name** and value on the screen?

10. Which **blocks** ask the user for their name and assign their name to the user_name variable?

11. Which block randomly chooses a job from the jobs list? *HINT List is NOT a variable, it is another way of storing and using data in a program*

Now mark this page using the investigate marksheet

photocopiable page

SUPPORTING INVESTIGATE

Whole class advice

Work in pairs, one device between the pair. Take it in turns every question to swap who runs code. You must work at the same pace as your partner and not move on to the next question until you have both written your answer down. If you disagree, write a different answer. You must mark your work before moving on to the next section.

Look in Kkraoke

Karaoke

Run the code to answer the questions

1. What is the value of the **user_name** variable at the start of the program?

   Dolly (1 mark)

   user_name

2. How many times is the user_name variable used in karaoke? *Hint*

   8 (1 mark)

3. Who **changes** the value of the user_name variable **halfway** through the program?

   Any answer that suggests it is the user or person running the programme (1 mark)

Stop karaoke running first using stop button 🔴

Problems will be created if two scripts are running at the same time

Look in quiz

quiz

Run the code to answer the questions

4. What value did you give to **user_name** in quiz when you first ran the program?

   Any answer (1 mark)

5. Does the value of **user_name** change after it has been assigned by the user in the beginning?

   No (1 mark)

6. How many joins blocks are used inside the first say block?

   2 (1 mark) Many joins can be combined

7. List the four different ways the programmer use the user_name variable in the first quiz question? *HINT Starts First Question*

   Add name to first question (1 mark) Add name to the question (1 mark)

   Add name to right answer (1 mark) Add name to wrong answer (1 mark)

Stop karaoke running first using stop button 🔴

Problems will be created if two scripts are running at the same time.

Look in Which Job?

Which Job?

Run the code to answer the questions

8. Which block stops the variable **user_name** and value being shown on the screen?

   Hide variable user_name (1 mark)

9. Which blocks display the **user_name** and value on the screen?

   Show variable user_name (1 mark)

10. Which blocks ask the user for their name and assign their name to the user_name variable?

    Ask what is your name, set user_name to answer (1 mark for all of this only)

11. Which block randomly chooses a job from the jobs list? *HINT List is NOT a variable, it is another way of storing and using data in a programme*

    Item random of jobs (1 mark)

Notes on the activity

Investigating the code encourages pupils to think deeply about how it works. Check that every pupil is filling in and marking the questions individually but at the pace of the slowest in the pair. Sometimes a pair decides not to mark to speed up their efforts. Marking gives valuable information, so I recommend sending them back to mark their work. A class instruction to come and talk to you if they have over half of the questions wrong or they do not understand the answer after they have marked it helps to check progress is being made correctly. There is real value in collecting these scores to build up a summative picture of pupil progress.

Q1 HINT Point out the picture top left of the worksheet which names parts of variable in Scratch.

Q2 Count user_name

Q3 HINT Inputs information through typing

Q4 What did you type in?

Q5 Is there any other set user_name variable block after the first?

Q6 First time a say block is used.

Q7 Point out where the first question starts and ends. How is your name value being used?

Send advice

Support pairs of pupils who are poor readers by reading questions, reading code samples and covering up questions until they get to them.

Q8 HINT Hide.

Q9 HINT Show.

Send advice

Which Job can be used as an extension section and missed out if SEN pupils are working at too slow a pace to reach create in time.

Q10 HINT Two lines of code.

Q11 Hint random.

Q11 Lists are a totally different way to store data. They are not variables. Lists can have many entries and things can be added or taken away from a list.

PLACEHOLDER CHANGE

Start Scratch and load Placeholder

Work with a partner

Placeholder Variable

Look in all the sprites

Make small changes or additions to the code

1. Change the value of the user_name variable in the first half of the karaoke programme. What did you change it to?

   Karaoke

2. In the quiz first say block swap, the order of the variable and the text so that the variable with the users name goes first.

   ☐ Tick here when you have done it

   quiz

3. Add a simple quiz question to the bottom of the quiz. Make sure you personalise it using the user_name variable. Write an algorithm plan to show what you created.

   quiz

   Here is a simple quiz question algorithm plan without a variable

   Ask 3×3=?
   If user answer is same as 9
   　　　Say correct
   Else
   　　　Say wrong

4. In Which Job, change one of the jobs on the job list. What did you change and what did you change it to?

   Which Job?

   Lists are places we can store more than one value.

   Lists are **not** variables.

5. Add a new job on to the list. Which block did you use?

   Which Job?

Now mark the change section using the answer sheet

photocopiable page

SUPPORTING CHANGE

Whole class advice

Work in pairs, one device between the pair. Take it in turns every question to swap who runs code. You must work at the same pace as your partner and not move on to the next question until you have both written your answer down. If you disagree, write a different answer. You must mark your work before moving on to the next section.

Notes on the activity

Changing or modifying code is a core part of this module, so I suggest you do not leave it out. It is an important step towards creation of their own code, as parts they have modified they will feel more ownership of. Recording marks will help with assessment.

Look in all the sprites

Make small changes or additions to the code

1. Change the value of the user_name variable in the first half of the karaoke programme. What did you change?

   Change Dolly to another name (1 mark)

Karaoke

Q1 HINT Set.

2. In the quiz first say block, swap the order of the variable and the text so that the variable with the users name goes first.

   Tick here when you have done it (1 mark for the tick)

quiz

Q2 You might need to cut and paste the text into a new join box (ctrl C ctrl V).

3. Add a simple quiz question to the bottom of the quiz. Make sure you personalise it using the user_name variable. Write an algorithm plan to show what you created.

quiz

Q3 You can create this quiz question in any way you want, as long as it uses the user_name variables in lots of ways.

THERE ARE LOTS OF WAYS TO DO THIS!

EXAMPLE
Ask **user_name** what is 3x3=?
If answer = 9

   Say correct **user_name**
Else

   Say wrong **user_name**

Has the algorithm got a question with user_name in it (1 mark)

Has the algorithm used user_name in the right and or wrong answer (1 mark)

> Here is a simple quiz question algorithm plan without a variable
>
> Ask 3×3=?
> If user answer is same as 9
>
>   Say correct
> Else
>
>   Say wrong

Q3 Remember when you planned a quiz in Year 5.

4. In Which Job, change one of the jobs on the job list. What did you change and what did you change it to?

   Change add (existing jobs) to jobs to add (your choice) to jobs (1 mark)

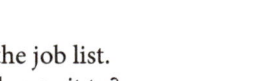
Which Job?

Q4 Is there a job that you don't like and a better one you can change it to?

5. Add a new job on to the list. Which block did you use?

   Add (new job your choice) to jobs (1 mark)

Which Job?

Q5 Which blocks add something to the list?

Send advice

Support pairs of pupils who are poor readers by reading questions, reading code samples and covering up questions until they get to them.

Send advice

Q4 & Q5 can be used as an extension section and missed out if SEN pupils are working at too slow a pace to reach create in time.

Now mark the change section using the answer sheet

PLACEHOLDER CREATE

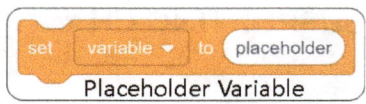

Work on
your own

Placeholder Variable

CREATE

Do one or more of these create challenges

1. Use a variable to personalise a previously created program. Make sure you save it with a new name.

2. Create a few quiz questions that have been personalised using a variable. Use the planning sheet underneath to think through your design.

3. Get the user to personalise a passage of text from a favourite book or your own writing using variables. Remember a variable can be a placeholder for any word or words not just a name. You can create as many variables as you need. Use the planning sheet underneath to think through your design.

4. Personalise a new program which is not a game using a variable. Use the planning sheet underneath to think through your design.

Idea Level *My app will... My characters will be... The aim of the app will be....*

Design Level Planning Algorithm

Teacher and Pupil Assessment

Circle one column on each row to show what you think you have achieved

	Not used **a variable as a placeholder**-through the program	Used user_name in exactly same way as shown in placeholder	Created own placeholder variable or use more than one placeholder variable for own use
Placeholder Variable	0 marks	1 mark	2 marks
		Not used previous programming concepts for real purpose	Used previous programming concepts for real purpose
Used previous programming concept such as loops or conditions correctly		0 marks	1 mark
		No theme in planning or code	Has a theme in planning or code
Has a project theme in create second		0 marks	1 mark

SUPPORTING CREATE

Whole class advice

Work on your own, one device each. You can discuss the work with your former partner but you are responsible for creating your own projects. Save your work regularly. Read the instructions carefully. Assess your own work by circling where you think you are in the assessment grid at the bottom of the page.

Notes on the activity

The make part of a project is really important and teachers should always make sure that pupils have time to make their own project, even if that means reducing the time spent on other stages for pupils who work slowly. It helps if pupils work on their own for this while supporting their partner.

CREATE

Do one or more of these create challenges

1. Use a variable to personalise a previously created program. Make sure you save it with a new name.

2. Create a few quiz questions that have been personalised using a variable. Use the planning sheet underneath to think through your design.

3. Get the user to personalise a passage of text from a favourite book or your own writing using variables. Remember a variable can be a placeholder for any word or words, not just a name. You can create as many variables as you need. Use the planning sheet underneath to think through your design.

4. Personalise a new program which is not a game using a variable. Use the planning sheet underneath to think through your design.

Q1 The ideal programs to personalise would be any created using Making Choices or Wizards Choices made in Year 5. However, if pupils missed this module, there is a simple maths quiz script they could add to here.

https://scratch.mit.edu/projects/622837919/

Q2, 3 & 4 all have planning elements, so check that pupils are thinking through what they are going to make in a plan before creating it.

Q3 This is a really fun project, but it will need careful planning and multiple variables. The author will also need to understand how to get the user to input a variable using the ask and answer input blocks.

Q3 & 4 It is good to have open choice, but check the progress of any pupil who has chosen 3 or 4, as it is easier to go off track.

Idea Level *My app will... My characters will be... The aim of the app will be....*

IDEA LEVEL Is there a clear aim to the programme?

Assessment

Do a preliminary assessment halfway through their creation time, as this will give them time to improve their projects. You can also ask them to self-assess their creations first.

Design Level Planning Algorithm

Design level

Has at least a part of the project been designed using an algorithm? See change for an example algorithm.

Send support

Q1 is an easier project to make and if pupils have struggled, it may be worth limiting their choice to this.

Teacher and Pupil Assessment

Circle one column on each row to show what you think you have achieved

	Not used **a variable as a placeholder** through the program	Used user_name in exactly same way as shown in placeholder	Created own placeholder variable or use more than one placeholder variable for own use
Placeholder Variable	0 marks	1 mark	2 marks
		Not used previous programming concepts for real purpose	Used previous programming concepts for real purpose
Used previous programming concept such as loops or conditions correctly		0 marks	1 mark
		No theme in planning or code	Has a theme in planning or code
Has a project theme in create second		0 marks	1 mark

PARSONS MARKSHEET

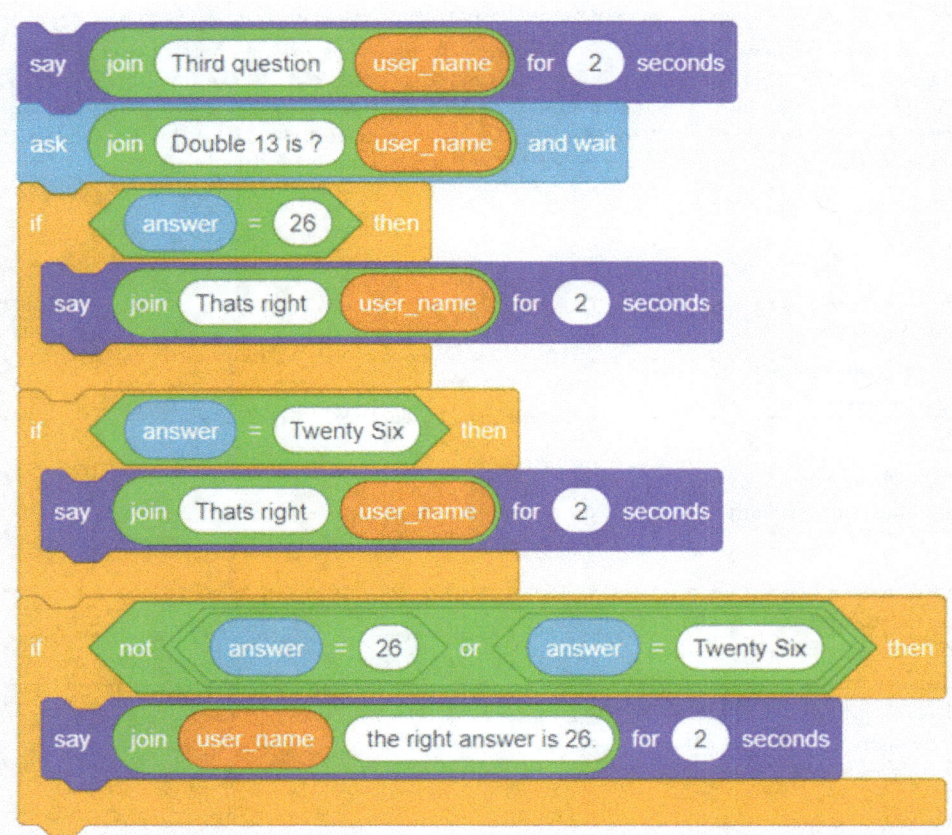

PREDICT MARKSHEET

> This line will say
> Second question Bob (1 mark)

Tick the most accurate prediction of what all the code does

- Asks a two question quiz and gives answers if the quiz answers are correct or wrong.
- Asks a personalised two question quiz and gives personalised answers if the user's answers are the same as the programmer's correct answers (1 mark).
- Asks a two question quiz and gives answers if the user's answers are the same as the programmer's correct answers.

INVESTIGATE MARKSHEET

Look in ;araoke

1. What is the value of the **user_name** variable at the start of the program?
   Dolly (1 mark)

2. How many times is the user_name variable used in karaoke? *Hint*
   8 (1 mark)

3. Who **changes** the value of the user_name variable **halfway** through the program?
   Any answer that suggests it is the user or person running the programme (1 mark)

Look in quiz

4. What value did you give to **user_name** in quiz when you first ran the program?
   Any answer (1 mark)

5. Does the value of **user_name** change after it has been assigned by the user in the beginning?
   No (1 mark)

6. How many joins blocks are used inside the first say block?
   2 (1 mark) Many joins can be combined

7. List the four different ways the programmer use the user_name variable in the first quiz question?
   HINT starts First Question
   Add name to first question (1 mark)   Add name to the question (1 mark)
   Add name to right answer (1 mark)   Add name to wrong answer (1 mark)

Look in Which Job?

8. Which block stops the variable **user_name** and value being shown on the screen?
   Hide variable user_name (1 mark)

9. Which blocks displays the **user_name** and value on the screen?
   Show variable user_name (1 mark)

10. Which blocks ask the user for their name and assigns their name to the user_name variable?
    Ask what is your name, set user_name to answer (1 mark for all of this only)

11. Which block randomly chooses a job from the jobs list? *HINT List is NOT a variable, it is another way of storing and using data in a programme*
    item random of jobs (1 mark)

CHANGE MARKSHEET

Look in all the sprites

Make small changes or additions to the code

1. Change the value of the user_name variable in the first half of the karaoke programme. What did you change?

    Change Dolly to another name (1 mark)

Karaoke

2. In the quiz first say block swap the order of the variable and the text so that the variable with the user's name goes first.

    ☐ Tick here when you have done it (1 mark for the tick)

quiz

3. Add a simple quiz question to the bottom of the quiz. Make sure you personalise it using the user_name variable. Write an algorithm plan to show what you created.

quiz

THERE ARE LOTS OF WAYS TO DO THIS!

Has the algorithm got a question with user_name in it (1 mark)

EXAMPLE
Ask **user_name** what is 3x3=?
If answer = 9

        Say correct **user_name**

Else

        Say wrong **user_name**

Has the algorithm used user_name in the right and or wrong answer (1 mark)

Here is a simple quiz question algorithm plan without a variable

Ask 3×3=?

If user answer is same as 9

        Say correct

Else

        Say wrong

4. In Which Job, change one of the jobs on the job list.

    What did you change and what did you change it to?

    Change add (existing jobs) to jobs to add (your choice) to jobs (1 mark)

Which Job?

5. Add a new job on to the list. Which block did you use?

    Add (new job your choice) to jobs (1 mark)

Which Job?

photocopiable page

www.ingramcontent.com/pod-product-compliance
Lightning Source LLC
LaVergne TN
LVHW082339070326
832902LV00043B/2706